The Spirit of the Matter

The Spirit of the Matter

D. L. WATSON

RESOURCE *Publications* · Eugene, Oregon

THE SPIRIT OF THE MATTER

Copyright © 2022 D. L. Watson. All rights reserved. Except for brief quotations in critical publications or reviews, no part of this book may be reproduced in any manner without prior written permission from the publisher. Write: Permissions, Wipf and Stock Publishers, 199 W. 8th Ave., Suite 3, Eugene, OR 97401.

Resource Publications
An Imprint of Wipf and Stock Publishers
199 W. 8th Ave., Suite 3
Eugene, OR 97401

www.wipfandstock.com

PAPERBACK ISBN: 978-1-6667-3549-9
HARDCOVER ISBN: 978-1-6667-9262-1
EBOOK ISBN: 978-1-6667-9263-8

JANUARY 17, 2022 2:52 PM

Scripture taken from The Scriptures, Copyright by Institute for Scripture Research. Used by permission.

To my wife, Kendra, and my friend James Lee.

> It is the esteem of Elohim to hide a matter,
> And the esteem of sovereigns to search out a matter.
>
> —PROVERBS 25:2

Contents

Note on Translation | 1
Before You Feast on This Book | 3

Part 1: Set-apart Gatherings

Before You Feast on This Part | 13
The Beginning of the Weird | 15
Knocking It Out | 17
The Sabbath | 19
The Feasts | 22
Passover | 23
Unleavened Bread | 25
Firstfruits | 30
Weeks | 32
Trumpets | 37
Stuck on Trumpets | 41

Part 2: The Beginning and the End

Before You Feast on This Part | 49
Humor Me | 50
The Basic Idea | 53
Day 1 | 57
Day 2 | 60

Day 3 | 64

Day 4 | 66

Day 5 | 69

Day 6 | 71

Day 7 | 74

Immediate Questions | 77

Why 2028? | 79

I Ended Up Reading Ansley's Book | 82

Part 3: THE LAW OF RELIGION

Before You Feast on This Part | 87

Wrestle with God | 89

Considering Our Holy Days | 92

Back to the Source | 95

"The Detestable Mob of Jews" | 100

Dining In or Taking Out? | 108

45,000 and Counting | 112

Religion Versus God's Word | 116

Part 4: THE GREAT LIGHT

Before You Feast on This Part | 125

Yeshua, the Torah, and Lovers of Truth | 128

The Gift of Righteousness and the Call to Obey | 131

Loving Expectation | 137

Part 5: THE LAW OF GOD

Before You Feast on This Part | 143

Legalism, Games, and Technicalities | 146

Sabbath Legalism | 153

Sabbath Law | 157

The "New Sabbath" Argument | 161

Those Two Verses | 168
　　Is the Torah a Good Thing for Christians? | 172
　　New Testament Scriptures Containing "Torah" | 174
　　So . . . Is It Good? | 193
　　The Torah Sets Up the Gospel | 199
　　Why So Much Torah? | 206
　　The Galatian Situation | 210

Part 6: THE END AND THE BEGINNING
　　Before You Feast on This Part | 217
　　Cents and Sensibility | 218
　　Science, Creationism, and the Spirit of the Matter | 223
　　The Astronaut, the Aliens, and the Politics | 232
　　Voluntary Humiliation | 241
　　The Realized but Unknown Creator | 245
　　The Final Chapter | 249
　　Trust the Lighthouse | 258

Part 7: SET-APART REGATHERING
　　Before You Feast on This Part | 265
　　God's Pleasure Versus Man's Pleasure | 266
　　Beastly Pleasure Versus Godly Law | 270
　　Revelation . . . Oh Man | 275
　　The Great Hour of Pre-Wrath Tribulation Rapture and Trial | 278
　　The Mark of the Beast at Four A.M. | 282
　　The Beast and the Horn | 290
　　The Hundred-Dollar Intention | 294
　　Authority Complex | 299
　　Back to the Sixth Day | 304
　　Chiastic Love | 308

Closing Content

Are You Saying . . . | 315

What If I'm Wrong? | 320

What If I'm Right? | 322

Either Way, the World is in Trouble | 326

So What Should We Do? | 333

Gratitude | 335

Bibliography | 337

Note on Translation

WHILE WRITING THIS BOOK, I changed my mind several times about which translation or translations of the Bible to use. I ended up using The Scriptures 2009 (TS2009) translation exclusively, and I want to briefly explain why.

TS2009 is a free version available through eSword, which is also a free download. If you are coming from a Christian background with more traditional Bible versions, you will notice a few obvious differences in TS2009. The most notable difference is the preservation of the Hebrew lettering for the names of God and His son. Here is the Hebrew lettering for the name of God in the Bible:

יהוה

Several of the teachers I have been listening to read it out loud as "Yah", though I understand that to be a shortened form of God's name, whose pronunciation in full is a debated matter.

TS2009 also uses the Hebrew lettering for the name of God's son, which is translated into English versions as "Jesus". Here is his name in Hebrew:

יהושע

Aside from the use of Hebrew lettering for these names, you will also notice different names for almost every other biblical character, as well, even though they have been translated into English. The names have been translated to preserve the integrity of the Hebrew as much as possible. For example, you will find "Mosheh" instead of "Moses". This can make the reading process more challenging, but also more enjoyable in the way of feeling fresh and new. I have found it helpful to keep a more familiar version of the Bible nearby and cross reference the Scripture if I don't know what person or place is being referred to.

I wanted to point out these differences to give my reader a head's up before jumping in. But the main reason I chose to use TS2009 is because of its use of "Torah". TS2009 uses the word "Torah" when the writers are referring to the law of God instead of using the word "law" like many other English versions do. There are other Greek words in the New Testament that often get translated into English as "law", even though they are not referring explicitly to the Torah. Therefore, if the Torah also gets translated as "law", we lose the ability to distinguish when the writers of the New Testament are referring to God's law and when they are referring to something else. The significance of this will become very clear in Part 5.

When I decided to use TS2009 for a specific reason (for the use of "Torah"), I felt unsettled at the idea of using other versions for other reasons. I didn't want to pick and choose versions based on which one best proved my point. I wanted whatever points I was making to align with the Bible as a whole and not be dependent upon the particular language of a singular, translated verse of Scripture. That's why I chose to use TS2009 throughout the whole book. I believe that all the points I have made in this book could be defended with any other reasonable English translation and that they are not dependent upon the specific wording of TS2009, with possible exception to Part 5.

Again, I wanted to address these points to give my reader a head's up and a quick understanding of why I went with TS2009 for this book. If you haven't read this version before, I pray it's a blessing to you.

Before You Feast on This Book

Not long ago, I watched a YouTube video posted by THE BEAT by Allen Parr questioning whether certain mainstream Christian teachers were false teachers. He used the illustration of how federal agents don't learn to spot counterfeit money by studying all the counterfeits out there. Instead, they study the real thing, and when they know what real money looks like, they can spot a counterfeit.

Parr went through each individual, explaining what the accusations against them were. I really appreciated how he concluded the video. He said he believes that our focus is off in the way of being so eager to create a list of false teachers. He said that instead of creating that list, we should be concerned with understanding truth, and then we can have the freedom to listen to whomever we want, because we will be able to distinguish truth from false teaching for ourselves.

He went on to say that one of the dangers of eagerly labeling people "false teachers" is potentially blocking a blessing they may have for someone else. That teacher might have a piece of truth to share that is really good, but if we write them off as a "false teacher", we could be shutting down some beneficial truth, as well. He said that when we know what truth looks like, we can then "eat the meat and spit out the fat"—in other words, we can identify and appreciate a nugget of truth and throw out any mistruths that may have been communicated along with it.

I appreciate this message because nobody is Jesus except for Jesus. If we're waiting for perfect truth before listening to anything, then we're not going to listen to anything, and we're not going to learn how to distinguish truth.

It is important to understand the spirit of the matter in order to distinguish false *teachers* from false *teaching*. I suggest that a false teacher is a person whose life is not aligned with truth, whereas a false teaching is a message that is not aligned with truth.

So what is the practical importance here?

Do not engage in an argument with a false teacher about their message. They are not seeking truth, and they do not love God and people. Engaging with them in an argument about their message will not be fruitful and will only lead to wheels spinning, at best. They need something deeper than a convincing argument, and that is a heart change.

For example, some people desire a preeminent role. They crave the adoration and respect of others even more so than truth. Other people are concerned with their comfort or pride. They will argue against truth, whether or not they realize they are doing so, if their comfort or pride is on the line. And some people simply have a combative spirit that reveals a thirst for argument. They don't care about truth, they just enjoy the recreation of an argument.

All those sorts of people need a heart change before they can begin hearing truth through reasoning. The spirit within us (not our ability to logic and reason) determines whether we have eyes that see and ears that hear. That is a large part of why this book is called *The Spirit of the Matter*.

It's useless to engage with false teachers in an argument around what they are teaching. There is no point in addressing their false teaching, because their false teaching is just a symptom of a false heart, and the false heart is the real problem that should be addressed. Put another way, the real problem is the spirit of the matter, which goes deeper than the content being argued.

A false teaching, on the other hand, should be addressed if it is coming from someone who has had that heart change and is genuinely seeking truth. If they are not seeking preeminence, comfort, pride, or argument for the sake of sport, then they are capable of receiving correction. Proverbs is ripe with evidence for this. Proverbs 9:8 says:

> Do not reprove a scoffer, lest he hate you; Reprove a wise one, and he loves you.

Discerning the spirit of the matter in the heart of another person is often not a simple thing, but Jesus tells us in Matthew 7:15-20:

> "But beware of the false prophets, who come to you in sheep's clothing, but inwardly they are savage wolves. By their fruits you shall know them. Are grapes gathered from thornbushes or figs from thistles? So every good tree yields good fruit, but

a rotten tree yields wicked fruit. A good tree is unable to yield wicked fruit, and a rotten tree to yield good fruit. Every tree that does not bear good fruit is cut down and thrown into the fire. So then, by their fruits you shall know them – "

Jesus says that we will know false prophets by their fruits. Before we start determining for ourselves what good fruit looks like, let's see what Scripture says about it. Paul writes in Galatians 5:22–23:

> But the fruit of the Spirit is love, joy, peace, patience, kindness, goodness, trustworthiness, gentleness, self-control. Against such there is no Torah.

This is the fruit we should look for when assessing the spirit of the matter in another person. We don't assess the spirit of the matter to judge a person. We do it so that we have proper discernment in listening to the things they are telling us. If the fruit of the Spirit isn't present in a person's life, then that gives us incentive to pump the brakes before digesting their words as truth.

I have come to realize that, for many Christians, discussing Scripture, doctrine, and theology is the fastest way to have them show their fruits. When there is total agreement, you find all the good stuff—love, joy, peace, patience, kindness . . .

The real test is when the disagreement surfaces. If they are genuine, the fruit of the Spirit remains. If not, the fruit of the Spirit melts away. Suddenly the joy and the kindness that were there before are strangely absent.

I understand that there is a place for zeal in defending the truth. If you hear someone smearing the truth, it can be easy to jump to righteous indignation. After all, even Jesus went into the temple courts and overturned the tables. But we need to be mindful of where our indignation is coming from and how we're displaying it.

John 2:16–17 says:

> And He said to those selling doves, "Take these away! Do not make the house of My Father a house of merchandise!" And His taught ones remembered that it was written, "The ardour for Your house has eaten Me up."

Jesus's indignation was a fulfilment of Scripture (Psalm 69:9). Also, he was Jesus, and he knew how to act out of pure love.

In my experience, arguments over Christian doctrine are usually steeped in much more than love. I have witnessed hate, pride, arrogance, self-righteousness, pre-eminence, and condemnation all in the name of God.

I don't know when it happened, but there came a point when I just stopped buying it. I stopped buying that church leaders were acting like bullies because they just cared so much about the Gospel. I stopped buying that pastors were gorging on pre-eminence for the purpose of reaching the lost. And I stopped buying that the Christian religion wanted me to read the Bible for myself. What I discovered was that the Christian religion wanted me to read the Bible for myself to the extent that I came to the same conclusions as they did about certain doctrines. Otherwise, they told me I needed to be cautious about getting into the Bible, as if my soul was in danger.

I stopped buying all these self-righteous, altruistic justifications when I started seeing people for their fruit. They loved me when I agreed with them, and they became some dark, sinister character when I didn't.

To be clear, this wasn't the case for most Christians I knew. In fact, most Christians I knew were genuinely kind, loving, and concerned.

You see, the reason this stuff can be so difficult to address is because the Christian religion tends to attract people who realize it is right to do good and love others. Many Christians are motivated to do wonderful things for others and to serve with profound passion.

So what's the problem? The problem is exactly that—Christians are profoundly motivated people and the Christian religion has taken advantage of that motivation. When well-meaning people want to please God, they seek understanding. People assume that, if there is truth about God out there, the most reliable dispensary must be the established institution, particularly the leaders within it. Church leaders, then, are given immense amounts of trust.

Many people believe that good institutional leadership necessarily translates into good church leadership. The result is that many, if not most churches today are filled with good institutional leaders. What's the problem with this? Good institutional leadership prioritizes the institution. Good church leadership prioritizes the people.

I don't want to get lost in semantics here, but this is a very important point to understand. We can call church an institution, but it's more appropriate to call it a body of believers. It's similar to how you can call someone a slab of meat, but it's more appropriate to call them a human being. There's something dehumanizing in calling them a slab of meat, just like there's something dehumanizing in thinking of the church as an institution instead of a body of believers. Technically, you could call it either way. But the way you choose to think about it will carry implications going forward.

People decided long ago to think of the Christian church as an institution rather than a body of people. Not everyone, but enough to get the ball rolling. That gave Satan a powerful foothold among church leadership. At that point he could influence man's heart to look after the institution before looking after the people. This has led to a Christian religion that is filled with good intentions, complex doctrines, surface-level understandings, and a real deficit of truth.

Christians today defend their institution by calling contrary ideas false teachings. If someone brings forth a message that doesn't align with some piece of doctrine that has gone into the structural integrity of their specific institution, then that messenger must be a false teacher. This labeling creates a fear within others who may otherwise be open to hearing truth.

A false teacher is not someone who disagrees with *you*. A false teaching is not a message *you* disagree with. False teaching disagrees with *truth*. We must understand truth before we can make claims of false teaching.

Sadly, Christianity has not done enough to teach Christians about the whole Bible. I never realized this until I started listening to teachers who could talk about the Bible in a holistic way, presenting a cohesive narrative, without having to write off sections as "not meaning what they're saying". That seems to be the way Christianity has survived for some time now, explaining away certain biblical portions that don't line up with its doctrines as "figurative" or "metaphorical".

You may be skeptical reading that, thinking, "Okay, but I'm sure whatever narrative you have to present will be taking just as many liberties as anyone else."

As Christians, we've been conditioned to think that. We look around at all the factions and distinctions within the church. We feel confident that the Bible offers a lot of different options for understanding a lot of different subjects, and we think that's why there are a lot of different churches today. But that's not why.

As you begin this book, I want you to understand something: the Bible teaches one cohesive narrative. It is consistent, and every book of the Bible has a part in it. The Bible is not responsible for the church division in our world today.

Think of it like this. Every book of the Bible is like a puzzle piece, and when we put all the pieces together correctly, it is obvious, because they all work together to form one clean, corroborative, and beautiful picture. As Christians, we've been conditioned to think that these puzzle pieces don't all fit together into a single, clean picture. We think that some of the pieces are supposed to be unconnected, garnishing the sides, almost stylistically, with justifications that it's part of God's pleasure for certain pieces to not cleanly connect. We feel like we do pretty well with putting the Gospel pieces together and the pieces of Paul's letters together. We may even have a pretty good outer border with the Psalms. But then we get those weird pieces like Ezekiel and Revelation, and we do our best with placing them around the pieces we've already connected. We never actually get all the pieces connected, so we just do our best with what we can and call it a day. Most Christians even put certain pieces underneath the already connected pieces, saying that not all the pieces are relevant anymore, anyway. And then, when someone comes along saying that all the pieces fit together to make one picture, we doubt it, because there are already so many attempts out there that have failed.

The problem is not that the Bible is unclear, inconsistent, self-contradictory, or containing any other shortcoming. The problem is us. The Bible is God's Word. It is so far beyond our ability to understand. The only way we can make sense of it is with the help of the Holy Spirit.

In this book, I hope to help show you how the pieces of the Bible all fit together. Before I proceed, though, I want to warn you about two things.

First, in order to see how the pieces of the Bible all fit together, you have to let the Bible mean what it says. You can't read something in the Bible, think, "It says this but it clearly doesn't mean *that*," and then expect to understand the Bible as a whole. The Bible says what it says on purpose. If you're not willing to consider that the Bible means what it says, even if it goes against what *you* think is reasonable, you're going to end up with a bunch of disjointed pieces.

Just like the pieces of a puzzle fit *together*, the pieces of the Bible work together, as well. If something in Scripture appears to contradict something else in Scripture, assume *you* are not understanding it correctly. Don't leave it unresolved. Work to understand what you might be missing. Why would the Bible say *this* here and *that* there? Figure out a way to connect the two pieces. When you do, you may then come across another piece that breaks the connection you found. That just means you have to go back to work, figuring out a new connection for all three pieces.

When you put a puzzle together, you don't end up with a hole in the middle and a piece that doesn't fit. It all has to work together.

Read the Bible.

Ask yourself, "What does it say?"

Take it at face value until you come across some other piece that challenges your understanding.

Seek reconciliation.

Reconcile.

Repeat.

When we read through the Bible in this way, we are allowing it to be the cohesive picture it is as opposed to the disjointed pieces we often make it out to be. I warn you about this upfront, because I know a lot of people might consider this kind of process exhausting and daunting. I, personally, find it fun and invigorating. I enjoy games, and this process feels like a giant Sudoku puzzle to me. If you are someone who finds this process daunting, though, that's one of the reasons I'm writing this book. I want to help people see that there's more to the Bible than many of us have been taught. Way more.

Second, I want to warn you that you might not like the whole picture. I think this is one of the main reasons we've ended up with chunks of the puzzle put together and a bunch of pieces disconnected around it. Humanity has slowly shied away from the whole picture over time because, when they see the way certain pieces fit together, they don't like it. This is because, for a sin-fallen humanity, this picture is challenging, absurd, offensive, and scary. If you want to see the entire picture, though, you must be willing to put the pieces together that challenge and offend you. You might not like it, and you ultimately might decide you don't believe it. I'm not trying to sell the Bible here. I'm only trying to show how it offers us a much more cohesive picture than most of us have ever known.

I'm not trying to sell the Bible here. But I will say, for someone who believes in it even after all its pieces are put together, it's a beautiful picture. I hope you'll stick with me through this.

Part 1

SET-APART GATHERINGS

Before You Feast on This Part

I WAS BORN IN Omaha, Nebraska on October 22, 1987. My mom tells me this story from when I was a toddler. Our family went to a Christmas pageant at our church. During the pageant, I fell asleep in her lap. When I woke up at the end, amid everyone getting up and clearing out, I looked around, confused, and started saying, "More baby Jesus, more baby Jesus!"

We moved to South Carolina when I was four. My dad was the preacher of our church. I grew up in a small town called Six Mile. In the summers, I attended VBS and Bible camp. In the winters, our youth group went to a Christian conference called Winterfest in Gatlinburg, Tennessee. When I was thirteen, my heart broke from hearing the Gospel. When we returned from Winterfest that year, my dad baptized me at our church. We had a big yard, so in the springtime we would have the church over for Easter picnics and egg hunts. In the fall, I had Halloween-themed birthday parties.

During my high school summers, I traveled to Mexico with a group from my church to build houses for families in poverty.

I went to Florida State University. Throughout my four years there, I stayed involved in a campus ministry called Ambassadors for Christ. One year I was the president of the group. During my college summers, I went to Oklahoma to be a counselor at a Bible camp for inner-city children. I studied abroad in London during the fall of 2008. While I was there, I attended Hillsong Church.

After graduating college, I moved to Montgomery briefly, attended a church there, and then I moved to Greenville, South Carolina. At my church in Greenville, I served as a youth leader for two years, and then I moved to New York City. I attended a church in lower Manhattan for about three years before I met my wife, Kendra, online (Coffee Meets Bagel, for those of you who are curious).

Kendra and I continued attending church in New York for about two years after we got married, and then in June of 2019, we left New York.

I'm telling you all this upfront because I want you to know that my life has not just been affected, but completely shaped by the culture of church. Church is one of a few things about which I feel comfortable calling myself a subject matter expert, not in the way of academia, but in life experience. As you read this book, you will understand why I am telling you this, and that all of this is not me boasting. Far from it.

We moved to North Carolina, where we lived for two years. Then, in June of 2021, we packed up and moved to Colorado. This book covers a timeline of about two years. It mostly represents my thoughts from our time in North Carolina.

The Beginning of the Weird

KENDRA AND I were living on the Upper West Side of Manhattan in 2018 when things started getting weird at our church in Tribeca. It was one of those weirds where some people said, "This is a good weird," and other people said, "This is a bad weird." Nobody was denying that it was weird. People just assessed the weird differently.

Our pastor was going through some stuff. Spiritual, Holy Spirit stuff. He told the congregation that he had not been letting God have total control, and that this needed to change. He started giving sermons without preparing for them in advance, to let the Holy Spirit speak through him as opposed to him speaking for God. He said things were going to change, and he told us that if we weren't on board with that, then it would be best to find another church.

Remarkably few people found another church at first. I say "remarkably" because a large portion of the congregation didn't seem to be on board. Even so, our pastor powered through, changing things up and telling people to leave if they didn't like the new direction.

When January 2019 rolled around, Kendra and I experienced our hardest month of marriage, for a slew of reasons. As much as it all hurt, though, it was a good thing. It hurt because walls that we had built around our hearts were being destroyed. We ripped them down and cleared out the rubble. It was not fun, but we would come to find that it was very beneficial.

Right in the midst of this, in early 2019, our church had its annual retreat. This event exacerbated the already exasperated crowd. There was much grumbling afterward. Things were getting too "charismatic" for some people's tastes. They didn't understand why this was happening. They loved the church the way it had been—the people, the community groups, and even the pastor. I completely understood this. I had been a part of the church for five years, and it had come to be my family.

Even so, there was truth in what the pastor was saying. We certainly didn't understand everything that was going on, but Kendra and I both felt a confidence that what was happening was from God. So we opened ourselves to it.

When springtime rolled around, Kendra and I were starting to feel better. We were healing and moving forward. We had decided that we were going to leave New York that summer.

Things at our church, meanwhile, continued to escalate. Sometime in May, our pastor called a meeting at his apartment. He told us that he and his family would be moving to Rwanda, and he doubled down on everything that had been happening at the church, saying that it would continue in the direction of giving God control.

In the weeks that followed, the pastor and his family moved to Rwanda, and Kendra and I left for Raleigh, North Carolina, our heads spinning. We didn't know exactly why we felt so compelled to move to Raleigh. Neither of us had a job there. Neither of us knew anybody there. The only reason we picked Raleigh was because it was exactly four hours from both of our parents, mine in South Carolina and hers in Virginia. Other than that, we didn't know why we were moving there. We just knew we felt led in that direction.

So we moved down there, not sure what to expect.

This was the beginning of this weird story.

Knocking It Out

AFTER EVERYTHING THAT took place at our church in Manhattan, I had resolved to write a book called *The Spirit of the Matter*. What had become so clear to me was a breakdown in humanity's understanding of "spirit", whether it was the Spirit of God, some other spiritual entity, or the general spirit of any given situation. Like so many other words in the English language, we throw the word "spirit" around haphazardly without a clear idea of what we are intending to say.

I wanted to write a book on this. I believed it could help Christians recognize when others were not being genuine in their words and actions. This was an important issue to me because I had already seen the damage that such people could do to both believers and non-believers. It broke my heart to realize that the church was so congested with individuals who said the right words and acted the right ways to gain trust and influence, only to use that trust and influence for self-serving purposes.

When Kendra and I moved to Raleigh, I had some summer pay from being a teacher, so my plan was to job search while that lasted. During my job search, I determined that I was going to write my book, *The Spirit of the Matter*. I kept telling Kendra, "I'm just going to knock it out." I had several other writing projects I wanted to work on, as well, so I wanted to get *The Spirit of the Matter* completed so that I could consolidate my focus.

As you may suspect, I did not knock it out. The phrase, "Just knock it out," developed into a joke between Kendra and me. "I'm gonna do laundry before I go to work," I might say. "Just gonna knock it out." It was a testament to my silliness.

I am convinced that God did not want me to knock it out, at least not at that point. The book was not ready to be knocked out. Put more appropriately, I was not ready. The months of July and August passed, and

I was still knocking it out. September, October, and November went by, and I was still knocking it out. By the end of 2019, I could no longer be knocking it out with a straight face. Suddenly I found myself in November of 2020, a few days before Thanksgiving, largely starting from scratch, and continuing to knock this sucker out.

The Sabbath

I started working at a rescue mission for homeless men, women, and children in Raleigh in August of 2019. I met James shortly after I started working there. We bonded over discussing the Bible. At first, I wasn't sure what to make of James. While I thoroughly enjoyed discussing certain subjects with him, he also gave off a crazy vibe.

I remember James asking me at work one day, "You know about the feasts in Leviticus?"

"Kind of," I told him. "Not really," I then admitted. I have since come to learn that most Christians who believe they know the Bible well will answer this question in a similar fashion.

"Man, I'm tellin' ya, it's all about those feasts," James said.

This is what I mean when I say he gave off a crazy vibe. In my mind I was thinking, "Okay, James, sure. It's all about those feasts." On the surface though, I just laughed and said, "Okay."

"Read about them," he said. "Leviticus 23. Ask the Spirit to open your eyes."

I listened to him, and I went back and read Leviticus 23. Before I even got into the feasts, though, I read about the Sabbath. Leviticus 23:3 says:

> "'Six days work is done, but the seventh day is a Sabbath of rest, a set-apart gathering. You do no work, it is a Sabbath to יהוה in all your dwellings.'"

The chapter goes on to talk about each of the feasts that God ordained for the Israelites, but the Sabbath had caught my attention.

I knew that honoring the Sabbath was the fourth commandment. I also had recently noticed how prevalent the Sabbath is brought up in Scripture while reading through the Bible.

The next time I saw James, I told him, "You know, before even getting into the feasts, I feel like I need to think more on the Sabbath." What I found particularly interesting about it was the fact that all the other Ten Commandments are essentially intuitive moral logic for Christians. In other words, modern-day Christians really wouldn't question whether or not we should follow each of the other nine Commandments. Just think about it. It's as if modern-day Christians treat the Ten Commandments like this:

1. Have no other gods before God.
2. Do not worship idols.
3. Do not take the LORD's name in vain.
4. ~~Honor the Sabbath.~~
5. Honor your mother and father.
6. Do not kill.
7. Do not commit adultery.
8. Do not steal.
9. Do not lie.
10. Do not covet.

I mean, honestly, all the other nine Commandments are engrained within us as assumed moral virtue. If you're a Christian, I challenge you to go back up to that list and find another one that you would feel comfortable crossing out. I wouldn't feel comfortable crossing out any of the others. But when it comes to the Sabbath, that's when Christians eagerly adhere to verses like Colossians 2:14 that, depending on the version, say things like "the law was nailed to the cross".

When I told James this, he took a deep breath, and then he said, "Yeah, man, I know what you mean."

I decided that I wanted to try keeping the Sabbath. I learned that the calendar God gave the Israelites was based on the moon. Each month is a full cycle of the moon, and each day starts at sundown. So the Sabbath day, which is the last day of the week, starts at sundown on Friday, and goes through sundown on Saturday. That's what I wanted to try observing.

To be clear, I wanted to observe the Sabbath as instructed by the Bible. I knew a lot of Christians considered themselves to be keeping the Sabbath commandment by observing Sunday. At the time, I didn't have particularly strong feelings about this distinction one way or another, but I knew that the Bible was very clear that the Sabbath was the seventh day of the week, not the first. There are no Scriptures that explicitly (or otherwise) tell us that the Sabbath changed from the seventh day to the first day. This idea was instituted by the Christian religion and not the Bible. That's why I wanted to try observing the Sabbath on the seventh day, to just see what it was like to remember the Sabbath based on what the Bible said.

I told Kendra about all this, and she was onboard. So that's what we did—on Friday at sundown, we said a prayer, took communion together, and then we rested for the next 24 hours. At sundown on Saturday, we prayed and took communion again. We did not make any of this out to be obligatory or act legalistic about it. We just wanted to do something to acknowledge the day in itself, and to tell God, "Thank You for this day, God. It is Your Holy Sabbath."

We just wanted to *honor* the day as God commanded in the Bible, not submit ourselves to some burdensome law. In fact, it was quite the opposite of burdensome. We quickly started looking forward to the Sabbath each week. It became our favorite day. It was *fun*.

It wasn't long after we started honoring the Sabbath that God really started opening my eyes.

The Feasts

SHORTLY AFTER KENDRA and I started observing the Sabbath, I went into the feasts. In Leviticus 23:2, God tells Moses:

> "Speak to the children of Yisraěl, and say to them, 'The appointed times of יהוה, which you are to proclaim as set-apart gatherings, My appointed times, are these:'"

He then begins with the Sabbath in verse three, proclaiming it to be a day of rest, a set-apart gathering.

After that, He begins laying out the annual feasts that the Israelites are to observe. There are eight of them (though a couple of them are often counted together) in Leviticus 23. I've listed them below:

1. The Passover
2. Unleavened Bread
3. The Feast of First Fruits
4. The Feast of Weeks
5. The Feast of Trumpets
6. The Day of Atonement
7. The Feast of Tabernacles
8. The Eighth Day

It is important to note that the first four feasts occur in the spring of the calendar year, and the last four feasts occur in the fall of the calendar year. Before going to the next chapter, I encourage you to read Leviticus 23, all the way through.

Passover

Assuming you listened to my encouragement from the last chapter, you have now read through Leviticus 23. If you're like I was at this point, you're skeptically wondering, "It's all about those feasts, huh?" I mean, I knew that Jesus became our Passover lamb, I guess, but that still didn't give James the right to make flippant claims like, "It's all about those feasts, man." After I read through Leviticus 23, I still didn't understand.

I told James I read through the chapter and still didn't get how "it's all about those feasts".

He told me, "Look at the timing of each feast."

I opened a Bible right there and went through each feast again, reading out when they occurred. Leviticus 23:5 says:

> "'In the first new moon, on the fourteenth day of the new moon, between the evenings, is the Pĕsaḥ [Passover] to יהוה.'"

I looked up at James. He had on his crazy smile and was nodding.

Finally he asked me, "Do you remember any particular time they were celebrating Passover in the Gospels?"

I told him it was happening around the time Jesus got arrested and was crucified.

With a little more prompting, I came to realize that when Jesus had the Last Supper (the Lord's Supper) with his disciples, the day of Passover had just begun, since their days started at sundown. That same day continued through the night with the Garden of Gethsemane, Jesus's arrest, and eventually his crucifixion. I had never really connected it, but Jesus shared the Lord's Supper with his disciples on Passover and he died on that same day (the day of Passover) even though there was a whole night separating the events.

In Exodus 12:6, we can read about the institution of Passover, how the Israelites had to slaughter a lamb *between the evenings* on the day of Passover and put its blood over their doors to be saved from the condemnation that was being brought upon Egypt. Jesus became our Passover lamb—his blood saves us from the condemnation of sin, just like the Passover lamb's blood saved the Israelites.

But Jesus did not simply become our Passover lamb by dying on the cross—he became our Passover lamb by dying on the cross *on the exact day* of Passover. Out of all the days of the year that Jesus might have shed his blood to save humanity, he died on the one day that commemorated the shedding of blood to save the Israelites, a day that had been celebrated for hundreds of years before Jesus's life on earth.

"Okay," I told James. "That's pretty cool. But I still don't understand the other feasts."

Unleavened Bread

I read the timing of the Feast of Unleavened Bread. Leviticus 23:6 says:

> "'And on the fifteenth day of this new moon is the Festival of Matzot to יהוה – seven days you eat unleavened bread.'"

James had on his crazy, nodding smile again. I knew the unleavened bread also commemorated the Israelites' escape from Egypt. In Exodus 12, God instructs that no leaven should be found in the Israelites' households for seven days. But I still wasn't clear on the connection.

"So when's the timing of Unleavened Bread?" James asked.

"It starts on the fifteenth day, which would have been the day after the Passover, and goes for seven days, a full week."

"So what happened the day after the Passover when Jesus was crucified?"

That's when the dots started connecting for me.

"He was buried."

I realized that Jesus's body was placed in the tomb, but it never spoiled. Bread without leaven does not spoil in the same way that leavened bread does. Unleavened bread lasts much longer.

When Jesus shared the Lord's Supper with his disciples before his death on Passover, he broke the bread and said, "'Take, eat; this is My body,'" (Mark 14:22). He did the same thing with the cup, telling them to drink, and that it was his blood.

I started seeing how these feasts and the Lord's Supper are intimately connected. The blood of the Passover Lamb and the unleavened bread point to the blood of Christ as he was crucified on the cross and his unspoiled body as it lay in the tomb. I was beginning to see that the events of Jesus's life that I had learned so often in church were intimately tied to the feasts God had laid out in Leviticus 23—more than a thousand years before Jesus ever walked the earth. In this way, Jesus was fulfilling these feasts.

James went on to point out that Jesus's body was taken down from the cross when evening came. If one day ends at sundown and the next one begins that evening, then Jesus was put in the tomb at the very beginning of the fifteenth day of that month, which was the very beginning of the Feast of Unleavened Bread.

Therefore, if we consider Jesus's unspoiled body to be the unleavened bread, Jesus not only fulfilled the Feast of Unleavened Bread by being buried in the tomb and not rotting—he fulfilled the Feast of Unleavened Bread by being buried in the tomb and not rotting *on the exact days* of the Feast of Unleavened Bread. Out of all the days of the year that Jesus's body could have been laid to rest in the tomb, it happened on the very feast commemorating the bread which he had previously told his disciples was his body, the very bread that didn't spoil like the bread made with leaven.

I've come to learn of a dual significance in this feast. Not only is Jesus's body the unleavened bread, but he took all the "leaven" with him to the tomb. The leaven represents our sin and disobedience, anything in or about us that is opposed to God. In Leviticus 23, God tells the Israelites to prepare for the Feast of Unleavened Bread by throwing out any and all leaven from their household. This is not a random request but serves as a representation of the spiritual leaven (sin) that we are to remove from our lives. Our spiritual leaven is to be put to death, buried with Jesus in the tomb.

One other interesting piece I learned about this feast is that the first and last days of the feast were to be "set-apart gatherings", which basically means honorary Sabbaths. In other words, even if these days did not fall on the seventh day of the week, they were still to be treated as if they were Sabbath days, meaning everyone was expected to do no work. You can read this in Leviticus 23:7–8.

This sheds new light on the possible timing of Jesus's death in relation to his resurrection. At least it did for me.

You may be familiar with the idea that Jesus was buried for three days and three nights. Jesus says in Matthew 12:40:

> "For as Yonah was three days and three nights in the stomach of the great fish, so shall the Son of Adam be three days and three nights in the heart of the earth."

From what I have experienced growing up, it is common Christian knowledge that Jesus was buried for three days and three nights.

That said, it is also common Christian tradition to honor Good Friday as the day that Jesus was crucified, and to celebrate Easter Sunday as the day he rose from the dead. But when you pause for a moment and try to line up what Jesus said in Matthew 12:40 with the idea that he was crucified on a Friday, it starts becoming mental gymnastics to try and reconcile Friday as the day he died with Sunday as the day he resurrected. I have heard ideas based on the way the Jews kept time, but even if you subscribe to the idea that Friday and Sunday both counted as days, it's still hard to make sense of the statement that Jesus was to be buried for three days and three nights as stated in Matthew 12:40.

How do we reconcile this? Let us start with what is stated clearly in the Gospels. All four Gospels mention the first day of the week as the day he resurrected. So how did we get Friday as the day he died?

Mark 15:42–43 says:

> And when evening had come, because it was the Preparation Day, that is, the day before the Sabbath, Yosĕph of Ramathayim, a prominent council member, who was himself waiting for the reign of Elohim, came, boldly went in to Pilate and asked for the body of יהושע.

Scripture tells us that Jesus was crucified the day before the Sabbath. We know that the weekly Sabbath takes place on what we now call Saturday. If we have no knowledge of the set-apart gatherings during the feasts of יהוה, then this leaves us with no alternative to thinking Jesus's crucifixion took place on a Friday, based on what is written in the Gospels. However, many people do not know that the feasts of יהוה include these set-apart gatherings (which are, in essence, Sabbath days) and that these days could occur on any day of the week. One of those set-apart gatherings took place on the first day of the Feast of Unleavened Bread. Since Jesus was crucified on Passover, and the first day of Unleavened Bread is the day after Passover, the day after Jesus's crucifixion would have been regarded as a Sabbath day regardless of the day of the week.

If we go back to Leviticus 23 and skip ahead for a moment to the Day of Atonement, we read that the Day of Atonement is called out as a set-apart gathering on which "you do not work", just like the first and last days of Unleavened Bread. The Day of Atonement takes place on the tenth day of the seventh new moon, which means that it, like the other feast days, is not tied to any particular day of the week. It could fall on the first day, the seventh day, or any day in between. With that in mind, we read in Leviticus 23:32, still addressing the Day of Atonement:

> "It is a Sabbath of rest to you, and you shall afflict your beings. On the ninth day of the new moon at evening, from evening to evening, you observe your Sabbath."

God Himself refers to this day, which does not necessarily fall on the seventh day of the week, as a Sabbath day. Therefore, it's not a stretch of the imagination to think that the Gospel writers could have been referring to the first day of Unleavened Bread, a set-apart gathering, as the Sabbath when talking about Jesus's crucifixion taking place on "the Preparation Day".

There is certainly more to the argument around what day of the week Jesus was crucified. But my concern here is less about a certain day of the week and more about how tradition may be stunting our understanding around the Bible.

The word "holiday" comes from "holy day", and so embracing a holiday is, to a certain extent, considering it a holy day. I know the instinctual reaction is to say that "holiday" means something different now and we don't necessarily consider every holiday to be a holy day. But holy just means "set apart".

The reality is, if a culture recognizes one day as a holiday and other days as regular days, then that culture is, in essence, proclaiming that holiday as set apart from the other days. We can talk our way around it, but that is the truth of what's going on: it is acceptable to take off from work or school on a holiday, but on other days it is not. Why? Because the holiday is considered set apart and therefore more important than the other days, and even if we want to say that we don't hold it that way in our minds, when we take off work on the one day and go into work on the next, we confirm that truth by our actions and lifestyles.

So what's the big deal, then, with Good Friday? It's simply a question of loving truth and seeking God. God explicitly lays out certain days that He considers holy (or set apart) days in Scripture. Is Good Friday explicitly one of those days? From what I've been able to gather through reading the Bible, it is not. It is, instead, a product of church tradition. This may not seem like a bad thing in itself, but when I think about Jesus saying, "so shall the Son of Adam be three days and three nights in the heart of the earth," in Matthew 12, I wonder why there are not more Christians doing the basic math and at the very least wondering why there seems to be a disconnect between what Jesus said and what we hold as truth. Why does church tradition carry more weight than Jesus's words?

I was saddened upon realizing that I had blindly accepted this tradition. I hadn't known about the feast days and the set-apart gatherings, so I never thought there was anything further to discuss. I guess I thought that perhaps Jesus was just being cryptic in Matthew 12. I honestly hadn't given it much thought.

But when these things were brought to my attention, I realized that I had blindly accepted a manmade holiday, partly because I was ignorant of the set-apart days given by God. In other words, if I had been familiar with the feasts and the set-apart gatherings, I may not have so easily swallowed the idea that Jesus was crucified on a Friday simply because Scripture says the next day was a Sabbath. The bottom line was that I had relied more heavily on what people told me than I had on the Word of God, and while this may be a fine approach for a baby in Christ, I had for some time considered myself an adult in the faith. This was humbling.

I still wrestle with the question of what day of the week Jesus was crucified on, and I can see why some people may thoughtfully arrive at the conclusion it was a Friday. But again, for me, this wasn't an issue about a day of the week. This was a spirit of the matter issue. My spirit had complacently accepted certain "truths" even though there were obvious questions to be raised, questions that I was more than capable of formulating with my own logic and reasoning. Instead of raising those questions, I chose willing ignorance and deferred to religion's better judgment. If I had so eagerly and dismissively overlooked such a simple discrepancy because religion made me feel assured and secure about doing so, what else was I overlooking?

This is what I was beginning to think as I learned about these feasts with James. The Christian faith that I had been a part of my entire life was much more heavily influenced by church tradition than I realized. To be clear, I had always known the Christian faith was influenced by church tradition, but I had no idea the extent to which even my understanding of God's Word was affected by it. That realization made me all the more thirsty to go back to the text and read it for myself.

Firstfruits

I read THE TIMING of the Feast of Firstfruits. Leviticus 23:10–11 says:

> "Speak to the children of Yisraěl, and you shall say to them, 'When you come into the land which I give you, and shall reap its harvest, then you shall bring a sheaf of the first-fruits of your harvest to the priest. And he shall wave the sheaf before יהוה, for your acceptance. On the morrow after the Sabbath the priest waves it.'"

I looked up to James' crazy, nodding smile, only this time I was wearing a bit of a crazy smile of my own.

"The feast of Firstfruits takes place the day after the Sabbath," I said. "The feast of Firstfruits is on Sunday."

"And what happened on the Sunday after Jesus was crucified?" James asked.

"He resurrected."

If we consider Jesus's resurrected body to be the firstfruits, Jesus not only fulfilled the Feast of Firstfruits by resurrecting from the dead—he fulfilled the Feast of Firstfruits by resurrecting from the dead *on the exact day* of the Feast of Firstfruits. Out of all the days of the year that Jesus could have resurrected, it happened on the very feast commemorating a new harvest taking place in the Promised Land.

Paul explains this straightforwardly and clearly in 1 Corinthians 15:22–23:

> For as all die in Aḏam, so also all shall be made alive in Messiah. And each in his own order: Messiah the first-fruits, then those who are of Messiah at His coming,

Paul also explained the fulfillment of Passover and Unleavened Bread. In 1 Corinthians 5:7–8, he writes:

> Therefore cleanse out the old leaven, so that you are a new lump, as you are unleavened. For also Messiah our Pěsaḥ was slaughtered for us. So then let us celebrate the festival, not with old leaven, nor with the leaven of evil and wickedness, but with the unleavened bread of sincerity and truth.

Passover entailed the blood of a slaughtered lamb saving those who slaughtered it. This feast was celebrated on a specific day of the year given to Moses by God for more than a thousand years before Christ came to earth. Christ fulfilled the Feast of Passover by becoming the Passover lamb *on the day of Passover*.

Unleavened Bread entailed clearing the household of leaven and eating only unleavened bread for seven days. This feast was celebrated more than a thousand years before Christ came to earth on specific days of the year given to Moses by God. Christ fulfilled the Feast of Unleavened Bread by becoming the unleavened bread *on the days of Unleavened Bread*.

Firstfruits entailed the Israelites bringing forth the firstfruits of their harvest once they entered the Promised Land and presenting it to the priest. This feast was celebrated more than a thousand years before Christ came to earth on specific days of the year given to Moses by God. Christ fulfilled the Feast of Firstfruits by resurrecting to become the spiritual firstfruits *on the day of Firstfruits*.

This is ridiculous. Either God divinely orchestrated these events, or Moses, Paul, and the writers of the Gospels were all in cahoots.

They weren't in cahoots.

This is what is so fascinating about the Bible. It is God's Word, and it is self-justifying, meaning that we have one of two "reasonable" conclusions upon understanding its content. Either it is God's inspired Word, or the people who wrote it were collaboratively literary geniuses shadowing all the other literary geniuses who have thus far walked this earth. I respect the writers of the Bible, but it was not their collaborative literary genius that produced this annual best-seller that has not just survived but thrived some 2,000 years after their existence.

These were the thoughts that were on my mind as James wore his crazy smile.

To make things crazier, we weren't even halfway through the feasts presented in Leviticus 23.

Weeks

I READ THE TIMING of the Feast of Weeks. Leviticus 23:15–16 says:

> "'And from the morrow after the Sabbath, from the day that you brought the sheaf of the wave offering, you shall count for yourselves: seven completed Sabbaths. Until the morrow after the seventh Sabbath you count fifty days, then you shall bring a new grain offering to יהוה.'"

I looked up at James with a crazy, nodding smile of my own. It was crazy because I didn't know what was going on, but I was expectant.

"I got nothing," I told him.

"Look at Exodus 19:1," he said.

I hurried over there and read:

> In the third new moon after the children of Yisra'ěl had come out of the land of Mitsrayim, on this day they came to the Wilderness of Sinai.

I looked up at him quizzically. "What, is this supposed to be the Feast of Weeks?"

He started chuckling. "Well hold up a second. What's going on there?"

I looked back at the page. The Israelites had left Egypt a few chapters back, and now they were coming to Sinai, the place where Moses went up on the mountain and received the Ten Commandments and the rest of the law from God.

"They're about to get God's law."

"Right. So look back at the timing of Feast of Weeks."

I went back and processed. "And you shall count for yourselves from the day after the Sabbath, from the day that you brought the sheaf of the wave offering . . . "

"Okay," I said, "so start counting from the Feast of Firstfruits. '. . . seven completed Sabbaths. Until the morrow after the seventh Sabbath you count fifty days, then you shall bring a new grain offering to יהוה.'" I thought for a moment. "Okay, so it's basically saying, the Feast of Weeks takes place fifty days after the Feast of Firstfruits."

James nodded. "And if the Feast of Firstfruits took place in the second half of the first month, what month would that put Feast of Weeks in?"

It took me longer to calculate than I care to admit.

"The third month. Wait, so you're saying Moses got the Ten Commandments on the exact day of the Feast of Weeks?"

James threw up his hands in surrender. "I'm not saying that. What's the Bible say?"

I went back to Exodus 19 and scanned. Eventually, I told him, "I don't see any more clarity here. It just says they came to Sinai in the third month."

"Yeah. We don't know exactly when some events took place. But let's recap for a moment. The Israelites celebrated the first Passover in Egypt, killing a lamb and putting its blood over their doors. They also celebrated the first Feast of Unleavened Bread by only eating unleavened bread for seven days. And then they came out of Egypt, out of slavery, into new life. Now, in the third month, they come to Sinai, where they get God's law.

"Flash forward to Leviticus 23. God tells Moses that they should celebrate Passover on the fourteenth day of the first month, the same day when the original Passover took place. It also ended up being the same day Jesus was crucified. Then they should celebrate Unleavened Bread, the same way the Israelites did when they were preparing to leave Egypt. That ended up being the same day Jesus was laid in the tomb. Then they should celebrate the Feast of Firstfruits, which was the day Jesus resurrected. Now, we've got the Feast of Weeks, fifty days after the Feast of Firstfruits. You remember what happened on the Feast of Weeks following Jesus's resurrection?"

"Wait, a minute," I said, "Is the Feast of Weeks the same thing as Pentecost?"

"Yeah," James told me politely, "it's the same thing. Pentecost became a Greek name for it because it was fifty days after the Feast of Firstfruits. It's called that and Weeks, because it was seven weeks after Firstfruits. You remember what happened on Pentecost in Acts?"

"The Holy Spirit came down on the apostles who were gathered together."

"Yep," he said. "Go to Acts 2. Read the first few verses."

I flipped there. Acts 2:1–4 says:

> And when the Day of the Festival of Sha<u>b</u>uʻoth [Weeks] had come, they were all with one mind in one place. And suddenly there came a sound from the heaven, as of a rushing mighty wind, and it filled all the house where they were sitting. And there appeared to them divided tongues, as of fire, and settled on each one of them. And they were all filled with the Set-apart Spirit and began to speak with other tongues, as the Spirit gave them to speak.

When I looked up, I found James was reading along in his own Bible.

"Okay," I said, "so what is the Feast of Weeks, or Pentecost, *supposed* to be celebrating? I'm a little confused."

"Well that's the thing," James said. "In Leviticus 23, when it talks about Feast of Weeks, it gives the timing, and then it lays out the offerings for the day. It also says that it's another set-apart gathering. It's another honorary Sabbath, like the first and last days of Unleavened Bread. But it never explicitly says what the feast is commemorating."

I flipped back to Leviticus 23 and read verses 15 through 22.

"Wait a minute," I said. I read out verse 22:

> "'And when you reap the harvest of your land do not completely reap the corners of your field when you reap, and do not gather any gleaning from your harvest. Leave them for the poor and for the stranger. I am יהוה your Elohim.'"

James pointed at me in his nonchalant way. "Yeah, I think you may have something there."

"Huh?"

"Okay, so we got the Feast of Weeks taking place fifty days after Firstfruits. That's the third month. We got Moses and the Israelites coming to Sinai, where God gives them His law, in the third month. And then you got the Holy Spirit coming upon the apostles on the exact day of Feast of Weeks, or Pentecost, following the Feast of Firstfruits when Jesus resurrected. You tracking?"

"I think so."

"Okay, so go to Jeremiah 31."

I felt like a detective as I furiously flipped the pages. Jeremiah 31:31–34 says:

> "See, the days are coming," declares יהוה, "when I shall make a renewed covenant with the house of Yisra'ěl and with the house of Yehuḏah, not like the covenant I made with their fathers in the day when I strengthened their hand to bring them out of the land of Mitsrayim, My covenant which they broke, though I was a husband to them," declares יהוה. "For this is the covenant I shall make with the house of Yisra'ěl after those days, declares יהוה: I shall put My Torah in their inward parts, and write it on their hearts. And I shall be their Elohim, and they shall be My people. And no longer shall they teach, each one his neighbour, and each one his brother, saying, 'Know יהוה,' for they shall all know Me, from the least of them to the greatest of them," declares יהוה. "For I shall forgive their crookedness, and remember their sin no more."

I looked up.

"Also check out Ezekiel 36," James told me.

I was there. Ezekiel 36:26–27 says:

> "And I shall give you a new heart and put a new spirit within you. And I shall take the heart of stone out of your flesh, and I shall give you a heart of flesh, and put My Spirit within you. And I shall cause you to walk in My laws and guard My right-rulings and shall do them."

"Okay, so what do you take from that?" James asked.

"Well," I said, "the part in Jeremiah is about God writing His law on the heart, and the part in Ezekiel is about Him giving a heart of flesh and putting His Spirit within us so that we walk in His statutes."

James was nodding. I thought to myself, "What's the connection here?" Then I realized.

"All of this has to do with God's law."

James was smiling.

"It all makes sense," I said. "Let's say God gives Moses His law on the Feast of Weeks. He then promises through Ezekiel to replace our hearts of stone—stone, which the law was first written on—with hearts of flesh, and He promises through Jeremiah to write His law on our hearts, which He did on the Feast of Weeks, or Pentecost, in Acts when the Holy Spirit came upon the apostles. From that point forward, when we are baptized and receive the gift of the Holy Spirit, God writes His law on our hearts, causing us to obey Him."

"Isn't that something?" James said.

I spent several minutes flipping between the different portions of Scripture, revisiting each piece.

"That's crazy," I said. "I mean, there's a lot going on with that one, but when you connect the dots, it's incredible."

James shrugged. "That's the Father, you know?"

"Okay, so what's next?" I eagerly asked, heading back to Leviticus 23.

James started chuckling. "Well hold up. That's the end of the spring feasts. I don't know if you're ready for the fall feasts yet. Besides, we need to pass out these dinners."

The food cart had arrived for the men's evening meal, so we went to hand out supper.

Trumpets

James wasn't joking when he said, "I don't know if you're ready for the fall feasts yet." We didn't jump right back in or anything. It ended up being a busy night, so we let it sit.

It was another week before we worked together again, and as soon as I had clocked in, I told him, "Okay, the next one is Feast of Trumpets. What do you got?"

James started laughing. "You been reading over it, huh?"

"Of course I've been reading over it. This stuff is incredible."

We grabbed a couple Bibles and flipped to Leviticus 23:23. I read it out loud, and continued through verse 25:

> And יהוה spoke to Mosheh, saying, "Speak to the children of Yisra'ěl, saying, 'In the seventh new moon [month], on the first day of the new moon, you have a rest, a remembrance of Teru'ah [soundings, by instrument or human voice], a set-apart gathering. You do no servile work, and you shall bring an offering made by fire to יהוה.'"

I looked to James. "So what's up with that?"

"Well you gotta remember," James replied, "we're now looking at the fall feasts."

"Okay, so what does that mean?"

"Well, these ones might not be fulfilled yet."

I remembered when James had pointed out that half of the feasts were in the spring, and the other half were in the fall. This was not arbitrary—in fact, it was extremely significant. During the time of Jesus's ministry, including his death and resurrection, the events of his life fulfilled the four spring feasts—Passover, Unleavened Bread, First Fruits, and Weeks. After all this happened, Jesus ascended into heaven (Acts

1:9). Because Jesus now sits at the right hand of God in heaven (Hebrews 1:3), all these events necessarily influence how we interpret the fall feasts.

"Okay," I said, "so what's it talking about?"

"Go to 1 Corinthians 15."

I went there. First Corinthians 15:51–52 says:

> See, I speak a secret to you: We shall not all sleep, but we shall all be changed, in a moment, in the twinkling of an eye, at the last trumpet. For the trumpet shall sound, and the dead shall be raised incorruptible, and we shall be changed.

"The resurrection," I said.

"Now go to 1 Thessalonians 4."

First Thessalonians 4:16–17 says:

> Because the Master Himself shall come down from heaven with a shout, with the voice of a chief messenger, and with the trumpet of Elohim, and the dead in Messiah shall rise first. Then we, the living who are left over, shall be caught away together with them in the clouds to meet the Master in the air – and so we shall always be with the Master.

There were a few moments of silence after I finished. Then I asked, "So you're saying Christ will return on the Feast of Trumpets?"

He laughed. "I'm not trying to say anything. What's the Bible saying?"

I reread the passages. "Well, it's not technically saying this is the Feast of Trumpets."

James gave a nod. "Yeah, that's true. So what is it saying?"

"It's saying there will be a trumpet sound when Christ descends and the dead rise."

"Yeah, and if you read the next verse in Thessalonians it talks about those who are still alive being caught up."

"Okay," I said. "I see what these verses say. So do *you* believe Christ will return on the Feast of Trumpets?"

James took in a deep breath. "Yeah, I do. I see enough connection in Scripture to believe that. There's some interesting teachings out there about it." He smiled to himself, seemingly humored by something, and continued, "There's this guy who does a pretty good teaching. Well, it's interesting. I don't know if I agree with everything he says. But his name's Gabriel . . . Gabriel Ansley. He's got a teaching about Jesus returning in 2028."

I wasn't expecting that. I guess what I mean is, I wasn't expecting James to be "one of those guys". Conspiracy nut led on by a false prophet. I knew that just about every year brought forth a new "prophet" claiming that "this was the end" and "Christ is coming back" on such and such date.

But James was still being friendly and unaggressive, so I saw no reason to be mean about it.

"Doesn't Scripture say that no man knows the day or the hour of Christ's return?" I asked him.

The corner of his mouth twitched, as if he was holding back a smile. He took another deep breath and leaned against the doorframe beside him, relaxing. He nodded. "Yeah. Yeah, it does say that."

I stared at him for an uncomfortable moment, until I realized he wasn't saying anything more.

Finally, I smiled. "So . . . doesn't that mean nobody's gonna know?"

"Well, yeah, no one will know the day or the hour," James said. "But there may be more to what Jesus is saying there. Some teachers say that expression is an idiom, like an expression in Hebrew, and it refers to the Feast of Trumpets. See Feast of Trumpets is the only feast day that happens on the first day of a month. It's the first day of the seventh month.

"Remember God's calendar works off the moon cycles. So every new month starts with the sighting of the new moon. They never knew exactly when the new moon would show itself. There was usually a window of one or two days when they would expect the new moon to appear and so they would have people watching for it, and if they saw the new moon in the sky, they would blow their shofars, which were like their trumpets, to announce they saw it. That announced the first day of the new month, and that designated the start of the Feast of Trumpets. So the Feast of Trumpets was known as the feast where no one knew the day or the hour. They didn't celebrate it until they actually saw the moon in the sky. Not until it actually came."

I didn't know that. I found it interesting.

"Okay," I said. "So what makes this guy so sure Christ is coming back in 2028?"

"Well he's got a whole thing on it, it's like ten videos on YouTube. Like I said, I don't know if I agree with all of it. I mean, it could be 2028. I hope it's 2028. I wanna see Messiah, you know?"

I couldn't help but chuckle. "Yeah, me, too."

"But he makes some interesting points. And there are some other teachers out there, too, who believe that Jesus is coming back pretty soon, and they go into it in their teachings. But the thing is, these feasts in Leviticus give us more insight than a lot of Christians think we can have. You gotta be open to the Father showing it to you through His Holy Spirit as you read through His Word."

I was dubious, but, then again, he had shown me some interesting things in Scripture already that I had never known. I had always considered myself relatively knowledgeable when it came to the Bible, at least on the "important" points. But here I was finding these fascinating connections between the feasts in Leviticus and Christ's death, burial, and resurrection that I had never realized before. What other sorts of connections lay within the Bible waiting to be discovered, connections that I had never seen before? I wanted to know.

Stuck on Trumpets

JAMES AND I TALKED about the next two fall feasts—Day of Atonement and the Feast of Tabernacles. He showed me some Scriptures and told me about some of his points of view around them. But at this point I was a bit transfixed with our discussion on the Feast of Trumpets, and I wasn't in a headspace to keep up with him on these special days in the same way I had been.

I understood the timing for each—the Day of Atonement takes place on the tenth day of the seventh month (Leviticus 23:27), and the Feast of Tabernacles starts on the fifteenth day of the seventh month and goes for seven days, and then there is an additional eighth day at the end (Leviticus 23:34–36). The Day of Atonement, the first day of the Feast of Tabernacles, and the eighth day after the Feast of Tabernacles are all set-apart gatherings. Also, the Day of Atonement is a day of fasting.

I also understood some of the general concepts that Scripture pointed to with these ideas. The Day of Atonement, among other things, appears throughout Scripture to be "the day of יהוה", a day of wrath and judgment. The Feast of Tabernacles points to God dwelling among His people.

But even with these basic ideas to start with for these special days, I couldn't really move forward in thinking about them. I suppose a large part of this was due to the idea that when Jesus said, "No man knows the day or the hour" (Matthew 24:36), that could be a reference to the Feast of Trumpets. I looked it up on my own, and I did find multiple sources connecting the two.

I was stuck on Feast of Trumpets because I had always assumed we could know nothing about Jesus's return. But here I was seeing that my assumptions may have been off base. I didn't particularly like the prospect of being wrong in this way, but if I wanted to maintain integrity in pursuing truth, I knew I couldn't simply discount the things I was hearing just because I didn't like the implications they carried. I had to see these ideas through before discounting them.

I also took it upon myself to revisit some other Scriptures. I knew that, in addition to the fact that Jesus said, "No man knows the day or the hour," the Bible also said that that day will come like a thief in the night. So even if "No man knows the day or the hour" was pointing to Feast of Trumpets, that still didn't explain the concept of that day coming like a thief in the night.

But when I looked into those verses, something registered for me in a way that it never had before. In 1 Thessalonians 5:1–3, Paul writes:

> Now, brothers, as to the times and the seasons, you do not need to be written to. For you yourselves know very well that the day of יהוה comes as a thief in the night. For when they say, "Peace and safety!" then suddenly destruction comes upon them, as labour pains upon a pregnant woman, and they shall not escape.

So *there* was the thief in the night piece.

But then I continued into verses 4–6:

> But you, brothers, are not in darkness, so that this Day should overtake you as a thief. For you are all sons of light and sons of the day. We are not of the night nor of darkness. So, then, we should not sleep, as others do, but we should watch and be sober.

Paul had continued in that section to say that "you, brothers, are not in darkness, so that this Day should overtake you as a thief."

Had I totally been misinterpreting this idea of Jesus's coming back being like a thief in the night?

I went back to Matthew 24 and reread that chapter. In the first half, Jesus talks about the signs of the times and the end of the age, the Great Tribulation, and the coming of the Son of Man. So even before I got into the piece where he tells us that no man knows the day or the hour, I had to ask, Why did Jesus spend so much time telling us about all these things? Did he want us to read about them and think about them?

In Matthew 24:36–44, Jesus says:

> "But concerning that day and the hour no one knows, not even the messengers of the heavens, but My Father only. And as the days of Noaḥ, so also shall the coming of the Son of Aḏam be. For as they were in the days before the flood, eating and drinking, marrying and giving in marriage, until the day that Noaḥ

entered into the ark, and they did not know until the flood came and took them all away, so also shall the coming of the Son of Adam be. Then two shall be in the field, the one is taken and the one is left. Two women shall be grinding at the mill, one is taken and one is left. Watch therefore, for you do not know what hour your Master is coming. And know this, that if the master of the house had known what hour the thief would come, he would have watched and not allowed his house to be broken into. Because of this, be ready too, for the Son of Adam is coming at an hour when you do not expect Him."

Mark 13 has a similar structure, and in Mark 13:32–37, Jesus says:

"But concerning that day and the hour no one knows, not even the messengers in heaven, nor the Son, but only the Father. Take heed, watch and pray, for you do not know when the time is – as a man going abroad, having left his house and given authority to his servants, and to each his work, and commanded the doorkeeper to watch. Watch therefore, for you do not know when the master of the house is coming – in the evening or at midnight, or at the crowing of the cock, or in the morning, lest, coming suddenly, he should find you sleeping. And what I say to you, I say to all: Watch!"

In Luke 21, after speaking on the coming of the Son of Man and the parable of the fig tree, Jesus says in verses 34–36:

"And take heed to yourselves, lest your hearts be weighed down by gluttony, and drunkenness, and worries of this life, and that day come on you suddenly. For it shall come as a snare on all those dwelling on the face of all the earth. Watch then at all times, and pray that you be counted worthy to escape all this about to take place, and to stand before the Son of Adam."

In all of these accounts, Jesus tells us to watch. I found it fascinating that he told us to watch so quickly after he told us that no one knows the day or the hour. Why would he tell us to do that right after telling us we don't know the day or the hour?

After reading these Scriptures carefully, it seemed clear to me. We don't know the specific day or hour that the Master will return, but if we watch, we may see indication that the time is drawing near. Not only that, but immediately before telling us that we should watch, Jesus lays out a whole bunch of stuff for us to specifically watch *for*.

Jesus tells us to watch because we do not know when the Master is coming. I realized I had been getting it backwards, from a "spirit of the matter" perspective. I knew that I didn't know when the Master is coming, but I had chosen to *not* watch in light of that. I regularly associated with Christians who would say we should always be watching. But if I'm honest, that was never truly the spirit of the matter within me, one that was watching eagerly for Christ's return.

Now I came to find that "no man knows the day or the hour" didn't necessarily mean "no man can know anything." I also came to understand that I wasn't supposed to be considering myself one upon whom the day of the Lord comes as a thief in the night. And finally, I came to realize I should *actually* be watching, not just saying, "We should always be watching," bearing in mind the things that Jesus told us in those portions of Scripture.

In a way, discovering these things came as a bit of a spiritual shock to my system. But it was in no way a bad one. It was like a jolt of joy, a renewed excitement in discovering new facets of my faith that I had been neglecting.

I decided I was going to watch that guy's videos, the one who was saying Jesus would return in 2028. Whereas before I would've succumbed to the disapproving Christian spirit immediately labeling such a teaching as "heresy", I now had a renewed appreciation for the importance of watching. I wanted to watch. I wanted to pay attention. Even if I didn't agree, perhaps there was something I needed to hear.

I wanted to be watchful, and here was an opportunity to be so. From what I had heard about the guy's teaching up to that point, there was nothing explicitly unbiblical about it. After all, the year 2028 is neither a day nor an hour.

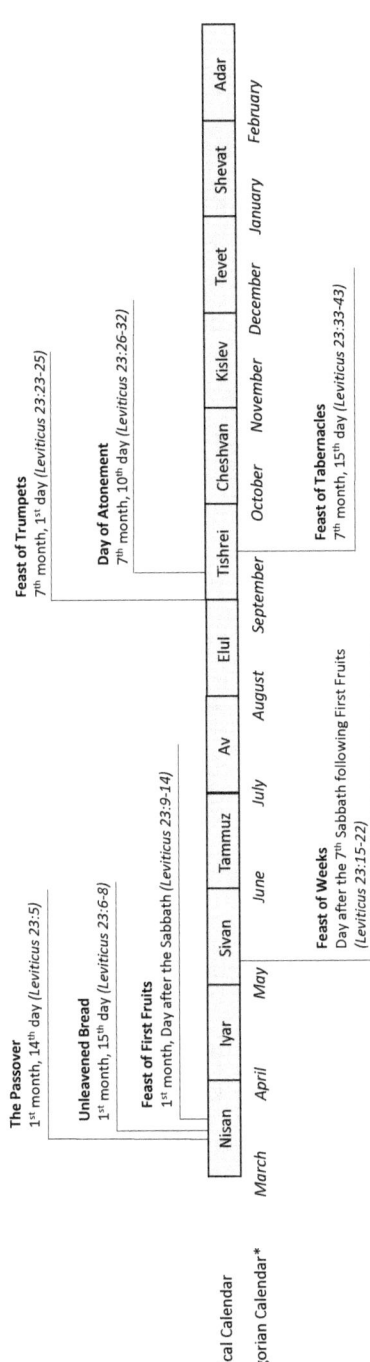

*The above schematic shows how the Biblical and Gregorian calendars overlap for the year 2021. However, since the Biblical calendar is on the lunar cycle, the months tend to be shorter (~28 days), so the overlap shifts accordingly each year.

Part 2

The Beginning and the End

Before You Feast on This Part

When you are listening to someone at a piano, there is a distinction that your mind makes between the person pressing random keys and the person playing an actual song. It is a bit of a spectrum. At the one end, you have nothing but random notes being played by the pressing of arbitrary keys. On the other, you have a classical masterpiece that so clearly carries an intentional melody. And then you have everything else in the middle, from "Silent Night" to Bill Murray blowing bubble gum in *Groundhog Day*.

This is how faith works for everybody. We each choose the point on the spectrum at which we decide we are listening to a song versus the random pressing of piano keys. There are some who might listen through the entirety of a perfectly performed "Canon in D" and still deny the existence of any melody. Others will insist that a song is being played upon hearing a single note. That is just the way it works with people and faith.

And that is the way the ideas I am going to present in this part seem to work, as well. Some may say these ideas are so clearly a 1+1=2 situation, and others will say they are a stretch of the imagination. All I am trying to say is, consider them for yourself. Consider them through this lens of random notes versus a song. I am not asking you to jump immediately to calling anything a masterpiece. I am not even asking you to ultimately accept any set of ideas as a song. I am only asking you to consider whether you can detect any sort of melody within all the ideas presented here. I am only asking that you approach with a spirit that is genuine and honest, and that you would be a lover of truth.

Humor Me

Part of me was laughing at myself as I started watching the first video.

I had looked up Gabriel Ansley and found his website, 2028end.com. I had scrolled to the first of ten videos in his video series, *2028 End of the World*.

And then I started it.

Fire formed the words, "2028 End: Are you ready for the end of the world?" Then Ansley appeared, and he asked, "Have you ever wondered when Jesus is going to return to planet earth? I mean it seems like every year someone is coming up with some reason why *that* will be the year."

He proceeded to list various people in recent history who predicted the end. Then he said none of that worried him, because he knew. He said the truth about when Jesus would return has been known since 2008, and it is contained in a book he wrote called *UNDENIABLE BIBLICAL PROOF THAT JESUS CHRIST WILL RETURN TO PLANET EARTH EXACTLY 2,000 YEARS AFTER THE YEAR OF HIS DEATH*.

I wondered if this was all a marketing campaign for his book. I determined that I wasn't going to buy anything, but if he was willing to give me an overview of his thoughts for free in these videos, I'd be willing to listen. I'm a pretty good listener, and I've always been able to listen respectfully and hear someone out fully even if I'm not on board with what they're saying.

I knew that if I told certain Christian friends and family that I was thinking about watching these videos it would be met with warnings and disapprovals. This in itself bothered me when I realized that I would feel more comfortable admitting in certain Christian circles that I had watched some graphic show or movie or even pornography than I would saying I had watched a video about a guy talking about Jesus Christ coming back in 2028. The Christianity I had been a part of had a selective grace and tolerance for those former things while maintaining a stringent condemnation and intolerance for the latter. That didn't sit well with me, particularly knowing that my heart on the issue was genuine in the way of wanting to seek out truth, knowing that there can be a process of sifting through falsity involved in order to glean grains of truth. I had spent my life guiltlessly watching all sorts of garbage prior—horror movies, reality TV, *Game of Thrones*. Why would I start pretending to be super prudent with what my mind consumed when it came to someone who was at least claiming to be basing his words on the Bible?

These were some of the thoughts going through my mind as I continued watching.

Now I am not intending to summarize his videos here, mostly because you can watch his videos for yourself, and I do not want to misrepresent what he says in any way. However, I am going to summarize the understanding I took away. Some of the points I am going to make come from my own understanding and not Ansley's videos. His videos include much of the information I will be sharing in this part, but there are some differing details, primarily within Days 6 and 7. For this reason, I encourage you to actually watch his videos before forming any kind of judgment about Ansley. I am more interested in considering the ideas than I am in considering Ansley.

If you are anything like most people I know (including myself not long ago), you are already done. Christian or non-Christian, you likely have your go-to reason or couple of reasons why you would go ahead and discount whatever I have to say next. I am plenty aware that there have been thoughts, claims, and theories all throughout the past two thousand years related to Jesus Christ returning. I am also aware that this reality presents a real challenge to the mind in terms of having a desire to hear yet another theory.

That is why my appeal to you, at this point, is nothing more than this: humor me for a few minutes. Please. Just allow me to pass along the things that I have heard and read thus far, and then you can test them for yourself.

I am asking you to humor me because I feel compelled to share these things. Not because of some doomsday mindset within me, but because I have grown closer to the Bible as a result of the process I have been going through. Consequently, I have been more driven to connect to God through prayer. Perhaps that is a "shame on me" kind of situation in which I have been weak in my faith. I am not trying to justify myself in any way. I am just trying to be genuine about my experience over the past two years.

And so I feel compelled to share these things with others because I believe simply taking the time to think through them will more often than not lead others to considering the Bible with a more thirsty spirit and connecting with God in a more desperate way.

I also believe that the circumstances of this world will become increasingly haywire leading up to Jesus's return (whenever that is), and it will only become more and more difficult to process these matters in the midst of increasing craziness.

So please, humor me for now. I know it sounds ridiculous. I know it sounds like conspiracy theory to some and apostacy to others. But I am not trying to argue with anyone. I am only trying to share out of love.

If you feel caught up on any specific point that would have you immediately discount everything, I encourage you to at least try and hear me out, that I might have a chance to get to and address that point. And if, by the end, I don't, then you have every liberty to reject it all. I know well the human tendency to respond by jumping around within our minds to different thoughts that we feel justified by or concerned about. I just encourage you to exercise patience and allow me to share with you the things which I have received through exercising patience on my own behalf.

If you do humor me for a bit, I think you will, among other things, enjoy this.

The Basic Idea

OKAY. SO HERE'S THE BASIC IDEA.

The days of creation in Genesis are both literal accounts of earth's creation and prophetic accounts of earth's timeline.

Wowza. Glad I got that Band-Aid ripped off.

I know, I know—science and stuff. Yes, we will talk about that, but let's just get through laying the foundational ideas for this belief first, just so we can say we have heard it out and have been fair to it before we simply dismiss it.

There are seven days in the creation account of Genesis. When we jump ahead to the end of the Bible, specifically to Revelation 20, we read about Jesus reigning for one thousand years on earth. Now again, this is one of those things that many Christians are prone to immediately discount, labeling the millennial reign as something figurative. I'm asking you to suspend any automatic dismissal in order to pay attention to the cohesion we find within the Bible when we begin to take it at its word, when we read it for what it says.

In Revelation 20, we read in verses 1–6:

> And I saw a messenger coming down from the heaven, having the key to the pit of the deep and a great chain in his hand. And he seized the dragon, the serpent of old, who is the Devil and Satan, and bound him for a thousand years, and he threw him into the pit of the deep, and shut him up, and set a seal on him, so that he should lead the nations no more astray until the thousand years were ended. And after that he has to be released for a little while. And I saw thrones – and they sat on them, and judgment was given to them – and the lives of those who had been beheaded because of the witness they bore to יהושע and because of the Word of Elohim, and who did not worship the beast, nor his image, and did not receive his mark upon their

> foreheads or upon their hands. And they lived and reigned with Messiah for a thousand years (and the rest of the dead did not come to life until the thousand years were ended) – this is the first resurrection. Blessed and set-apart is the one having part in the first resurrection. The second death possesses no authority over these, but they shall be priests of Elohim and of Messiah, and shall reign with Him a thousand years.

I would like to make note that these six verses call out "thousand years" five separate times, and there is another usage of "thousand years" in the next verse, as well. If we claim that this is a figurative period of time, we need to realize that we are explaining away as figurative something that is called out explicitly six times within seven consecutive verses. When we dismiss this as a figurative period of time, we set ourselves up to overlook some very striking connections elsewhere in Scripture that contribute to the Bible's overall cohesion.

Now when we look elsewhere in the Bible for the phrase "thousand years", we find two other verses that corroborate one another. Psalm 90:4 says:

> For a thousand years in Your eyes Are like yesterday that has past, Or like a watch in the night.

The second verse is in 2 Peter 3:8:

> But, beloved ones, let not this one matter be hidden from you: that with יהוה one day is as a thousand years, and a thousand years as one day.

I encourage you to read all the context around those verses, as well. Psalm 90 is Moses' psalm. When reading it, pay attention to the language around creation and the numbering of days. In 2 Peter 3, Peter is addressing the coming of the day of the Lord. The contexts for both verses play a role here.

But for the purpose of presenting the basic idea, I just want to highlight the use of the phrase "thousand years" in each. The idea in both these verses is that a thousand years are like a day in God's eyes.

Now even though this idea is presented twice, once in the Old Testament and once in the New Testament, by two different people, I know many Christians will do the same thing here and say, "It just means that God sees time differently than we do. It's not making a literal point about a thousand years." Once again, for the purpose of understanding the overall cohesion that the Bible has to offer, let's for now just pretend that it is supposed to be a literal point about a thousand years and see where it takes us. For the time being, let us suspend our immediate desire to write it off as figurative.

In Revelation we read about Jesus returning to reign for one thousand years. In Psalm 90 and 2 Peter 3, we read about a thousand years being like a day to God. Then, in Genesis 1 and 2, we read about the seven days within the creation account. Genesis 2:1–3 says:

> Thus the heavens and the earth were completed, and all their array. And in the seventh day Elohim completed His work which He had done, and He rested on the seventh day from all His work which He had made. And Elohim blessed the seventh day and set it apart, because on it He rested from all His work which Elohim in creating had made.

Then, verse 4 says:

> These are the births of the heavens and the earth when they were created, in the day that יהוה Elohim made earth and heavens.

Again, the basic idea is that the days of creation in Genesis are both literal accounts of earth's creation and prophetic accounts of earth's timeline. The key to understanding this idea is provided in 2 Peter 3:8 when it tells us that "with יהוה one day is as a thousand years, and a thousand years as one day."

To better explain what I mean by this, let's begin with the end.

When we look at Day 7, we're looking at the end of the timeline. It was the last day in the creation account. On Day 7, God ended His work and rested. He blessed the day and sanctified it. So if this is not just a literal account of creation but also a *prophetic account* of earth's timeline, then we can look at this day as being prophetic of the literal millennial reign of Christ, a thousand-year period that is blessed and sanctified by God.

Do you see what I'm getting at? The seventh day of creation (the set-apart day in which God rested) is prophetic of Christ's millennial reign spoken of in Revelation (a blessed and set-apart time for those who have been resurrected). Second Peter 3:8 gives us the key to understanding this connection, for to God "one day is as a thousand years."

The millennial reign has not occurred yet, not in the way that Scripture has presented it. This means that, according to this view, we are still living somewhere *within* this timeline.

It is not only Day 7 that is prophetic of events that are to happen on the earth. The idea is this: *every* day within the creation account provided in Genesis contains a prophecy about the most significant event to occur within a respective one-thousand-year period of earth's history. Day 1 contains prophecy about the first one-thousand-year period of earth's history, Day 2 contains prophecy about the second one-thousand-year period, and so forth. This means—and hold onto your hats for this one—that the total lifespan of the earth is presented in the Bible as being a period of seven thousand years. Do you see how we got there? A seven-day creation account provided by God, for whom one day is like a thousand years, and the seventh day representing Christ's millennial reign, means that the earth's history as we know it is existing in a period of six thousand years (six days of creation) leading up to the final (seventh) thousand-year period of Christ's millennial reign. Again, I know, science, and more science, and carbon dating, and things like that. But just go with me for a few more pages. This, to me, is where it really starts getting fun.

Day 1

I will italicize the prophecy piece in each verse for each creation day, as well as italicize prophecy fulfilment pieces in subsequent verses.

Genesis 1:4 says:

> And Elohim saw the light, that it was good. And *Elohim separated the light from the darkness.*

In Day 1 of the creation account, the prophecy piece is that God divided the light from the darkness. This is referring to Adam and Eve eating the fruit from the forbidden tree in the Garden of Eden. This event happened during the first set of one thousand years in human history according to the Bible. Light being separated from darkness in Day 1 of creation was prophetic of Adam and Eve eating the fruit sometime during the first one thousand years of earth's history.

Genesis 3:22–23 contains a direct fulfillment of this prophecy:

> And יהוה Elohim said, "See, *the man has become like one of Us, to know good and evil.* And now, lest he put out his hand and take also of the tree of life, and eat, and live forever..." *so* יהוה *Elohim sent him out of the garden of Ěḏen* to till the ground from which he was taken,

While it is true that we do not know how long Adam and Eve were in the Garden of Eden before eating this fruit, Genesis 5:5 reads:

> So all the days that Aḏam lived were nine hundred and thirty years, and he died.

I suppose one may argue that this number of years does not refer to Adam's time spent in the Garden of Eden leading up to eating the fruit. But why would we argue that? That mindset seems more eager to create questions needlessly than it is eager to seek understanding. Why would we not simply take "all the days that Adam lived" to mean "all the days that Adam lived"? Any reason for not taking it as it's written would be tied to human rationalization rather than what the Bible says.

Adam's age in Genesis 5:5 contributes to the belief that Day 1 of creation prophesied of the fall of man within the first one thousand years of human history. If Adam was the first man, and he did not live to be one thousand years old, then any event in his lifetime would be within the first one thousand years of human history according to the Bible.

What I found interesting about this creation day is the idea that Genesis 1:4 makes explicit mention of dividing the light from the darkness. As Ansley points out, "What's the point of that?" We intuitively know that light casts out darkness, so why explicitly say it?

We can get into a headspace of considering parts of the Bible to be esoteric or maintaining intentionally hidden meaning. I don't see a problem with that in itself. It becomes a problem when we insist that parts of the Bible are esoteric *only because* we feel threatened by someone else's explanation. If we don't know what something means, and someone tries to tell us what it means, we're not exactly in any position to tell them they're wrong about it. We can disagree with them. But if we can't come up with any possible explanation other than, "Some things aren't meant to be known," why would we feel so confident in insisting that somebody else is wrong?

Some things aren't meant to be known, but that is, grammatically speaking, a declarative statement. It is just stating a fact rather than commanding us to be a certain way. Seek after truth. That is, grammatically speaking, an imperative command. It's important to make this distinction, because when we get transfixed on the idea that the Bible holds intentionally hidden meaning, we get confused about what that means for us in terms of seeking truth. Some things aren't meant to be known, yes, but we should be seeking truth. The things that aren't meant to be known are determined by God, not us. Those things will remain unknown, no matter how hard we search. Our job is to discover the things that can be known and obey God when He commands us.

Sorry for that tangent, but I felt it was important.

Going back to the original question, then, why is this line about God dividing light from darkness part of the creation account in Genesis? The verses flow seamlessly when you take that piece out. While I am open to other explanations for why this verse is included, the most satisfying explanation I have heard is rooted in this prophecy idea, that God was making the point that in the first thousand years of human history, a distinction would be made within the human heart between good and evil, and this is exactly what happened when Adam and Eve ate the fruit.

I also have heard the idea that the phrase about God separating the light from the darkness is part of the text to demonstrate God's power, His omnipotence over everything. I understand the sentiment behind this explanation, but I also do not see what particular value that adds within the context of God already creating everything. I am not trying to be dismissive of it. I do think it is a good thought. But I do find further significance and meaning within the idea that the text might serve a prophetic purpose in addition to a statement around God's sovereignty.

As far as the idea of God using light and darkness to prophesy about good and evil, the first thing to note is the first half of Genesis 1:4. It says:

> And Elohim saw the light, that it was good.

This is the first thing the Bible calls "good", and it occurs immediately before God divided the light from the darkness.

Furthermore, we have many examples in the New Testament of light being associated with good, and darkness with evil. We read in John 8:12:

> Therefore יהושע spoke to them again, saying, "I am the light of the world. He who follows Me shall by no means walk in darkness, but possess the light of life."

Paul writes in Ephesians 5:8:

> For you were once darkness, but now you are light in the Master. Walk as children of light –

And again he writes in 1 Thessalonians 5:5:

> For you are all sons of light and sons of the day. We are not of the night nor of darkness.

These are all examples of the analogous relationship between light/darkness and good/evil, and they help connect this idea of God separating light and darkness in Genesis 1 with the idea of good and evil being separated in humanity's heart, and God sending sin-fallen man out of the Garden of Eden, out of His presence.

That is the Day 1 prophecy—God dividing the light from the darkness. It was prophesying the most significant event to occur during humanity's first one thousand years, which was the fall of man in the Garden of Eden.

Day 2

Genesis 1:6 says:

> And Elohim said, "*Let an expanse come to be in the midst of the waters,* and let it separate the waters from the waters."

If Day 2 is prophesying about the second one thousand years of earth's history, then that would be the period of time that started one thousand years after Year 0, the creation of Adam. This is where the genealogies in Scripture come into play. Many people look at these parts of Scripture as a drag, something to be waded through with no real clarity around why they are included in the Bible. I have heard explanations for why the genealogies are included in the Bible, explanations about the nature of historical oral history and about the idea of God loving His children so much He keeps a record of them by name.

Neither of these reasons, however, have ever done much to get me excited about reading the genealogies. I understand the reasoning, but at the end of the day, what am I supposed to be doing with the genealogies as an individual?

To be clear, I don't believe that our interpretation of Scripture should be based on the excitement of the particular interpretation. I just genuinely didn't know what to do with the genealogies. Was I supposed to read them, memorize them, know them in and out? Did God care if I just skimmed past them, or didn't even look at them at all?

When we look at this idea that God has a seven-thousand-year masterplan in mind for humanity on earth, suddenly there is a very clear reason behind the meticulous record keeping found in the genealogies of Scripture. While it does take a little work, you can read through the genealogies from Adam to Jesus and calculate an estimated number of years that takes place between the creation of Adam and the birth of Jesus based on Scripture.

When you do these calculations (and I invite you to), you will find that roughly 4000 years pass between the creation of Adam and the birth of Jesus. And based on our modern day calendar, we know that almost 2000 years have passed between the death of Jesus and where we are today (at the writing of this book in the year 2021). Thus, the Bible tells us the earth is approximately 6,000 years old.

I realize that this has become a point of ridicule from the world upon the Bible. People today who believe the earth is roughly six thousand years old based on literal interpretation of these genealogies are largely considered a joke among educated populations. I am not intending to affirm nor defend against that ridicule at this point, I only want to acknowledge its existence, and acknowledge that I am aware of the general perception.

That said, when we "humor" the idea that God has a seven-thousand-year masterplan (a one-thousand-year millennial reign of Christ preceded by a six-thousand-year history of earth) in mind for humanity on earth, these genealogies suddenly become more of a game than anything. I have personally found it fun finding the links of descendants, connecting the pieces, and adding up the numbers. But what I have found most interesting is the way in which the numbers within the genealogies line up with this seven-millennia idea.

So we've already presented Day 1 of creation, which prophesied about the first millennium, in which we see Adam and Eve eating the fruit. So what about Day 2? In Genesis 5:5, we read Adam lived to be 930 years before he died. If you continue reading Genesis 5 (and I encourage you to do so with a pen and paper, and maybe a calculator), you will read about Adam's descendants leading right up to Noah. If you do the math, calculating how old each descendant was when he had his subsequent son, you will find that, if Adam was created in Year 0, then Noah was born in Year 1056, officially within the next period of 1,000 years (Day 2). And then, if we jump ahead to Genesis 9:29, we read:

> So all the days of Noaḥ were nine hundred and fifty years, and he died.

If Noah was born in Year 1056 and he lived to be 950, then he died in Year 2006, nearly spanning the entirety of the second millennium, similar to Adam and the first millennium.

And yes, the prophesied event within creation Day 2 is the flood. The story of Noah's Ark and the flood is believed by many to be the first time it rained on earth. It certainly is the Bible's first account of rain. Genesis 2:4–6 tells us:

> These are the births of the heavens and the earth when they were created, in the day that יהוה Elohim made earth and heavens. Now no shrub of the field was yet on the earth, and no plant of the field had yet sprung up, for יהוה Elohim had not sent rain on the earth, and there was no man to till the ground, but a mist went up from the earth and watered the entire surface of the ground.

After the flood, God speaks to Noah. He tells Noah in Genesis 9:13:

> "I shall set My rainbow in the cloud, and it shall be for the sign of the covenant between Me and the earth."

God tells Noah using a rainbow that He will not destroy the earth again with a flood.

This brings up a couple questions.

First, why would it be important to establish this sort of covenant with Noah? We too often gloss over this as a "Hallmark moment" in the story—God was making a nice point, the rainbow is a nice thing, and it's all very nice. But there is a more visceral reason to this covenant. If this was the first time it ever rained on earth, can you imagine how terrified Noah and his family would have been the next time it started raining? They might have been tempted to book it back to the Ark, which was settled somewhere on top of Mount Ararat. God was comforting them with this covenant. It would rain again, but they need not worry about another flood. The appearance of a rainbow, either while it was still raining or after it had stopped, would have reminded Noah and his family that God wasn't flooding the earth again.

Second, if it had already rained on earth, what is the big deal about a rainbow? They would have likely already seen a rainbow in the sky—the rainbow is given by God as a natural phenomenon in our physical world. God's rainbow is a big event in this story, because this is the first time the "expanse", or sky, was "in the midst of waters" in this specific way. This is how Genesis 1:6 is prophesying about the flood during Noah's time.

So why is the flood the most significant event to happen during the second set of one thousand years recorded in the Bible?

Well, can you name any event during this time period that might compete with the flood in terms of significance? If you look at the genealogies for indication about what else happened during the second millennium of earth's history, according to the Bible, you will find Ham looking at the nakedness of his father, the birth of Abram at the very end of this one-thousand-year period, and, well, more genealogies. The birth of Abram is not the meat of Abraham's story, so by process of elimination, the flood seems to be our answer.

That still does not answer what is so significant about the flood. The answer is that the flood was in itself prophetic of Jesus Christ's second coming. In the same way that it was one family (Noah's family) being safe in the ark as the flood wiped out the rest of creation, there will be one family (Jesus's family) being safe in the heavens as fire wipes out the rest of creation. In the same way that the ark was laid back down on earth and Noah's family reinhabited the earth, Jesus's family will be laid back down on the earth and will reinhabit the earth during Christ's millennial reign (Revelation 20:1–6).

There is more to be said about the details of the flood story connecting it to Christ's second coming, but I just wanted to mention those few to give some understanding.

That is the Day 2 prophecy—God created an expanse (sky) in the midst of the waters. It was prophesying the most significant event to occur during humanity's second one thousand years, which was Noah's ark and the global flood.

Day 3

GENESIS 1:9 SAYS:

> And Elohim said, "*Let the waters under the heavens be gathered together into one place, and let the dry land appear.*" And it came to be so.

Day 3 prophesies the most significant event of the third set of one thousand years, which was Moses parting the Red Sea for the Israelites to pass through on dry land to escape the oppressive slavery of Egypt.

Exodus 14:21 says:

> And Mosheh stretched out his hand over the sea. And יהוה *caused the sea to go back* by a strong east wind all that night, and *made the sea into dry land*, and *the waters were divided*.

Also, Exodus 15:8 says:

> "And with the wind of Your nostrils *the waters were heaped up*, the floods stood like a wall, the depths became stiff in the heart of the sea."

To me, the connection for this day is very clear. Waters gathered, dry land appeared—this language applies to both the third creation day and the third set of one thousand years of human history, according to the Bible.

Perhaps it is a coincidence that the first day was about light/darkness and good/evil, the second day was about waters in the sky/the flood, and the third day was about waters gathering and dry land appearing. Separate from those connections, however, is this notion that each of those represents the most significant event to happen within its respective one-thousand-year span. So far, we have not had many events to choose from within the biblical accounts to be the most significant event of that millennium. The first millennium had a few, and the second had a few, as well. But now we have a lot of stuff happening during the third millennium, according to the Bible, starting with Abraham, going through Isaac, Jacob, and Joseph, and even including Moses and this business with the parting of the Red Sea.

So again, it may be just a coincidence that Day 3 mentions the waters gathering and dry land appearing, and the third millennium contains this miraculous event of the waters gathering and dry land appearing. But if this event is arguably the most significant event of the third millennium based on what we read in the Bible, are we still going to claim that it is all a coincidence? That is for you to decide, personally, whether you are hearing random notes or a song.

Is there any reason to believe that Moses parting the Red Sea is the most significant event of the third millennium? Yes, there is. Moses was freeing God's people from the bondage of slavery placed upon them by the Egyptians. Whereas the story of Noah prophesied Jesus's *second* coming, the story of Moses prophesied Jesus's *first* coming, in particular his death on the cross.

Back in Exodus 14:21, the first part of the verse says, "And Mosheh stretched out his hand over the sea." Jesus stretched out his arms on the cross. Moses parted the Red Sea, and Jesus's death tore the temple veil in two. Just like Moses was freeing God's people from the bondage of slavery placed upon them by the Egyptians, Jesus was freeing God's people from the bondage of slavery placed upon them by sin.

Through Moses, God was creating a physical picture of a spiritual reality that took place through Jesus. Hold onto this thought, because there is more to come on the story of Moses and the Israelites, and it is perhaps the most important matter of it all for us to be clear on. But because I want to be clear with all of this, I do not want to tangent here. I want to finish laying this foundation in order to be completely clear.

That is the Day 3 prophecy—God gathered the waters and dry land appeared. It was prophesying the most significant event to occur during humanity's third one thousand years, which was Moses parting the Red Sea.

Day 4

GENESIS 1:16 SAYS:

> And *Elohim made two great lights: the greater light to rule the day, and the lesser light to rule the night,* and the stars.

Before I even get into any explanation about this piece, can we just agree that this is a weird direction to take a creation story in at this point? I mean, I thought we dealt with the whole light thing in Day 1. After that, we got into the sky and the water, and then we saw the dry land appearing because the waters were gathered together. Why is it that *only now* we are revisiting light? It almost seems irresponsible of God, to divide light and darkness, switch His focus to the water, sky, and land, and then go back to dealing with light. Why not just take care of light, all the way through, before moving into focusing on smaller matters like water, sky, and land?

It is rather confusing, until we consider it to be a part of prophecy. And here is where I get really tickled by it all. Up until now, we might say that it has been Moses running the show. Tradition holds that Moses wrote the first five books of the Bible, which means that he would have written both Genesis and Exodus. So, technically, Moses could have been some literary genius orchestrating a collection of writings in which he both set up and fulfilled "prophecy". It would be like me writing a book that said, "He will be named Daniel," and then writing another book that said, "My name is Daniel." Basically, if we wanted to take on a humanistic skeptic approach up to this point, we could, because Moses was the one writing it all down. But at this point, the fourth set of one thousand years, we can no longer do that. Moses is not part of this period, and any writing that might fulfil the prophecy within Day 4 of creation cannot be attributed to Moses, who wrote down the creation account in Genesis 1.

So what is it? What is the prophecy in Day 4?

DAY 4

It is Jesus and John the Baptist. Again, based on biblical genealogies, we can estimate four thousand years between Adam and Jesus. If Jesus died on Year 4,000 after creation, that would put his and John the Baptist's lives in the fourth one thousand years (Day 4).

John 1:4–8 says:

> In Him was life, and the life was the light of men. And the light shines in the darkness, and the darkness has not overcome it. There was a man sent from Elohim, whose name was Yoḥanan [John]. *This one came for a witness, to bear witness of the Light,* that all might believe through him.

John 1:32 says:

> And *Yoḥanan bore witness*, saying, "I have seen the Spirit coming down from heaven like a dove and remain on Him."

John bore witness to Jesus. This is the relationship of the moon to the sun. As you may have learned in some astronomy or other science class in school, the moon is not a light source, in that the moon does not emit light. The only reason we can see the shining silvery glow of the moon at night is because it is reflecting the light of the sun. The moon bears witness to the sun's light.

In addition to what we just saw in John 1:3 about Jesus being light, we read in John 8:12:

> Therefore יהושע spoke to them again, saying, "*I am the light of the world.* He who follows Me shall by no means walk in darkness, but possess the light of life."

Just as the moon bears witness to the light of the sun, John bore witness to Jesus. Also, John 8:12 further supports the prophetic language in Day 1, in which God divided the light from the darkness—Jesus calls out that the one who follows him will have the light of life and will not walk in darkness.

Pay close attention to the two lights that God establishes in Genesis 1:16—the *greater* light to rule the day and the *lesser* light to rule the night. In John 3:30, John the Baptist speaks one of his few lines in all of Scripture:

> "It is right for Him [Jesus] to increase, but me [John] to decrease."

John explains that Jesus should be greater, and he should be less.

So, to review, the creation account includes a greater light and a lesser light being established on Day 4, and then during the fourth one-thousand-year period of human history, according to the Bible, we have John the Baptist bearing witness to Jesus, who calls himself the light of the world.

More notes, or any trace of a song here?

If you are still only hearing notes, then I have to ask, can you at least admit that this is turning into a very strange coincidence? Again, it'd be one thing if the days of creation in Genesis 1 just happened to be connected to those events that occurred in each of their associated millennia. But it's another level to add in the reality that these events are the most significant events to occur during their respective thousand-year period. And now that we've come to Day 4, there shouldn't be any argument about whether this was the most significant event of the fourth millennium—it's talking about Jesus.

That is the Day 4 prophecy—God made two great lights, the greater to rule the day, and the lesser to rule the night. It was prophesying the most significant event to occur during humanity's fourth one thousand years, which was John the Baptist bearing witness to Jesus Christ, and Jesus Christ, the promised Messiah, showing up, the light of the world.

Day 5

Genesis 1:20 says:

> And Elohim said, "*Let the waters teem with shoals of living beings*, and let birds fly above the earth on the face of the expanse of the heavens."

Acts 2:38 says:

> And Kĕpha [Peter] said to them, "Repent, and let each one of you *be immersed* in the Name of יהושע Messiah for the forgiveness of sins. *And you shall receive the gift of the Set-apart Spirit.*"

The prophecy within creation Day 5 is within the waters teeming with shoals of living beings, and it is fulfilled in the fifth set of one thousand years, the period immediately following Jesus's first coming, when the Holy Spirit comes upon new believers after they are baptized. In other words, those who repented and were immersed in water (baptized) in the name of Jesus Christ received the gift of the Holy Spirit, which is the gift of new life within. In this way, the waters during the fifth set of one thousand years in human history were teeming with living beings—Christians.

After his resurrection, Jesus says in Matthew 28:19–20:

> "Therefore, go and make taught ones of all the nations, immersing them in the Name of the Father and of the Son and of the Set-apart Spirit, teaching them to guard all that I have commanded you. And see, I am with you always, until the end of the age." Amĕn.

This prophecy described one large event that was actually a culmination of many events—baptisms of believers from all nations receiving the Holy Spirit. These baptisms all pointed to this idea that the waters would bring forth life.

Also, Mark 1:10 says (this is immediately after John the Baptist baptizes Jesus):

> And immediately, coming up from the water, He saw the heavens being torn open and the Spirit coming down on Him *like a dove*.

Genesis 1:20 includes the waters teeming with living beings *and* the birds that fly above the earth. I find it very interesting that the Holy Spirit is likened to a dove coming down upon Jesus after his baptism. We can see a full connection here with the creatures in creation Day 5—the waters teeming with living being (believers being baptized) and the birds that fly above the earth (the Holy Spirit coming upon the believers).

That is the Day 5 prophecy—God telling the waters to teem with shoals of living beings. It was prophesying the most significant event to occur during humanity's fifth millennium, which was the collective baptisms of repentant believers in Christ leading them to receive the gift of the Holy Spirit, new life.

Day 6

Genesis 1:24 says:

> And Elohim said, "*Let the earth bring forth the living being according to its kind*: livestock and creeping creatures and beasts of the earth, according to its kind." And it came to be so.

If you are keeping up with the respective dates, you realize we are now looking at the most recent one-thousand-year period of human history, according to the Bible, which is the sixth set of one thousand years. We have established some pretty major events along our timeline so far:

- Year 0–1000: The creation of Adam and the fall of man
- Year 1001–2000: The flood and Noah's ark
- Year 2001–3000: The parting of the Red Sea and the deliverance of the Israelites from slavery
- Year 3001–4000: John the Baptist pointing the way, the birth and death of Jesus
- Year 4001–5000: Many believers in Jesus receiving new life through baptism in the Holy Spirit

If Jesus died four thousand years after the creation of Adam (roughly around the year 30 AD), then that means we are looking at this most recent period of one thousand years to be roughly dated from 1030 AD to 2030 AD. I do not believe those to be correct specific dates. I am just trying to provide the general timeframe. Regardless which specific year we choose, though, we are currently living around the end of the sixth one-thousand-year period of earth's history.

So what is the prophesy within Day 6 that gets fulfilled in the sixth millennium? It is the earth bringing forth the living creature according to its kind.

I'm not quite ready to really unpack this one yet—there's quite a bit I need to cover first.

But there are some things I do want to share here about this one. Things that I find fascinating. I don't believe any of these things are the most significant prophetic fulfilment for creation Day 6, but we will get to that in time.

First, over the past thousand years, man has spread all throughout the earth in a more major way than in any time past. This one-thousand-year period is the first time in human history that mankind has ever circumnavigated the globe (roughly 500 years ago with Magellan's expedition). It is also the period during which humanity's population has sprung from millions to billions, an exponential leap unlike previous millennia. I encourage you to Google "human population growth throughout history" and scroll through the images. You'll find charts depicting exponential spikes in the last couple hundred years. I believe there is some prophetic meaning in the words, "Let the earth bring forth the living being . . . " related to this idea of human population growth and spread throughout the world during this millennia. But, again, I don't think this is the main prophecy of Day 6.

Also, we have the animals of the earth on Day 6, as well as man. I want to call particular attention to "the beast of the earth". Revelation 13 speaks of a beast from the sea and a beast from the earth. Revelation 13:11 reads:

> And I saw another beast coming up out of the earth, and he had two horns like a lamb and spoke like a dragon.

And then, in Revelation 13:18, it reads:

> Here is the wisdom! He who has understanding, let him calculate the number of the beast, for it is the number of a man, and his number is six hundred and sixty six.

It is interesting how the number of the beast, which is the number of man, is composed of 6, and it is creation Day 6 that speaks to the earth bringing forth beasts. It is something worth considering.

But why am I talking about the beast here? What is this all about?

It is all about "the end times", the days leading up to Christ returning to earth. When you read through Scripture, there is a lot of cryptic-sounding language throughout the prophets (such as Isaiah and Daniel), and the Gospels (Matthew and Mark), and Paul's letters (1 and 2 Thessalonians), and John's Revelation. When you start paying attention to the various details, you begin to see certain trends.

One of the major cautions you may hear from many Christians is to not get carried away with looking into these things. I agree with the idea of not getting "carried away", though I suppose we should consider what we are meaning when we say that. However, I do not think that is reason to not look into these things at all. I believe there is an appropriate level of attention we ought to be paying to these things, for they are in the Bible, the book that we hold to be God's Word.

That said, when you look at the trends that occur throughout various books concerning the end times, you begin to put some of the pieces together. The beast is part of this end-time narrative, having a role here on earth leading up to Christ's return.

I'm not trying to explain the beast here (who he is, what he looks like, etc.). The reason I'm talking about it is to make the point that the Bible speaks of a beast to come, and I believe that the coming of that beast is in connection with this Day 6 prophecy.

That's all I'm going to say for now about the Day 6 prophecy. Keep these things in the back of your mind, and we will revisit them later.

Day 7

AND SO NOW we're back where we started with this, at Day 7.
Genesis 2:2 says:

> And in the seventh day *Elohim completed His work which He had done, and He rested on the seventh day* from all His work which He had made.

So according to this paradigm, God has been working on this earth for the past six thousand years to accomplish this immaculately foretold story written in the Bible, and Genesis 2:2 is prophesying that He will end this work on the seventh day, or the seventh one-thousand-year period of earth's history.

Revelation 20:6 says:

> Blessed and set-apart is the one having part in the first resurrection. The second death possesses no authority over these, but they shall be priests of Elohim and of Messiah, and shall reign with Him a thousand years.

Paul writes in 1 Corinthians 15:22–26:

> For as all die in Adam, so also all shall be made alive in Messiah. And each in his own order: Messiah the first-fruits, then those who are of Messiah at His coming, then the end, when He delivers up the reign to Elohim the Father, when He has brought to naught all rule and all authority and power. For He has to reign until He has put all enemies under His feet. The last enemy to be brought to naught is death.

Read those portions of Scripture carefully. Those who belong to Christ will be made alive *at his coming*. This is the first resurrection. It takes place at Christ's second coming, and those who take part in it will reign with Christ a thousand years. Christ must reign until he has put all enemies under His feet. The last enemy to be destroyed is death. And then Christ will deliver the kingdom to God the Father.

If Christ's millennial reign begins at the beginning of Day 7, that means Christ returns at the end of Day 6/the sixth set of one thousand years. During Christ's millennial reign, he will put all enemies under his feet. The last enemy to be destroyed is death. At the end of his reign, Christ will hand the kingdom over to God, his Father. This will put an end to all the work he has done, and he will rest. This will be the fulfilment of Day 7.

So to recap, the sixth set of one thousand years is sometime around 1030 AD to 2030 AD, meaning that, as of today (2021), the beast will come (if it hasn't already) sometime during the next decade or so, and Jesus will return shortly thereafter to reign for one thousand years. According to this paradigm.

That is the Day 7 prophecy—God ended His work which He had done. It is prophesying the most significant event to occur during humanity's seventh one thousand years, which has not yet occurred. The most significant event will be God ending His work through Christ (destroying death) and resting.

Now one thing to note here is that this view of a literal millennial reign is not new. This is referred to today as "premillennialism", and many of the early church fathers maintained this view. Ansley goes into more detail with this in part three of his video series by looking at writings from some of the early church fathers—Barnabus, Irenaeus, Hippolytus, and Lactantius. I encourage you to look into this more on your own, but I just wanted to mention it here to let you know that this view is not something new or recently invented.

I believe most Christians (at least out of those who have a perspective on the matter) do not believe in a literal millennial reign. Some of them point to the idea that Christ already conquered death, and therefore the discussions about his reign are pointing to a more figurative idea. We need to be mindful, though, of the difference between conquering and destroying. Jesus did conquer death. But if we try to argue that death has already been destroyed, then we're kind of going out of our way to be figurative about everything. Death has not been destroyed, and we know this. People are still dying. If we try to make the claim that it's referring to spiritual death, I would say the same thing. Spiritual death has not been destroyed, and we know this, as well. People are still at risk of dying spiritually.

Death has not yet been destroyed. When we read these verses in 1 Corinthians and Revelation and say that it's all just figurative, we're taking some very audacious liberties. I wonder why we're doing that. I can't help but feel like it is tied to a lack of faith. There's no risk where there's no substance.

Immediate Questions

So this is the basic layout for the belief that the days of creation in Genesis contain prophesies surrounding their respective millennia (with Year 0 being the year of creation):

Day	Creation Account	Prophetic Timing in Earth's History	Prophetic Meaning
1	Light/darkness	Year 0–1,000	Fall of man, Good/evil
2	Sky in the waters	1,001–2,000	Noah's Ark, Flood
3	Waters gathered and dry ground appearing	2,001–3,000	Moses parting the Red Sea
4	Two lights to govern the day and night	3,001–4,000	Jesus, John the Baptist
5	Waters teeming with shoals of living beings	4,001–5,000	Baptism, Holy Spirit
6	Earth, living creature, beast	5,001–6,000	Humanity, The Beast, ???
7	God ended His work	6,001–7,000	Christ Destroys Death at the end of His Millennial Reign

The first question I had when being presented with this information was, Is there any biblical reason to think that each of the creation days may represent a period of one thousand years?

Then I recalled that yes, there is. Both Psalm 90:4 and 2 Peter 3:8 tell us that a day is as a thousand years to God.

The second question I had was, Is there any biblical reason to believe the first chapter of Genesis is prophetic of humanity's timeline?

Once again, the answer is yes.

Isaiah 46:9–10 says:

> "Remember the former events of old, for I am Ĕl, and there is no one else – Elohim, and there is no one like Me, declaring the end from the beginning, and from of old that which has not yet been done, saying, 'My counsel does stand, and all My delight I do,'"

It says that God declares the end from the beginning. Think through what that means—from the time of the beginning, God declared the end. The prophetic view of Genesis 1 not only aligns with this idea but supports it.

So yes, there is biblical *reason* to consider each day of creation to be a one-thousand-year period, and there is also biblical *reason* to believe the first chapter of Genesis is prophetic of humanity's timeline. I will concede that you or others may not find the reasons to be compelling. I am only trying to make the point that if God intended the days of creation in Genesis to be prophetic, He did not leave us with absolutely no reason to consider them in this way. Put another way, if He intended them to be prophetic, He also provided reason elsewhere in Scripture to consider the possibility that they might be prophetic.

The third question I had was, Why?

If God prophesied humanity's timeline from the very beginning, why are we only now finding out about it, right before it seems some really crazy stuff is going to happen? And what is the point of knowing about it if I am already a believer in Jesus Christ?

That question has been the most common one I've heard from people when we talk about this stuff: what is the point of all this if I'm already a Christian?

I have some strong feelings tied to my answer for that question. I only want to address it here to say that I intend to talk about it, but not quite yet, so please hold onto it for now.

Likewise with my next question, perhaps the most difficult one for many to move past: what about science and the age of the earth? This is another question I want to get into, but I'm trying to be orderly with how I present everything, and certain pieces of this require more than a quick couple of sentences. So please bear with me as I work towards getting there.

Why 2028?

AGAIN, REGARDING THE DAYS of creation being prophetic, this has been a presentation of my understanding that spring boarded from Ansley's video series. Most of what I have presented has been the understanding I have gained from Ansley's videos, with some exceptions.

That said, I need to point out that Ansley is very clear that Jesus Christ is returning on Feast of Trumpets 2028. Again, even with this proclamation, we don't know the day or the hour because we cannot know which day Feast of Trumpets is each year until it arrives. Remember, Feast of Trumpets occurs on the first day of the seventh month of God's calendar, and the first day of the seventh month is determined by the first sighting of the moon in the sky, which could be one of potentially three days.

So why does Ansley say it will be 2028?

In Matthew 24:32–34, Jesus says:

> "And learn this parable from the fig tree: When its branch has already become tender and puts forth leaves, you know that the summer is near. So you also, when you see all these, know that He is near, at the doors. Truly, I say to you, this generation shall by no means pass away until all this takes place."

This is the same section of Scripture in which Jesus is talking about the coming of the Son of Man, and the same place he says that no one knows the day or the hour.

Throughout Scripture, the nation of Israel is represented by or connected to figs or a fig tree. You can read Jeremiah 8:13, Jeremiah 24, Hosea 9:10, and Joel 2:21–25 for some examples.

Because of this representation, we can understand Jesus's words as meaning, "When we see the nation of Israel come forth again, we can know that the time is near."

Israel ceased being a nation before the time of Jesus, and for nearly two thousand years after Jesus there continued to be no nation of Israel. And then, on May 14, 1948, Israel was proclaimed a nation, and it has been a nation to this day.

In that same portion of Scripture, Jesus also says that "this generation" won't pass until these things take place. In other words, the generation that is alive when the nation of Israel returns will not pass away until all the things Jesus is speaking of take place.

When we go back to Psalm 90, the same psalm that tells us that a thousand years in God's sight are like a day, we read in verse 10:

> The days of our lives are seventy years; Or if due to strength, eighty years, Yet the best of them is but toil and exertion; For it is soon cut off, and we fly away.

Since Scripture tells us that by reason of strength our days might be eighty years, Ansley makes the case that 2028 will serve as the fulfillment of Jesus's words. If Israel became a nation in 1948, then 2028 would be eighty years later, and the generation that was alive in 1948 will not have passed away when 2028 comes. This would fulfill Jesus's words, "Truly, I say to you, this generation shall by no means pass away until all this takes place." In this context, "all this" is all the events leading up to the return of Jesus.

As a note, 2028 also is a feasible fulfillment of the seven-millennia structure with regard to our common calendar. If Jesus died on the cross around 28 AD, which is not a historical stretch of the imagination, then that would put his life and ministry (pre-death) and the life and ministry of John the Baptist in the fourth set of one thousand years (Day 4). The sixth set of one thousand years (Day 6) would then end two thousand years later, on 2028 AD.

Earlier I gave a more general timeframe, saying the sixth set of one thousand years is sometime around 1030 AD to 2030 AD. Ansley is very clear and straightforward about the year being 2028.

I presented the timeframe more generally because I don't want anyone to immediately write off the whole view simply because they may disagree with the specific reasoning around 2028. You may have doubts or reservations about the specific 2028 piece, but I hope, if that is you, that you can still see these fascinating connections that would otherwise have to be some pretty astounding coincidences.

I mean think about it. Israel wasn't a nation for more than two thousand years, and then, lo and behold, it is pronounced a nation eighty years almost exactly before the sixth one-thousand-year period ends, according to biblical genealogies. And according to this model, Jesus will return at the end of the sixth one-thousand-year period, and he said to look for the fig tree, when its branch becomes tender and puts forth leaves, to know that the time is near.

This model is either true or eerily coincidental. I hope we can at least agree on that.

When you start looking into these things more, you begin to find other teachers unaffiliated with Ansley teaching models with similar components. I say this to make the point that the framework here transcends any one person's ability to make creative claims. These fascinating connections are rooted in Scripture, not in isolated creative genius.

This is why I presented the general timeframe as opposed to 2028 specifically. Personally, I'm on board with 2028. And as far as I'm concerned, the sooner Jesus comes back, the better. But there is an entire structure at play here, revealed through the Bible, and the specific year in which Christ returns is just one piece of it. Granted, it is an extremely relevant and important piece to understand, but if you can't see the larger structure at play, then you won't have clarity around that specific piece anyway. You must have an appreciation for the overall framework before you can have an appreciation for any specific year.

Once you're able to appreciate the structure of this model, please go and watch Ansley's videos before coming to any conclusions about his ideas based on what I've said here. Test his words for yourself.

I Ended Up Reading Ansley's Book

AFTER I HAD watched the videos and had some conversations with James about them, I read Ansley's book: *UNDENIABLE BIBLICAL PROOF THAT JESUS CHRIST WILL RETURN TO PLANET EARTH EXACTLY 2,000 YEARS AFTER THE YEAR OF HIS DEATH.* It felt weird carrying that around.

I read it, and I really appreciated it. I'm not going to say much about it in a detailed way, because it's his book. I will say, though, that the overarching message was aligned with what the prophets throughout the Bible preached. Now don't put words in my mouth here. All I'm saying is that the message of the book was consistent with the message of the prophets.

Repent. Turn from evil and obey the commandments of God.

Ansley's book has a lot of really good stuff in it. He dives into the Bible and looks at how Jesus and the Ten Commandments and the Holy Spirit and other major themes are all connected. A lot of what he says runs counter to some mainstream Christian doctrine today. We will get into more of that later, but the point I'm trying to make here is we should take every teaching we receive and test it against the Bible for ourselves.

Reading his book was my way of testing his teachings. After watching the video series, I found his message intriguing. It was in reading his book, and comparing it to what the Bible said, that I found his message to be loving and truthful.

He emphasized the importance of following the Ten Commandments, and he went into each commandment individually, including the fourth commandment, remember the Sabbath and keep it holy.

It was strange to have just recently started observing the Sabbath. I felt like that decision started me on a journey that had now come full circle in a way. As I read through the book and contemplated the various ways in which his words differed from much of current Christianity, I began to realize that I had a lot of issues with today's mainstream Christian doctrine, myself.

By the way, in case you're thinking, "Ah, his marketing campaign worked on you. You did get his book," I'll just say this. I've had some email exchanges with him, and from what I've seen in our interactions, he is a man seeking to serve God. I realize that probably does nothing to convince you of anything, but I just wanted to share it, because I am very grateful for his service. When I reached out to him to ask if he was okay with me sharing his message in my book, this was the first line of his response:

> Sure, Daniel, no problem at all. This whole message is God's anyway. I'm nothing. So you can talk about it all you want.

In one of his videos, Ansley says, "The church hates me." I had already assumed it, but hearing him say it himself made me really sad. I continued to realize that I had some major issues with today's church. I believe that a lot of people out there, if they are honest, would say the same thing.

Part 3

THE LAW OF RELIGION

Before You Feast on This Part

WHILE I WAS working for the rescue mission in Raleigh, I also began working for a 24/7 prayer line. I would sign in from home and be available for my designated shift for any callers calling in to receive prayer.

I started working this prayer line towards the end of 2020, which made for a very interesting time to start this sort of thing. Not only was America wrapping up a year of COVID quarantining and social justice reckoning, but we were entering into one of the most bizarre presidential elections in American history. I could describe the sorts of calls I received, the obscure prayer requests and all the opinionated accusations, but I think the overarching narrative of that time speaks for itself. It was a weird and polarizing period.

The point that really got hammered home for me, though, was the fact that the most intense polarization of that time seemed to be coming from *within* Christianity. Understand what I mean here. I am not saying the most intense polarization came *from* Christianity. It came from *within*. One Christian furiously insisted on ABC, another demanded XYZ, and they hated each other for their difference in opinion.

For a while, I worked the prayer line from midnight to four A.M. I prayed with some incredibly kind people, but I also spoke with a lot of really mean Christians. I had spoken with mean Christians before, but there was something different about being on the other end of a prayer line, receiving calls from self-professed followers of Jesus who were out to pick a fight.

I don't believe we should make blanketing judgments about an institution based on individual outliers who subscribe to the institution. But when a certain behavior is no longer reflective of the outlier, and is instead reflective of the norm, it is reasonable to think that the cause of the behavior is rooted in the institution and not just the individual.

We need to be mindful of the Christian religion in this way. I am not talking about faith in Jesus. I am talking about the institution of Christianity. We celebrate the Gospel being spread and more and more people coming to know Jesus. But while this religion is swelling up with angry people who are looking for a fight, are we willing to be critical of the institution for the purpose of correcting the spirit of the matter? Or is the institution in our eyes on the level of God, blameless and beyond reproach?

Wrestle with God

NOT LONG AFTER I watched Ansley's videos on the prophetic days of creation, I came across another video on YouTube: *#1 – Torah Parashah Bereshit – Hidden Prophecies in Creation!* posted by Assembly of Called-Out Believers. In this video, the teacher, Pastor Isaac, gives a teaching that includes the prophetic account of the days of creation. As far as I could tell, he was in no way affiliated with Ansley, but, with a notable exception which I will address below, his message was strikingly aligned. This made it all the more intriguing for me.

In his teaching, Pastor Isaac broke down some of the Hebrew in Genesis and unpacked even further prophetic meaning within the first chapter of the Bible.

The notable difference in Pastor Isaac's teaching on the days of creation prophecies is regarding Day 4. Remember, Day 4 speaks of two lights, the greater to rule the day, and the lesser to rule the night. Pastor Isaac indicates King David as the lesser light (as opposed to John the Baptist), one who foreshadowed and thereby witnessed to the coming of the greater light, King Yeshua (Jesus).

I find both views on the lesser light compelling. I wanted to point this out to further the idea I was making in Part 2 around taking issue with the specific year. Even though Ansley and Pastor Isaac differed on a specific point, the overall structures of their teachings were more aligned than not. Even though there was technically a discrepancy between them, I came away with the bigger idea that their teachings corroborated rather than discounted one another.

Why am I bringing this up? Because the Bible offers a journey for every person, and none of us can simply jump to the end of that journey by listening to the right preacher or reading the right commentary. I believe that God used the name He gave to Jacob (Israel) for His people because of the name's meaning. In Genesis 32, Jacob wrestles with God through the night, after which Jacob is given the name "Israel", meaning "wrestles with God" or "struggles with God". We often think of wrestling with God to be something God wouldn't want us to do. But that is the name He chose to give to His people, the ones who were to be a light to the rest of the world.

I believe that's a clear message to us. Why would God want people to wrestle with Him? Because that is how we grow and develop. That is how we reconcile the spiritual hardship of being caught between our yearning for abundant life and our sin-fallen reality.

If God is perfect holiness, perfect set-apartness, and we are living in a sin-fallen world, then engaging with God is, at its very essence, wrestling with God. Sin has caused us to be blinded to truth, and God is truth. Therefore, when we read truth from God's Word, the Bible, it doesn't immediately line up with what we understand truth to be. Choosing faith means choosing to believe that we are deceived in some way and that God's Word is truthful and is the solution to our deception.

There is a whole other discussion to be had about translation and version issues, but here I'm getting at the overall essence of the Bible. Just like Ansley and Pastor Isaac might disagree on particular points, their teachings point to the same big ideas. This is the same truth when applied to different translations, or versions, of the Bible. Different versions lead to different conclusions about the more granular details. But when you read the entire Bible *for what it says*, and you do this with multiple versions, you find consistency and repetition around the broader, more overarching teachings. The Bible calls us to repent of sin, obey God, and put our trust in Jesus.

It is not always easy to repent, obey, and put our trust in something or someone other than our own understanding. That is why it is a wrestling match. God is calling us to engage with Him through His Word, which He has given to us to be a beacon of light in the midst of a darkened reality.

When I read the Bible, I recognize the areas in which it differs with the messaging of the world around me. I wrestle with God by seeking to understand why the Bible says what it says in those areas. I may never reach a full understanding, but I commit myself to wrestling through the whole night.

God's people are those who will wrestle with Him. He has the truth and He is trying to tell us the truth, but He knows our minds are misled into believing false truths. So He challenges us with His Word to wrestle with Him. The only options are wrestling with Him or walking away from Him. We're not going to beat Him either way. But if we wrestle with Him, He will bless us, and the truth will set us free.

Considering Our Holy Days

I WATCHED ANOTHER YOUTUBE video around this time called "Why Hanukkah IS Biblical" from Triumph in Truth ministries. The teacher, Gary Simons, used Scripture to make the case that Hanukkah is biblical. He also addressed the Roman holidays celebrated by Christianity (like Christmas and Easter) and talked about how believers in Yeshua (Jesus) should not celebrate those holidays.

I had known Christians who didn't celebrate Christmas or Easter, but I had never taken time to consider that point of view. Whenever I encountered that perspective, I had written it off as some form of religious extremism, but I had never given it any real thought.

I loved Christmas. I loved Easter. They were my two favorite days of the year, and I had no desire to stop celebrating them. I could go on for pages gushing over my favorite Christmas and Easter memories, all of the Christmas Eves and egg hunts, all of the presents and goodies.

But I was in the middle of a spiritual journey at this point. I wanted to know what was pleasing to God and, therefore, what the Bible said, even if it meant revealing certain truths that I had been wrong about. Everything I have talked about so far (the Sabbath, the biblical feasts, the prophetic days of creation) had all been brought to my attention within a matter of months. It felt like the more I determined to lean into what God wanted instead of what I wanted, the more He opened my eyes.

That didn't make things any easier with Christmas and Easter, but it did help me determine how I was going to approach the subject: if it became clear that God was pleased with one course of action over another, then that was the path I would take.

I knew Christmas and Easter evolved, somehow, from pagan roots and that the Roman Catholic Church had a part in integrating them into Christianity. I also knew that these holidays had changed so much throughout time, and now they look nothing like they used to. So I never understood what the big deal was. Christians weren't worshipping other gods or anything. In fact, we were honoring God by recognizing the birth and resurrection of His son.

Understanding the feasts in Leviticus offered me my first glimpse into how we may not be honoring God with these holidays as purely as I assumed. After all, Passover, Unleavened Bread, and Firstfruits beautifully and prophetically pointed to Christ's death, burial, and resurrection. God gave these specific days with their specific timings to Moses. In this way, God had already provided humanity with an occasion for honoring Christ's resurrection (the Feast of Firstfruits) that served as a testament to God's divine power and knowledge. Basically, God called out the specific day that Christ would resurrect over a thousand years before it happened, and when He called out this day, He made the point that it was to be celebrated, as if to say, "You'll see."

So why would Christianity have taken it upon itself to scrap that day and create the holiday of Easter with the incorporation of pagan elements? The word "Easter" derives from the pagan goddess Ishtar. In the past, I had always brushed over or rushed through questions like these. Knowing the feast days in Leviticus prompted me to consider these sorts of questions more thoroughly.

Considering those questions led me to new questions (beyond those related to holidays) about the history of Christianity. I believe this is why many Christians shy away from thinking about their customs and traditions more critically. When it comes to faith, it's uncomfortable coming face to face with questions that we don't know how to answer. It's uncomfortable, but I needed a better understanding of the history of the Christian religion.

When I lived in New York, I taught middle school history for a couple years. I enjoyed the curriculum I taught from the perspective that it was a high-level overview of world history and civilizations. Up until that point, I had never spent much time considering Constantine and the rise of Christianity within the Roman Empire. When we got to this unit in class, I started thinking about it a little more, but I still walked away with the overall understanding that Constantine was a champion of the Christian faith, with little knowledge of the details surrounding his story.

The basic narrative is that Christians in the first few centuries after Jesus were being martyred by the Roman Empire, and then Constantine came along, had a conversion experience, and legalized Christianity.

Overtime, Christianity went from being persecuted by the Roman Empire, to being legalized, to being the dominant religion in Europe.

With just those bullet points, the whole story sounds like a triumphant victory for the Christian faith. That's what I took away from the curriculum that I was given to teach with. But when I started digging into the history on my own about a year later, I began finding pieces that didn't add up.

It wasn't a problem that the history surrounding Constantine was messy. It was a problem that Christians today simplify the history to, "Good guys won, bad guys lost." As a 21st-century Christian looking back, it's easy to think like that. But when we really understand what the Christian faith is supposed to be all about according to Jesus and then compare that to the history of the Christian religion, we find the two narratives going in opposite directions.

This is what I mean when I say the pieces didn't add up. When we look at the Christian religion developing into a world power, we see a lot of transformation going on. We see the church transforming, which in itself is fine. We see traditions transforming, which I have mixed feelings about. But then we see the spirit of the matter transforming, the spirit of our core faith, and that is where I take issue. The transformation that occurred within the spirit of the Christian faith throughout the first millennium A.D. gives me reason to say, "I'm devoted to God, and I'm devoted to Jesus. But do I really want to be devoted to this Christian religion?"

I've discovered that, in the eyes of many Christians, this kind of questioning is blasphemy. That's what concerns me—Christians have elevated the Christian religion to the level of the Christian God.

I wanted to understand why and how this happened, and so I continued digging into history, seeking to find the source of the error.

Back to the Source

Since as early as I can remember, my favorite movie has been *Back to the Future*. By that, I mean the whole trilogy as one movie. I enjoy all three films because they each offer a mental puzzle to complete. They're not enormously challenging, but they are fun, and you have to invest at least a little thought to understand what's going on with the plot.

For example, in *Back to the Future Part II*, Doc and Marty took the time machine from 1985 into the future (2015) to resolve a problem with Marty's future children. While they were taking care of that, the villain of the movie, a guy named Biff, stole the time machine and used it to give a sport's almanac from the year 2015 to a younger version of himself in the year 1955, so that young Biff could bet on future sporting events and get rich. Old Biff then brought the time machine back to 2015 and snuck away before Doc and Marty realized it was missing.

When Doc and Marty returned to the year 1985, everything had changed. Biff had become filthy rich and, as a result, was pretty much a dictator running the show. When Doc and Marty figured out what was going on, Marty said something along the lines of, "Great, we just need to go back to the future and stop old Biff from stealing the time machine."

Doc told him, however, that they couldn't do that. At this point, if they went into the future, it would be an extension of the warped reality they were in with Biff in charge. The only way they could fix the situation was by figuring out when, in the past, old Biff gave the almanac to young Biff, and then go there and take the almanac back from young Biff.

In the movie, Doc draws a little diagram to make this easier to understand. If you haven't seen the movie and aren't really following, don't worry about it. It's pretty ripe with paradoxical plot holes, anyway, regardless how enjoyable it is.

The point I'm wanting to draw out of this illustration is that Doc and Marty were trapped in a corrupted reality that couldn't be set right by moving forward within that corrupted reality. They had to understand the source of the corruption and go back to correct it, not forward.

I believe that is where we stand today within Christianity. Something happened in the past that created a new religion within which the authority of the Scriptures took a backseat to the authority of culture. I am referring to the Christian religion that evolved out of Roman Catholicism. I am not saying that all Christians who have been part of this Christian religion throughout the ages have been corrupt and devious. I am saying that the institution of Christianity within the Roman Empire created "an alternate reality", resulting in a lot of confusion around what it means to have faith in Jesus. Now, if we want to free ourselves from the influence of this confusion surrounding our faith, it does us no good to move forward within the context of this confusion. The only way out of this "alternate reality" is going back to where things went wrong and correcting it at its source. (I'm putting "alternate reality" in quotes because I don't believe our situation to actually be an *alternate* reality—it is our reality. I am only trying to clarify my point by connecting it to the illustration.)

Moving forward within the understanding that has been given to us by Roman Christianity will not help clear things up, as evidenced by the ever-increasing number of Christian denominations today. Moving forward within the context of Roman Christianity only creates new problems seen through the same confusing lens. We have to go back to get rid of this lens that is coloring our perspectives. We have to locate the point at which Biff handed off the almanac. We must understand how the seed of confusion was planted.

When I read through the Bible, I see a reverence for the Scriptures within its very pages that I don't see today within Christianity. I meet a lot of Christians who *say* they believe in the Bible and who seem to genuinely believe they do. But, especially when it comes to the Old Testament, there is a clear difference between how Christians today *interpret* the Scriptures and how major figures throughout the Bible *submit to* the Scriptures. Let's just consider some figures from the New Testament.

In Matthew, Jesus quotes from the Torah while being tempted by Satan. Matthew 4:4 says (Jesus is quoting from Deuteronomy 8:3 here):

> But He answering, said, "It has been written, 'Man shall not live by bread alone, but by every word that comes from the mouth of יהוה.'"

Paul writes in 2 Timothy 3:16–17:

> All Scripture is breathed out by Elohim and profitable for teaching, for reproof, for setting straight, for instruction in righteousness, that the man of Elohim might be fitted, equipped for every good work.

The writer of Hebrews writes in Hebrews 4:12:

> For the Word of Elohim is living, and working, and sharper than any two-edged sword, cutting through even to the dividing of being and spirit, and of joints and marrow, and able to judge the thoughts and intentions of the heart.

James 1:22 says:

> And become doers of the Word, and not hearers only, deceiving yourselves.

First Peter 1:25 says:

> "but the Word of Elohim remains forever." And this is the Word, announced as Good News to you.

First John 5:2–3 says:

> By this we know that we love the children of Elohim, when we love Elohim and guard His commands. For this is the love for Elohim, that we guard His commands, and His commands are not heavy,

While each Scripture here poses a different idea, all of them express a reverence for the Word of God and a sincere belief that it should be trusted and put into practice.

Many Christians today will say they believe in the Bible and say that they put it into practice. However, it does not take much digging to reveal that many such Christians are quick to justify the common practice of discounting certain portions of the Bible, particularly the Old Testament.

As an example, I'd like for you to recall Part 2 of this book in which I presented the days of creation. It is a common practice and belief among Christians to take the days of creation as a metaphorical presentation: "I know the Bible says the earth and all that was in it was created in seven days but, you know, science! Therefore the seven-day creation account must be poetic or metaphorical. We can't possibly be expected to take it literally."

This is one example of how many Christians will be quick to say they believe the Bible, but just as quick to discount or interpret away what the Bible actually says.

Again, many Christians today will *say* they believe in the Bible and *say* that they put it into practice, but there is a real breakdown between 1) how they justify themselves for interpreting or even discounting certain portions of the Bible, particularly the Old Testament, and 2) how these figures in the New Testament held their ground regarding the integrity of *all* of God's Word.

What is more, in our time, it is a burden simply trying to have this discussion with Christians, because many are eager to point out verses from Paul that address the legalism of the first-century Jews. These Christians want to argue that the law has been abolished, even though Jesus instructed us explicitly in Matthew 5:17 to *not* think that he has come to do that:

> "Do not think that I came to destroy the Torah or the Prophets.
> I did not come to destroy but to complete."

Even so, Christians make this argument and are often quick to label those who wish to discuss the matter further "Judaizers" or "heretics".

The New Testament is filled with quotes from and references to the Old Testament. Yet today, many Christians don't want to hear about the Old Testament being actively relevant to our faith. It's not hard to understand why this is—if you enjoy your life and believe there's no real harm in the way you're living, why bother stirring up the waters? To return to the previous example, if you learned a long time ago that the seven-day creation account was metaphorical and poetic, and you feel comfortable with the explanation, why would you now reconsider the issue? Especially when reconsidering the issue would appear to make things more complicated, and especially if you might find something that runs contrary to how you're living?

This is the confusion I'm referring to. Something happened at some point between the time of these New Testament figures and now, and it warped how we, believers today, guard and obey the Word of God. We cannot understand this clearly by attempting to move forward within our present confusion. Much of the world has been deceived in this way.

The first thing we must do is understand the deception *instead of* trying to work out the issues that have come as a result while still operating within the deception. So many churches and individuals with loving intentions have tried to work out the issues we see in Christianity today *while still in the context of the Christian religion.* What has been the result? More divisions, more factions, more arguing over doctrines. There is an infection at the heart of the religion, and it does us no good to fight the symptoms.

We must fight the infection. To do that, we have to move backwards: back through the history of America, back through the Age of Enlightenment and the Age of Exploration, back through the Reformation, back through the Renaissance, back through the Middle Ages, back through the Dark Ages, back before the fall of Rome, and back through the Roman Empire, to the time when Christians were still being martyred by Rome for their faith. We have to understand what happened from that point moving forward in order to understand why we're in the situation we are in today.

"The Detestable Mob of Jews"

ABOUT A YEAR after Kendra and I moved to Raleigh, while I was right in the midst of wrestling with all these topics, George Floyd was killed. I began writing some blog posts on the topic of race in America, which evolved into a short book I self-published called *A Formal Repentance on Behalf of White American Christianity*. The process of writing this book revealed to me a few truths that tied in closely to the spiritual journey I was on.

I spent much time pondering the history of racism in America and why we still have such a divided nation on this issue. It baffled me how much of Christianity either remained silent on the topic or insisted that it was no longer an issue. I was struggling with how a population of people claiming to believe in the Bible as God's Word could so aggressively maintain some of the political perspectives they did.

And then, suddenly, it clicked. I had been going along on this spiritual journey while considering racism in America, and I realized that the two areas were very connected.

Constantine legalized and ushered Christianity into the Roman Empire in 313 AD. Not long after he did so, he made a decisive effort to separate Christianity, the new faith of Rome, from the faith and religious practices of the Jews. One of the main ways that Constantine created this distinction and separation was to dictate that Christianity would not observe the biblical feast days. Constantine not only did away with the biblical feast days but instituted a replacement in establishing and commanding an observance of Roman holidays in their place. You will recognize these Roman holidays as the chief holidays that Christian culture now observes, namely Easter and Christmas.

As I read into these decisions and decrees made by Constantine, I was taken aback by the tone with which Constantine spoke about the

Jewish faith. Constantine's derogatory statements towards the Jews were particularly notable.

Here is a selection from Eusebius' *The Life of Constantine*, taken from Book III, Chapters XVIII and XIX, in which Constantine is making statements regarding the separation of Easter (a Roman holiday) from Passover (a biblical feast):

> In the first place it was decreed unworthy to observe that most sacred festival in accordance with the practice of the Jews; having sullied their own hands with a heinous crime, such bloodstained men are as one might expect mentally blind. It is possible, now that their nation has been rejected, by a truer system which we have kept from the first day of the Passion to the present, to extend the performing of this observance into future periods also. Let there be nothing in common between you and the detestable mob of Jews! We have received from the Saviour another way; a course is open to our most holy religion that is both lawful and proper. Let us with one accord take up this course, right honourable brothers, and so tear ourselves away from that disgusting complicity. For it is surely quite grotesque for them to be able to boast that we would be incapable of keeping these observances without their instruction.[1]

When I read those statements from Constantine, I cringe at the overtly disgusted accusations. These don't sound like the words of a man who has given his heart to the pursuit of loving others as Jesus loved us. These words convey hatred and pride.

When we continue reading right where we left off, we find Constantine saying:

> What could those people calculate correctly, when after that murder of the Lord, after that parricide, they have taken leave of their senses, and are moved, not by any rational principle, but by uncontrolled impulse, wherever their internal frenzy may lead them? Hence it comes about that in this very matter they do not see the truth, so that nearly always they get it wrong, and instead of the proper calculation they observe the Pascha a second time in the same year. Why then do we follow those who are by common consent sick with fearful error? We would never allow the Pascha to be kept a second time in the same year. But even if that argument were absent, your Good Sense ought to make it the continual object of your effort and prayer, that the purity of

---

1. Eusebius, *Life of Constantine*, 128–129.

your soul should not by any resemblance appear to participate in the practices of thoroughly evil persons.[2]

We find more disgust toward the Jews here, but I want to point out specifically Constantine's accusation regarding their observance of the Passover "a second time in the same year". First, let's answer the question of why the Jews may have been observing the Passover a second time in the same year.

Numbers 9:5-13 says:

> So they performed the Pĕsaḥ on the fourteenth day of the first new moon, between the evenings, in the Wilderness of Sinai. According to all that יהוה commanded Mosheh, so the children of Yisraĕl did. But there were men who were defiled for a being of a man, so that they were not able to perform the Pĕsaḥ on that day. So they came before Mosheh and Aharon that day, and those men said to him, "We are defiled for the being of a man. Why are we withheld from bringing near the offering of יהוה at its appointed time among the children of Yisraĕl?" And Mosheh said to them, "Wait, let me hear what יהוה commands concerning you." And יהוה spoke to Mosheh, saying, "Speak to the children of Yisraĕl, saying, 'When any male of you or your generations is unclean for a being, or is far away on a journey, he shall still perform the Pĕsaḥ of יהוה. On the fourteenth day of the second new moon, between the evenings, they perform it – with unleavened bread and bitter herbs they eat it. They do not leave of it until morning, and they do not break a bone of it. According to all the laws of the Pĕsaḥ they perform it. But the man who is clean and is not on a journey, and has failed to perform the Pĕsaḥ, that same being shall be cut off from among his people, because he did not bring the offering of יהוה at its appointed time – that man bears his sin.'"

We find here in Numbers 9 that God did institute a second celebration for Passover for those who were unable to take part in the first celebration. To be clear, God is direct in that this is not an alternative option for the sake of preference. The expectation is that all the people celebrate the Passover on the fourteenth day of the first month, and the second Passover is strictly for those who could not celebrate it because they were unclean or on a journey.

---

2. Eusebius, *Life of Constantine*, 128–129.

Now, with that in mind, let's revisit Constantine's words. Leading up to his qualm with the Jews keeping the Passover twice in the same year, Constantine accused the Jews of having "taken leave of their senses" and being moved "not by any rational principle, but by uncontrolled impulse, wherever their internal frenzy may lead them". Reread that selection of Constantine's words, noting how all his accusations there seem to be pointing to this idea of Passover being celebrated a second time. He even says, "We would never allow the Pascha to be kept a second time in the same year."

Constantine didn't seem to be aware of a second Passover celebration given by God in Scripture. If he was aware, he gave no indication. Instead, he made accusations about the Jews acting nonsensically and irrationally, celebrating, instead, on impulse.

If it was the case that the Jews were celebrating a second Passover in such a way that was unbiblical and displeasing to God based on what was written in the Torah, then that could have been addressed in a completely different manner. However that doesn't appear to be Constantine's qualm here. Constantine wasn't attempting to clarify Scripture and correct misguided behavior. He was accusing the Jews of celebrating flippantly and without any reason whatsoever. In doing so, Constantine revealed himself as being ignorant of what the Scriptures actually say, particularly in boasting, "We would never allow the Pascha to be kept a second time in the same year," without any acknowledgement of the account in Numbers 9.

What is more, Constantine's accusation ends up being ironic in that it ultimately leads to his edict to celebrate Easter over the biblical feast days. It is ironic because the accusation claimed that the Jews were making flippant decisions concerning the celebration, and yet he was the one who made a mandate on the matter without looking into and understanding why the Jews were celebrating the Passover twice in the same year. In other words, he acted flippantly after accusing the Jews of doing just that.

Later in that same section, Constantine states:

> But let your Holiness's good sense reflect how dreadful and unseemly it is, that on the same days some should be attending to their fasts while others are holding drinking parties, and that after the days of Pascha some should be busy with feasts and recreations while others are dedicating themselves to the prescribed fasts. That is the reason therefore why divine Providence intends that this matter should achieve the proper settlement

and be brought under one regulation, as I presume all are aware. Since therefore it was proper that the matter should be adjusted in such a way that nothing be held in common with that nation of parricides and Lord-killers ... and to put the most important point concisely, by unanimous verdict it was determined that the most holy feast of Easter should be celebrated on one and the same day, since it is both improper that there should be a division about a matter of such great sanctity, and best to follow that option, in which there is no admixture of alien error and sin.[3]

When the Roman Empire legalized Christianity, the authority of Constantine's government claimed precedence over the authority of the Scriptures, as seen here. (I propose that this was the handing off of the almanac to young Biff, if that analogy was jiving with you.) Constantine claimed that "divine Providence" intended to replace certain feast days previously given by God in the Torah with the Roman holiday of Easter, whose name comes from a pagan goddess of fertility. To be clear, at this point in history, the holiday of Easter, which originated as a pagan springtime celebration, had already begun seeping into Christian culture. It was Constantine's edict, though, that essentially tossed out the observance of the biblical feasts. He mandated a prioritization of the Easter holiday, a celebration formerly dedicated to a pagan goddess, "rebranding" it as a day unto God. In doing this, he made no effort to conceal a resentment towards the Jews, who had "sullied their own hands with a heinous crime".

Now I imagine many Christians today might read Constantine's words and adamantly agree, pointing to some of the things Jesus and Paul said throughout the New Testament. I encourage those Christians to consider the difference between the position of Jesus and Paul and the position of Constantine (and us). To begin with, Jesus and Paul were Jews. They were speaking to and of their own people. Constantine was a Roman, claiming that the Jews were "bloodstained men" and "mentally blind" and that there should be nothing in common between Christians and "the detestable mob of Jews". It's not an issue of whether Constantine's words here are true or false. It's the spirit of the matter. The spirit I see in Constantine's words reminds me of Romans 11:17–21, when Paul was addressing Gentiles, specifically *Romans*:

---

3. Eusebius, *Life of Constantine*, 128–129.

> And if some of the branches were broken off, and you, being a wild olive tree, have been grafted in among them, and came to share the root and fatness of the olive tree, do not boast against the branches. And if you boast, remember: you do not bear the root, but the root bears you! You shall say then, "The branches were broken off that I might be grafted in." Good! By unbelief they were broken off, and you stand by belief. Do not be arrogant, but fear. For if Elohim did not spare the natural branches, He might not spare you either.

Israel was God's family. They were His people. The people of Israel had turned their backs on God, and so God, through Jesus, invited the Gentiles (those who were not part of Israel) to become part of the family of God to provoke Israel to jealousy (Romans 11:11). Paul, in this portion of Romans, warned the Gentiles to not become haughty and prideful about being brought into the family of God, because if God removed some of the natural branches, He might remove them (the Gentiles), also.

As believers who have been brought into the family of God through Jesus, we should be paying more attention to these verses in Scripture and spending less time using other verses to blast the Jews for being unfaithful to God.

I believe Constantine set a precedent when he legalized the Christian faith in Rome and began creating edicts about how to go about worshipping God—edicts that notably, and intentionally, went against how God commanded His people to worship Him in Scripture. Constantine claimed a salvation through faith and then called the Jewish people—the *people* through whom the salvation had come—"detestable". Though God created a way for everyone to receive salvation, salvation was of the Jews (John 4:22). Constantine set the precedent of taking the blessing and degrading the people. Does that sound familiar? This is precisely what white American Christians did with black slaves—they took the fruit of the slaves' labor and degraded the people.

Clearly there are major differences between our situation and the one surrounding Constantine and the Jews, but I hope you see the connection.

Take particular note of how Constantine called the Jews detestable. Jesus and Paul may have rebuked the Jewish religious leaders, but that's not the same thing as labeling a people group "detestable". In fact, Constantine's labeling was in direct contrast with the Gospel. We are not called to label anyone detestable (Acts 10:28), but rather to love everyone as Christ loved us (Matthew 5:44).

I know that some people argue against the feast days using Romans 14. However, these verses aren't addressed at the Torah, but rather at manmade beliefs. Romans 14:2–3 says:

> One indeed believes to eat all food, but he who is weak eats only vegetables. He that eats, let him not despise him who does not eat, and he that does not eat, let him not judge him who eats, for Elohim received him.

These verses aren't distinguishing between pork and no pork, or between anything that is called unclean in the Torah and anything that is clean. These verses are distinguishing between food and vegetables. The Torah never commands that people should only eat vegetables. This was a belief some people held that was distinct from the Torah. In this way, Paul doesn't seem to be addressing an issue with obeying the Torah, but rather with having one's own convictions unrelated to what the Torah says.

With this in mind, let's continue in Romans 14, but rather than using these verses to accuse the biblical feasts, let's consider them in light of what Constantine said. Romans 14:4–6 says:

> Who are you that judges another's servant? To his own master he stands or falls. But he shall be made to stand, for Elohim is able to make him stand. One indeed judges one day above another, another judges every day alike. Let each one be completely persuaded in his own mind. He who minds the day, minds it to יהוה. And he who does not mind the day, to יהוה he does not mind it. He who eats, eats to יהוה, for he gives Elohim thanks. And he who does not eat, to יהוה he does not eat, and gives Elohim thanks.

Let's revisit Constantine's words:

> In the first place it was decreed unworthy to observe that most sacred festival in accordance with the practice of the Jews . . . [1]

Constantine was referring to Easter as "that most sacred festival". Why would Constantine refer to Easter, a day named after a pagan goddess, as the most holy feast rather than the biblical feasts given by God Himself, which all point to Jesus?

Constantine didn't understand the Scriptures, and he preferred his culture to God's culture. This was the man laying the foundation for the Christian religion as we know it today.

Constantine set a precedent that was not biblical when he established Easter. If you have a Bible that mentions Easter (Acts 12:4), it is because it was translated after Christianity had been subjected to Roman authority for centuries, and the translators replaced "Passover" with "Easter". When Martin Luther posted his Ninety-five Theses in 1517, he was just beginning to scratch the surface of all the ways in which the church and the Bible were not aligned.

Dining In or Taking Out?

CHRISTIANS TODAY NEED to understand a foundational distinction and then determine how they want to move forward. Either Jesus brings us into his culture, or we bring Jesus into our culture. Think of it like this: we are either dining in or taking out. The Bible does not teach both of these ideas, though mainstream Christianity may have us believing that it is a good thing to mix Jesus in with our culture.

I want to take a quick tour of some passages in the Bible to show how God expects us to come into His family, and therefore His culture, rather than the other way around.

Leviticus 18:1–5 says:

> And יהוה spoke to Mosheh, saying, "Speak to the children of Yisraěl, and say to them, 'I am יהוה your Elohim. 'Do not do as they do in the land of Mitsrayim, where you dwelt. And do not do as they do in the land of Kena'an, where I am bringing you, and do not walk in their laws. Do My right-rulings and guard My laws, to walk in them. I am יהוה your Elohim. And you shall guard My laws and My right-rulings, which a man does and lives by them. I am יהוה.'"

Israel was intended to be a light to the world, and God told Moses that they were not to do the doings of Egypt (where they were coming from) or the doings of Canaan (where they were going to). God did not want Israel to act like the Egyptians or the Canaanites—they were supposed to be different from the rest of the world in that they obeyed God's commands, which lead to life.

Deuteronomy 12:8 says:

> "Do not do as we are doing here today – each one doing whatever is right in his own eyes."

And then Deuteronomy 12:29-32 says:

> "When יהוה your Elohim does cut off from before you the nations which you go to dispossess, and you dispossess them and dwell in their land, guard yourself that you are not ensnared to follow them, after they are destroyed from before you, and that you do not inquire about their mighty ones, saying, 'How did these nations serve their mighty ones? And let me do so too.' Do not do so to יהוה your Elohim, for every abomination which יהוה hates they have done to their mighty ones, for they even burn their sons and daughters in the fire to their mighty ones. All the words I am commanding you, guard to do it – do not add to it nor take away from it."

God was very clear with Israel—do not do what is right in your own eyes, and don't even ask about how the other nations worshipped their gods. God hated how they worshipped their gods, and He did not want to see His people doing the same thing.

Leviticus 19:33-34 says:

> "'And when a stranger sojourns with you in your land, do not oppress him. Let the stranger who dwells among you be to you as the native among you, and you shall love him as yourself. For you were strangers in the land of Mitsrayim. I am יהוה your Elohim.'"

And then Leviticus 24:22 says:

> "'You are to have one right-ruling, for the stranger and for the native, for I am יהוה your Elohim.'"

God was painting a picture for all of humanity using Israel. Israel was God's family. They were His people. He didn't want them to do the same things that the nations were doing. In fact, that is the very reason God called them an adulterous people—because they ended up doing the same things that the nations were doing. God wanted them to stand out as a light, showing the world what was pleasing and acceptable to God. And if a foreigner came to live among them, the Israelites were to accept them as their own, and the foreigner was called to obey the same law that Israel was called to obey.

Do you see how this is a picture for us today? God's people today are those who have put their faith in Christ and seek to obey him, and the same truths apply. God does not want us doing the same things the nations are doing. He wants us to stand out as a light, showing the world what is pleasing and acceptable to God. And when someone who was once outside the people of God becomes part of God's family, they are accepted, and God wants them to live by His commands, which lead to life.

If you are someone who can't accept these principles because they come from the Old Testament, I would ask if your feelings about the Old Testament come from your own understanding of what the Bible says or from what the Christian religion has told you to feel about it.

Either way, consider Paul's words in 2 Corinthians 6:11—7:1:

> Our mouth has spoken openly to you, O Corinthians, our heart is wide open. You are not restrained by us, but you are restrained by your own affections. But for the same reward – I speak as to children – open wide your hearts too. Do not become unevenly yoked with unbelievers. For what partnership has righteousness and lawlessness? And what fellowship has light with darkness? And what agreement has Messiah with Beliya'al? Or what part does a believer have with an unbeliever? And what union has the Dwelling Place of Elohim with idols? For you are a Dwelling Place of the living Elohim, as Elohim has said, "I shall dwell in them and walk among them, and I shall be their Elohim, and they shall be My people." Therefore, "Come out from among them and be separate, says יהוה, and do not touch what is unclean, and I shall receive you." "And I shall be a Father to you, and you shall be sons and daughters to Me, says יהוה the Almighty." Having, then, these promises, beloved, let us cleanse ourselves from all defilement of the flesh and spirit, perfecting set-apartness in the fear of Elohim.

Paul is quoting from Leviticus, 2 Samuel, Isaiah, Jeremiah, and Ezekiel here, and the point he is making is not new. What fellowship has righteousness with lawlessness?

First Peter 4:3–5 says:

> For we have spent enough of our past lifetime in doing the desire of the nations, having walked in indecencies, lusts, drunkenness, orgies, wild parties, and abominable idolatries, in which they are surprised that you do not run with them in the same flood of loose behaviour, blaspheming, who shall give account to Him who is ready to judge the living and the dead.

While I was in college, I was in a student circus. One summer, I traveled with the circus to Georgia to work at a family resort. There were about twenty-five of us, and we all lived in a dormitory together. Every weekend felt like an extended party until hangover Monday came, except for three of us who chose not to partake in the drinking that summer. Now please don't think I was being super righteous. My reasons for not drinking were more legalistic than anything, and that time is reflective of a spiritual disposition I have since repented of. I was twenty, I had never drunk before, and I didn't want to drink underage because I liked the idea of being able to say that I never drank underage. So I didn't drink. The three of us who didn't drink stuck out like a sore thumb together, even though we all had different reasons for not drinking. We all got put together into the same group—the ones that didn't drink.

Regardless of each of our reasons, all the others were "surprised" that we did "not run with them". They were surprised because we were in the minority, and when you are in the minority, you are set apart from the rest.

I have experienced this from both sides. I once found it surprising that some Christians didn't celebrate Easter or Christmas. I felt very comfortable being in the majority and thought *they* were strange for being in the minority. If you are on the fence, or confused, or anything other than convinced, I urge you to reread the verses above. Meditate on them. Ask God to reveal to you what they mean. To me, the meaning is clear: God calls those who believe in Him to be set apart. We are not to look like everybody else. We are called to look like the nation of Israel, as prescribed by God. If looking like the nation of Israel offends you, I encourage you to dig into that and ask yourself why. I'm coming to realize that believing in the God of the Bible (the one who calls us to be set apart) while celebrating "holy days" that originated in a pagan society and have since been adopted by a secular society, is a very strange thing.

The more I came to understand this, the more I realized that, while I may have been believing in Jesus, I had been effectively living as a stranger to God's people, according to God's Word. If God's people are those who are set apart from the way of the world, we can't simultaneously call ourselves God's people while being steeped in the world's culture.

I professed a love for God all my life, but I was not exempt from deception. I wasn't really doing the things He told His people to do through His Word. Instead, I was doing the things some guy had declared to be holy a couple hundred years after Revelation was written, things that evolved out of pagan customs, acting like it would be silly to take issue with what I was doing. I can't help but feel like the spiritual forces opposed to God had a laugh at my expense.

45,000 and Counting

PAUL QUOTES ISAIAH 52:11 in 2 Corinthians 6:17:

> Therefore, "Come out from among them and be separate, says יהוה, and do not touch what is unclean, and I shall receive you."

In instituting Easter, Constantine did the exact opposite of this call to action. Rather than bringing himself out of the customs of the nations (the worship of Roman gods and goddesses), he instead applied the message of salvation to preexisting pagan practices. During the Dark Ages to follow, very few people had access to the Bible and could read, so they just relied on what the authorities within the church told them. When Martin Luther challenged the church on certain practices like indulgences, he started a ripple effect that has continued to this day, in which people convicted by God have decided to look into what the Bible has to say for themselves rather than rely on what someone in authority is telling them to believe.

I hope you are beginning to see that the Christian religion, as molded by Constantine during the age of the Roman Empire, worked great deception within the faith, encouraging Christians to embrace cultures and practices that were loved by the world but strangely absent from the Bible. The unfortunate effects of this on the Christian church today are painfully obvious. Did you know that there are an estimated 45,000 denominations within Christianity? I know some people might consider this a good thing in that "the gospel of Christ is being preached to all sorts of people". But honestly, if this number doesn't point to confusion, I don't know what does. Furthermore, do we really think all 45,000 versions of the gospel being preached are the true Gospel?

When I look back at the history of Christianity being brought into the Roman Empire and mixed with pagan customs, I don't see a love of

God and His Word, but rather a love of culture. Culture can be very appealing, and the message of salvation through faith in Jesus is also very appealing.

Unfortunately (I say this facetiously), that message of salvation comes with a moral standard already in place, given to humanity by God. Wouldn't it be nice if we could have that message of salvation without having to give up all the worldly things that we've grown so fond of? If you're the emperor of the most dominant empire in the world, you can make that happen. And that is what Constantine did.

Sadly, our reality is an ongoing extension of what Constantine did with the Christian faith. We won't look to the Old Testament to course correct because we consider it the law of the Jews rather than the law of God, and we think of the Jews as "bloodstained" and "detestable", never minding that Jesus was a Jew who obeyed those laws. And we can't look to the New Testament to course correct—we can't really understand it because we're not willing to look to the Old Testament, and roughly a third of the New Testament is made up of quotes from and references to the Old Testament. So rather than recognize that there is something seriously wrong going on here, we are satisfied with creating new denominations every year, dismissing large portions of Scripture as irrelevant, metaphorical, or just plain confusing, tweaking doctrines as needed, all to appease what is right in our own eyes.

This doesn't seem too problematic until we put it into a real context. As an example, let's revisit the topic of racism that has plagued America since the country's inception. The Christianity that came to America was and is an extension of Roman Christianity. The slavery practiced in America was justified by many Christians with claims that the white man was evangelizing to the black man. But the slavery practiced in America didn't even resemble the slavery talked about in the Bible. The Torah explicitly addresses slaves' rights, none of which seemed to have found their way into American slavery. Instead, we can find the American version of slavery in a section of the Torah covering general violence. Exodus 21:16 says:

> "And he who kidnaps a man and sells him, or if he is found in his hand, shall certainly be put to death."

That describes the kind of slavery practiced in America, and clearly tells us God's feelings about it.

This is one of the reasons why it is problematic to write off the Old Testament as not relevant. The New Testament gives us clarity on what all of God's law was about: loving God and loving people. But without the Old Testament, we leave it up to each of the 45,000 denominations to determine for themselves what it means to love God and love people on a granular level. History has shown us that some Christians believe loving people means taking them from their homes and subjecting them to forced labor in the name of Jesus. We look at that now and say, "Yeah, that was definitely an abuse of interpretation," but if we're satisfied just going along with whatever mainstream doctrine is out there, we're no different.

The beauty of God's law as laid out in Torah (the first five books of the Bible) is that it doesn't leave it up to every person to decide for themselves what loving God and loving people looks like. It tells us. If you kidnap a man and sell him, or if you're found with him, you should be put to death, because that is not loving your neighbor.

Christians today are eager to then ask, "Okay, so we're supposed to follow the law, huh? So are you saying we should be putting people to death?" No, I'm saying we should not do the things the law says are punishable by death. Jesus took the death penalty for us, and it is not the responsibility of the Christian to play the role of judge. That is God's role. Sadly, though, Christianity has gotten things all mixed up, and the result has been Christians who carry on as if Jesus died for us so that we no longer have to obey God. We are often much more concerned with judging matters than we are with taking the plank out of our own eye, and I believe that is yet another result of the arrogance injected into the Christian faith when the Roman Empire laid claim to it.

When we look at history and see how Christianity took a stark turn when it was embraced by the Roman Empire, we are then confronted with the question, "Do we really want to do whatever it takes to please God, or do we prefer the version of Christianity given to us by the Roman Empire?"

If we really want to please God, then it's going to take some work getting back to His truth. The Bible itself has been shaped by Roman Christianity, both in structure and translation. Furthermore, the 45,000 Christian denominations available to you today have also inevitably been influenced by this same history, so seeking out truth on the matter can be quite tricky. We live in a reality in which the Gospel has been taken, mutilated, and repackaged as the Christian religion, and now moving forward within this Christian religion will still have us trapped, in some way, within its mixed messaging. The only way to really free ourselves from its deception is to go back to the Scriptures and pray for God to show us truth.

Religion Versus God's Word

THE SCRIPTURES TELL us to look at Jesus as our example. Paul says in Philippians 1:21:

> For to me, to live is Messiah, and to die is gain.

And then he says in verses 29–30:

> Because to you it has been given as a favour, on behalf of Messiah, not only to believe in Him, but also to suffer for His sake, having the same struggle which you saw in me, and now hear to be in me.

Paul is saying that, if he is alive, he is going to suffer in the same way Jesus did, and he is telling the Philippians that this call has been given to them, as well.

The Scriptures, particularly those of the New Testament, call us to be humble servants. Jesus has already come once as a servant. He will come again as a conquering king, but until that time comes, we are called to serve and even suffer in the way he did, demonstrating our love for God and people.

If you consider yourself a Christian and you've never looked into the history surrounding Constantine's conversion, you should. This event is a major turning point in the history of the Christian religion. When you investigate Constantine's conversion, there are a few important ideas you will likely come across.

To begin with, there is controversy about what really happened surrounding Constantine's conversion. This is not surprising, given the nature of history. I only bring this up to make the point that you can spend a lot of time reading about Constantine's history and still not be sure about what exactly happened.

Also, there are only two primary sources documenting Constantine's conversion, provided by Lactantius and Eusebius. There are some discrepancies between these two accounts, but both point to the idea that Constantine had a vision. The generally agreed upon narrative today is that Constantine had a vision of a cross-like symbol and a subsequent dream in which he was visited by Jesus. In both the vision and the dream, Constantine was told to conquer his enemies.

With just that general information in mind, we can look at a very peculiar history playing out.

Nearly three hundred years after Jesus's first coming, we find an emperor claiming to have a vision and subsequent dream from Jesus telling him to conquer. That was the entire message of his vision: "In this sign, you will conquer," referring to the cross-like symbol.

Now, in order to believe that Constantine had a conversion experience as a result of meeting the true Jesus, I would have to accept two things:

1. The testimony of a man claiming he was given instructions from God through a dream.
2. That those instructions ran contrary to the instructions of Scripture.

In Scripture, Jesus told us to love our enemies.
In Constantine's dream, Jesus told him to conquer his enemies.
That doesn't sound like the same Jesus to me.

We should not pass over this point lightly. If we are willing to accept the testimony of a man who, through a dream, was given instructions that ran contrary to the instructions of Scripture, why are we not willing to accept the testimony of another man who began having visions in the year 610 A.D. (nearly three hundred years after Constantine), who also received instructions that ran contrary to Scripture? I am referring, of course, to Muhammad and the religion of Islam.

It is easy for modern-day Christians to accept the idea that Constantine was a champion for the Christian faith because we have come up in a Christian culture that is the result of certain foundations laid by Constantine. It's similar to Americans believing that communism is simply evil for no reason other than they've been brought up in a democracy.

When considering Constantine and his conversion, we can take the perspective of a 21st-century American Christian or that of a 1st-century Jewish Christian.

If we choose the perspective of a 21st-century American Christian, Constantine seems like a hero. He had a vision of a cross-like symbol that told him, "In this sign, you will conquer," and he went and conquered. He legalized Christianity, stopping the martyring of Christians, and he laid the foundations for the Christian religion that we know today.

If we choose the perspective of a 1st-century Jewish Christian, Constantine seems suspicious. The Scriptures tell us that Jesus came first as a humble servant and that, when he returns, he will be a conquering king. Jesus himself set an example of servitude and love, to the point of dying on the cross. He told us to turn the other cheek and to forgive our enemies. The time had not come for him to forcefully conquer. And then, a few centuries later, the emperor of a pagan nation says that this same Jesus came to him in a dream with instructions to conquer.

As a 21st-century American Christian, I could easily argue that this was God's will in order to stop the martyring of Christians. As a 1st-century Jewish Christian, I would have to ask, "Did Constantine really have an encounter with Jesus that led him to place his faith in Jesus?" Between what I read in the Scriptures and what I read about Constantine, I would be inclined to say, "No."

If you do your own research on Constantine, you'll find that some people love him, some people hate him, and many people find his story questionable. I agree that there are quite a few confusing pieces to the story, and it's probably an oversimplification to just say he was good or bad. But I am less interested in the person of Constantine than I am in the trajectory of the Christian faith, and that is why I am focusing on him here.

When I look at the difference in spirit between what's in the Bible and what's in the Christian faith today, I see this whole situation with Constantine as the singular most significant turning point in Christian history to account for the difference. Under Constantine, the Christian faith went from followers laying down their lives in the name of Jesus to followers justifying the taking of lives in the name of Jesus. The issue I see is not a discrepancy in a specific data point. The issue is a discrepancy in the fundamental spirit of the matter.

Jesus *defied* religion, *loved* his enemies to the point of death, and told his followers to do the same. A few centuries later, we see Constantine *establishing* religion and *conquering* his enemies. A few centuries after that, we see Muhammad, and a few centuries after that, we see the Crusades. The faith that claimed to follow Jesus turned into a religion that ended up in a series of religious wars some thousand years later. The Christianity that exists today is still a product of this religion. It has gone through some reformations and restorations and reparations, but it is still a product of that same religion that totally flipped the spirit of the matter on its head when Christians began *fighting* in the name of Jesus instead of *laying down their lives* in the name of Jesus.

Constantine is said to have had his vision and dream of Christ in the year 312 A.D. In 326 A.D., fourteen years later, Constantine had his own son and wife executed. I am fully aware that God uses imperfect people to do great things. But when we find ourselves faithfully taking part in a religion, we should learn about the people responsible for the institution of our religious practices to test for ourselves whether their discretion was trustworthy. We should understand what we are believing and why.

Again, the issue here isn't about some specific idea or practice within Christianity. The issue isn't even about Constantine. The issue is about the spirit of the matter. Does the Christian religion today maintain the spirit demonstrated by Jesus: serving (not just for the photo op, but even when it's humiliating), loving our enemies (including those who don't look or think like us), and willing to suffer for the truth, even to the point of death?

It's tempting to think that Constantine's conversion was all part of God's will for Christianity. I personally don't believe it was, but I am not arrogant enough to say that I am certain of God's ways. I don't think Constantine's conversion was based on him meeting Jesus, but I do believe God has used the circumstance to demonstrate His grace throughout history. The main problem I see in believing that Constantine's conversion was God's will for Christianity is the warped perspective which that belief inevitably leads to around the Christian faith. If we believe that Jesus appeared to Constantine and told him to conquer, even though Jesus's messaging throughout the Gospels is the complete opposite, then we are dividing our faith between God's Word and man's word. God's Word says, "Love your enemies," and man's word (Constantine's word) says, "Conquer your enemies." Lo and behold, this is the core problem in Christianity today—people valuing man's word (whether it is someone else's or their own) on equal or higher footing than God's Word.

Perhaps the best example of this is the Sabbath. The Christian religion worships on Sunday, even though the Bible makes it clear that God's Sabbath is the seventh day, what we now call "Saturday". I want to look at an article that was published in *The Catholic Record* of London, Canada on September 1, 1923. The article, called "Sabbath Observance", is presumed to have been written by an editor of the periodical. In the article, the editor writes:

> Now in the matter of Sabbath observance the Protestant rule of Faith is utterly unable to explain the substitution of the Christian Sunday for the Jewish Saturday. It has been changed. The Bible still teaches that the Sabbath or Saturday should be kept holy. There is no authority in the New Testament for the substitution of Sunday for Saturday. Surely it is an important matter. It stands there in the Bible as one of the Ten Commandments of God. There is no authority in the Bible for abrogating this Commandment, or for transferring its observance to another day of the week.[1]

In other words, the Bible clearly teaches that the Sabbath is the seventh day, that it should be kept holy, and Protestants do not have a valid explanation for why the switch was made from Saturday to Sunday (just summarizing the article here). The editor continues:

> For Catholics it is not the slightest difficulty. "All power is given Me in heaven and on earth; as the Father sent Me so I also send you," said our Divine Lord in giving His tremendous commission to His Apostles. "He that heareth you heareth Me." We have in the authoritative voice of the Church the voice of Christ Himself. The Church is above the Bible; and this transference of Sabbath observance from Saturday to Sunday is proof positive of that fact. Deny the authority of the Church and you have no adequate or reasonable explanation or justification for the substitution of Sunday for Saturday in the Third - Protestant Fourth - Commandment of God.[2]

The editor wrote, "The Church is above the Bible . . . " Now before we argue one way or another, let's read what was written next: " . . . and this transference of Sabbath observance from Saturday to Sunday is proof positive of that fact."

In other words, you can say whatever you'd like regarding the authority of the church and the Bible, but if you worship on Sunday, then your actions are proving that the church has more authority in your life than the Bible does.

I don't agree with this editor about the church being above the Bible, but I cannot argue against his logic. When we look to history, we find the

---

1. Anonymous, "Sabbath Observance," 2342.

Roman Catholic Church explicitly rejecting the seventh day in favor of the first day.

The following extract comes from Canon XXIX of the Council of Laodicea, which took place around 363–364 AD:

> Christians must not judaize by resting on the Sabbath, but must work on that day, rather honouring the Lord's Day; and, if they can, resting then as Christians. But if any shall be found to be judaizers, let them be anathema from Christ.[2]

The Roman Catholic Church is responsible for Sunday being the Christian day of worship, not the Bible. We'll look more at this later, but there are no verses in Scripture that tell us to disregard the seventh-day Sabbath and treat Sunday as the new holy day. On the contrary, the fourth commandment explicitly tells us to *remember* or *guard* the Sabbath day and to keep it holy. When I come to understand this clearly, it's really a simple matter—either I believe God has given the church (whether it's the Roman Catholic Church, the "universal" church, or any other view of "the church") the authority to override the commands He laid out for us in the Bible, or I believe that God's Word maintains its authority even when religious leaders contradict it.

Protestants often claim to base their beliefs on the Bible alone. But the editor of that article makes a good point in indicating that Protestant Christianity is unable to explain the substitution of Sunday for the Sabbath day as commanded in the Bible. The reason Christianity worships on Sunday is because the church took it upon itself to change the day of worship from what God instructed and modelled from the beginning. Regardless of what we say, the fact that Christianity worships on Sunday is a sign of the church's authority (in the eyes of Christians) over the Bible—the leaders of the church dictated that Sunday would be the day to worship, and Christianity obeyed, even though the Word of God says otherwise. Christianity's obedience was and is proof of the authority of the church.

This is religion versus God's Word in action. We come upon portions of God's Word that don't line up with what we profess to believe or how we do things. We justify, creatively interpret, or simply write off those things that muddy the waters. We look the other way and try to put it out of our minds, all the while reassuring ourselves that God is full of grace and therefore He's cool with whatever.

2. Schaff and Wace, *Nicene and Post-Nicene Fathers*, 148.

I'm calling out Christianity because I see more religion coming out of it today than Christ-like love. I know many Christians who do exhibit Christ-like love, and I have much gratitude for the grace and love that I have received from those Christians. But too many people have been deceived in the way of thinking that in order to really have faith in this man we call Jesus, you have to be part of the Christian religion, and that is where I have to draw the line for myself. That is not the message of the Bible.

The message of the Bible is at odds with the message of religion. The Bible says God saves. Religion says religion saves. If we are too fearful of upsetting the Christian religion to seek out real truth in God's Word, then we are living out the message of religion, not the Bible.

Part 4

The Great Light

Before You Feast on This Part

THROUGHOUT MY LIFE, I've been called "an Andrew" by different people at different churches.

John 1:40–42 says:

> Andri [Andrew], the brother of Shim'on Kĕpha [Simon Peter], was one of the two who heard from Yoḥanan [John], and followed Him. First he found his own brother Shim'on, and said to him, "We have found the Messiah" (which means the Anointed). And he brought him to יהושע. And looking at him, יהושע said, "You are Shim'on the son of Yonah, you shall be called Kĕpha" (which means a Stone).

I always enjoyed bringing my friends to church. This is why people called me "an Andrew". I found the comparison both flattering and humbling. On the one hand, what an honor to be considered someone who brings people closer to Jesus. On the other hand, say what now? Out of all the people in Scripture to be compared to, I made people think of the guy who brought his brother to Jesus, and then kind of ghosted? When I was younger, my pride tempted me to feel indignant about this. Why didn't people think of me as a Paul, or a David, or even a Daniel, for crying out loud?! I wanted to be the person encountering God, not the person pointing someone else in the direction of encountering God.

As I've grown, however, I've come to appreciate this role more and more, as well as realize the futility of trying to compare myself with others. Now, whenever I read this account of Andrew and Peter, I think to myself, "You the man, Andrew, reeling in that pillar of the church."

I find a real joy in connecting people with the Messiah, whatever may come of it. For me, doing this is a labor of faith. God called Abraham to leave his home and go to a strange land. For Abraham, doing that was a labor of faith. He had to do something to show that he believed God. Jesus tells us that if we love him, we will obey him, and he commands us to share the message of the Gospel. If we want to show that we believe him, we have to do something. More accurately, we have to share something.

We have to share something. That's not the same as saying we have to share *anything*. What is the Gospel? What is the Good News? We may be quick to say, "Jesus!" but that's not incredibly clarifying for someone who isn't familiar with the whole story.

Pretend a friend runs up to you and says, "I have good news. Not just good news, but *the* good news!"

"What is it?" you ask impatiently.

"Billy!" he announces.

You cock an eyebrow. "Billy? The good news is Billy?"

"Yep."

"Who's Billy?"

"He's the son of Santa, and he died for *you*."

You feel skeptical. "Oh he did now, did he?"

"Yep," your friend says.

When we come up in a Christian culture, things like, "Jesus is the son of God and he died for you," sound reasonable and almost intuitive. But when we think about how this sort of thing sounds to nonbelievers who did not come up in a Christian circle, it sounds more like nonsense or, at best, a hasty conclusion without a supporting argument.

When Andrew told Peter that they had found the Messiah, there was context. They were both Jews, and they were familiar with the Scriptures that we now call the Old Testament. The concept of the Messiah, or the Anointed, was already engrained in them. Their faith and their culture had already put them in a position of being expectant for this figure to show up. When the Messiah did show up, it may have been surreal or unbelievable for most Jews, but there had already been a foundation of expectation laid by the Scriptures.

When that foundation isn't already there, it's often insufficient to simply jump to a summary about the Good News.

"Jesus died for you and if you put your faith in him you will receive salvation."

"Dude, what are you talking about?"

If we want to bring people to the Messiah, we must go get them, not call them from afar. "Jesus is the son of God" might make sense to you, but what is going to make sense to them?

Our world of marketing gives us reason to think we can sell things with clever catchphrases and slogans. It scares me, the extent to which commercial jingles of the 1990s have stuck with me through the years. Hearts, stars, and horseshoes, clovers, and blue moons, pots of gold, and rainbows, and me red balloons. I wish I could get that sequence of words out of my head, but I can't.

Too often we treat Jesus like a product that we're supposed to sell to the world. We craft clever slogans and catchy jingles and compelling campaigns, hoping the world will buy our limited-edition Jesus. But Jesus is not a product to be sold.

If anything, we are the product, in need of being purchased. God is our buyer, and He purchased us with the currency of blood. Every person now has the decision of drawing near to their rightful owner or rejecting Him. Perhaps, for some, this makes a little more sense than simply hearing, "Jesus is the son of God." It doesn't answer every question, but it gets the ball rolling in the way of understanding.

If we want to bring people to the Messiah, we need to give them reason to come. If we hope to do that without compromising the integrity of the Gospel, then we need to understand the Gospel.

Yeshua, the Torah, and Lovers of Truth

"Huh. Interesting," I said.

I had just finished watching "Why Hanukkah IS Biblical", and I felt very curious about who this Gary Simons guy was. I returned to the Triumph in Truth YouTube channel and scrolled through his messages, until I came to one titled, "How A Sunday Mega-Church Pastor Came To Torah".

"Very interesting," I said.

I Googled him and unsurprisingly found accusations of heretical teaching, mostly centered around the idea that Simons teaches works-based righteousness. Just about every pastor that has any degree of celebrity has accusations against them posted online, so that did little to shape my opinion of Simons.

I went ahead and watched "How A Sunday Mega-Church Pastor Came To Torah". He had a fascinating story to tell. I thought he had a good spirit. He spoke of his journey going from preaching in the evangelical scene to obeying the law of God. Out of those from his congregation who stuck with him through this, some wanted him to be more pressing with teaching certain aspects of the law, to which he said, "You don't get to the heart by lopping off the head." I could appreciate that. I know I don't want to listen to anyone who is eager to lop off my head if I don't immediately obey them. God knows this, and I believe that is why He is so patient and loving with us. He desires that we would understand and mature in the ways of wisdom and that we would choose to love Him.

I also believe this is one of the reasons why some sects of Christianity have earned themselves a certain reputation. Have you ever heard a pastor preach about love with what appeared to be a hate-filled spirit?

Bear in mind there is a distinction between fervent love and hate. One can be intense and not hate-filled. But fervent love doesn't seek to back someone into a corner and pressure them into agreement. That's what I see in this idea, "You don't get to the heart by lopping off the head."

Simons also said something along the lines of, "We have to be lovers of Truth." I really appreciated this idea, as well. Pause and consider it for a moment. We have to love the Truth, and we have to love it more than culture, more than ourselves, more than our pride, and more than our comfort. When we submit to the idea that there are multiple "truths" out there, we are not being lovers of *the* Truth. We are being adulterous against the Truth. God is Truth. If we do not have a love for the Truth, then we do not have a real love for Him.

I also remember how Simons kept referring to Jesus as "Yeshua", and how Pastor Isaac had done the same thing. I'm not sure if I actually knew that Jesus was the English translation of the Greek form of the Hebrew name given to the Messiah. I knew that it was an English translation of something. I had never thought, though, of referring to Jesus as Yeshua. But the more I thought on it, the more I liked it. If Yeshua sounded closer to what his friends and family called him, that's what I wanted to call him, too. Also, Luke 2:21 says that the name "JESUS" (English translation) was given to him before he was conceived in the womb. If his name was given to him before he was conceived in the womb, it seemed like his name was important to God.

I decided I wanted to call him Yeshua. I wasn't of the mindset that it was bad or wrong to call him Jesus or anything like that. I just preferred Yeshua, given the information I had.

So I liked Simons' spirit, and I decided to start referring to my Savior as Yeshua. But neither of those ideas represented the larger point in his message, which was getting at the Torah. Again, the title of his message was "How A Sunday Mega-Church Pastor Came To Torah", and as I listened to him speak, I realized, *He is actually saying that we should obey the Torah.* I don't know if I thought there would be some interesting twist on it or what, but there was no twist.

He wasn't preaching the Jewish faith, as we understand the Jewish faith to be, because he acknowledged Yeshua as the Messiah who died for the sins of the world. Having been a product of Christian culture, I knew this was exactly what many Christians had in mind when they spoke of heretical false teachers, preaching to those who had been freed from sin in the name of Christ Jesus, leading them back under a yoke of slavery.

But as I listened to his message, it became clear to me that that was not what he was doing. In fact, I've heard Simons make a really good point on this exact accusation: "It's not bondage if you *want* to."

Over the three years leading up to that point, I had read through the Bible about four times, restarting every time I finished. I don't say this to boast. I say this to make the point that God had been leading me on a journey. The Scriptures of His Word were fresh and alive on my heart and mind. The words of the Bible were planted within me. Now, something was triggering a new activation of those words, revealing meaning to me that I hadn't known before. I needed to continue returning to the Bible, reading it, rereading it, praying along the way, to test the things I was hearing.

I wanted to be a lover of Truth, and if I was being honest with myself, after reading through the Bible, there were some troubling loose ends that didn't make a whole lot of sense through the lens of mainstream Christianity. For instance, the idea that the Old Testament was primarily for Israel and didn't apply to New-Testament-believing Christians raised the question, "So why did the writers of the New Testament constantly quote the Old Testament?" Or, if we are called to live our lives like Yeshua, and Yeshua fulfilled the law (meaning he obeyed God's law perfectly), why are we not living like him in this area? And why do some Christians get up in arms upon hearing that the law is a good thing when Paul wrote in 1 Timothy 1:8 that it is good if one uses it legitimately?

Things just weren't adding up, and since this was a matter of my core faith, I desired some reconciliation in my understanding. When I paid attention to the idea that God's law is a good thing, that's when the cogs really started turning.

The Gift of Righteousness and the Call to Obey

Imagine a stranger seeks you out and presents you with a ticket. He says it's a gift. He says he's going to leave for a little while, but he's going to return. When he returns, if you still have the ticket, he will reward you with eternal life in paradise.

"What's the catch?" you ask him.

The man tells you that you must love your creator and love people, otherwise the ticket will disappear as soon as he returns. Then the man leaves.

When we come to have faith in Yeshua, he gives us the gift of righteousness, just like the man giving the ticket. The man doesn't say, "When I return, I will give you the ticket if you have obeyed." That wouldn't be a gift given. That would be a reward earned. That is why we speak of righteousness as a gift from Yeshua. He's not waiting for us to do the right things before giving it to us. He has given it to us here in this life and told us to use it to love God and love people, just like the ticket would be a reminder and motivation to do the same.

Righteousness leads to eternal life, and that is why it is such a wonderful gift. However, while it is a gift that is given freely, we have the choice of rejecting it, and this is where we must clarify some misconceptions. The gift that Yeshua has already given us is righteousness, not salvation or eternal life. Righteousness *leads* to salvation, but that is not the gift Yeshua has *already* given us. Righteousness *leads* to eternal life, but that is not the gift Yeshua has *already* given us. If it were, then every person in the world would already be saved from death and living eternally, because the gift is freely given to all. But the gift that has already been given is righteousness, and every person in the world is offered this gift because of what Yeshua did. Our lives determine whether we receive and hold onto this gift or reject it.

Paul writes in Romans 5:17:

> For if by the trespass of the one, death did reign through the one, much more those who receive the overflowing favour and the gift of righteousness shall reign in life through the One, יהושע Messiah.

Yeshua tells us in Matthew 6:33:

> "But seek first the reign of Elohim, and His righteousness, and all these shall be added to you."

John 5:14 says:

> Afterward יהושע found him in the Set-apart Place, and said to him, "See, you have been made well. Sin no more, so that no worse matter befalls you."

We can also read in John 8:11:

> And she said, "No one, Master." And יהושע said to her, "Neither do I condemn you. Go and sin no more."

Sin ruined the righteous purity with which we were created. Our restored righteousness is a gift from Yeshua (Romans 5:17), but we must continue to seek after righteousness once we receive it (Matthew 6:33, John 5:14, John 8:11).

Proverbs 11:30 says:

> The fruit of the righteous is a tree of life, And he who is winning lives is wise.

Righteousness leads to salvation and eternal life. Yeshua gives us the gift of righteousness, but it must be maintained by continuing to seek after it.

It's like receiving a fruit tree as a gift. It will bear fruit, but it must be cared for and maintained until the fruit is produced. You need to put it in soil and make sure it receives sunlight and water. If you don't properly take care of it, it's not going to produce its fruit.

It's the same with the righteousness given to us by Yeshua. The righteousness, which was given to us as a gift (meaning we didn't earn it, deserve it, or create it on our own), will produce the fruits of salvation

THE GIFT OF RIGHTEOUSNESS AND THE CALL TO OBEY

and eternal life, but we are called to nurture and maintain the gift in the meantime. The Bible tells us how to do that properly.

Of course, we can (and do) say salvation and eternal life are gifts from Yeshua, because they are by extension. He gives us the righteousness that leads to salvation. But the way that Christianity has focused on the concept of salvation and neglected the reality around the necessity of righteousness has left a ton of Christians confused about the whole matter. We must understand that righteousness is our ticket to salvation. We failed at coming up with a ticket on our own. Yeshua died to purchase tickets for anyone in the world who will receive one through faith.

We have the *ticket* to salvation, but we literally are not at the venue yet. We should not focus on the salvation that is to come if it causes us to neglect the righteousness that is our ticket in. Imagine being so transfixed on going to a concert that you showed up to the venue, only to find you dropped your ticket somewhere along the way and didn't notice.

We get so caught up on salvation because we don't understand the role of righteousness, and rather than working out our own deliverance with fear and trembling (Philippians 2:12), we create convenient doctrines that allow us to skip over the substantial meat and go straight to the dessert.

Some people want to say, "Once saved, always saved," but the practical reality is we're not saved until we're saved. If a boy is drowning in a pool and there's a lifeguard sitting nearby, we don't consider the boy saved before the lifeguard even jumps in. Even though the lifeguard will be the one to save the boy, the boy is not saved until he is out of the water. In the same way, we don't have eternal life until we are living lives that are eternal. It is through the gift of righteousness that we *will* be saved from the evils of this world, but the evils of this world are currently still around us, trying to convince us to throw away our ticket. It is through righteousness that we *will* have a life that is eternal, but for now, look around—we currently have lives that end in death. Even Yeshua's earthly life ended in death. But Yeshua resurrected after he died into a life that is eternal. We call him the firstfruits because he experienced this resurrection into eternal life first, and those who have received the gift of righteousness that he offers us will one day experience this resurrection into eternal life, as well (1 Corinthians 15:22–23). That is when we literally receive eternal life.

Our righteousness is a gift from Yeshua, meaning that he earned righteousness by what he did and gifted it to us. We did nothing to earn it, but now we have it because it was a gift given to us. It is the ticket to our salvation and eternal life, and therefore we now must guard it and take care of it so that we do not lose it in this life.

I don't mean that if we commit a sinful action the gift of righteousness is taken away. I mean that if we turn our backs on the gift, if we neglect it altogether so that we don't even care if we're acting in ways that are destructive to the gift we've been given, then we reject the gift.

Think of the fruit tree that was a gift. If you forget to water it one day, it's not going to shrivel up and die immediately. But if you completely abandon the tree and consistently deprive it of what it needs to grow, the end result will not be fruit.

Pretend you forgot to water your fruit tree on Monday and then realized this on Tuesday. Now how silly would it be if you spent all of Tuesday having a nervous breakdown, running from room to room in your home, looking out the window at your tree, wondering if it was going to die, and never going out to water it that day, either? And how absurd would it be if you woke up on Wednesday completely overcome with sorrow because you didn't water the tree Monday or Tuesday, and you proceed to spend all of Wednesday moping around your home regretful, never going out to water the tree that day, either?

It's easy to see how irrational that would be in the context of taking care of a fruit tree, but that's exactly how so many people today are treating the gift of righteousness that Yeshua gave them. They realize that they failed in the past to properly care for the gift, and they allow that knowledge to determine how they move forward rather than do their best to take care of the gift starting today, regardless of how yesterday went.

This is the problem I see with the idea that "we're already saved". The idea may have begun as an encouragement to keep the faith and persevere. But religion and man's doctrine have twisted it into delusion and discouragement. It's delusion for those who believe they can go on sinning with no repercussions. It's discouragement for those who think they've missed the boat, because if the saved are already saved, well, then, why don't they feel saved? You see, the same logic for "we're already saved" can be used to conclude "I'm already damned".

It's like saying that if your fruit tree will ever produce fruit, it already has produced fruit. With that in mind, you look out your window, you don't see any fruit on your tree, you realize you didn't water it the past three days, and so you conclude it's all over.

Do you see the problem I'm getting at here? We need to spend less time freaking out over whether we've "lost our salvation" or we're "going to hell" because we committed a sinful action and more time focusing on continuously getting back on track, committing ourselves to the pursuit of righteousness. We need to know that God is patient, gracious, and forgiving, but we can't just call it quits because we've gotten off track. In the same way, we can't assume we're good to go just because we did the right thing that one time. We are called to nurture the gift of righteousness for as long as we are living. Our lives are the fruit trees, so as long as we're living, it's not too late to go out and water the tree. In other words, as long as we're living, it's not too late to start caring for the gift of righteousness that will be our ticket to eternal life.

Paul writes in Philippians 3:8–11:

> What is more, I even count all to be loss because of the excellence of the knowledge of Messiah יהושע my Master, for whom I have suffered the loss of all, and count them as refuse, in order to gain Messiah, and be found in Him, not having my own righteousness, which is of the law, but that which is through belief in Messiah, the righteousness which is from Elohim on the basis of belief, to know Him, and the power of His resurrection, and the fellowship of His sufferings, being conformed to His death, if somehow I might attain to the resurrection from the dead.

Paul makes it very clear that his righteousness comes from his belief in Yeshua. He then continues in Philippians 3:12–16:

> Not that I have already received, or already been perfected, but I press on, to lay hold of that for which Messiah יהושע has also laid hold of me. Brothers, I do not count myself to have laid hold of it yet, but only this: forgetting what is behind and reaching out for what lies ahead, I press on toward the goal for the prize of the high calling of Elohim in Messiah יהושע. As many, then, as are perfect, should have this mind. And if you think differently in any respect, Elohim shall also reveal this to you. But to what we have already attained – walk by the same rule, be of the same mind.

Do you see what Paul is saying there? He's not done. It's not over. He is still pushing forward because he understands there is still work to be done in order to attain the resurrection from the dead. Notice what he says in verse 16: "But to what we have already attained – walk by the same rule, be of the same mind." What have we already attained? The righteousness of Yeshua. What are we supposed to do with it? Walk by the same rule, be of the same mind. In other words, strive to embody righteousness.

With that said, let's go back to the ticket illustration. Suppose the man gives you the ticket, tells you to love your creator and love people, and then leaves. How long would it be before you asked yourself, "Do I know who my creator is? And do I know what the man meant by 'love'?" These are the sorts of questions we start asking when we're taking this gift scenario seriously.

Who is God? What does He consider love to be? Many Christians today either assume they know the answers to these questions or defer to church culture rather than the Word of God.

When we read about Yeshua in the Bible, it is clear he valued the Word of God over the word of religious culture. So if he is the one giving us the ticket, and if he is the one making the final assessment when he returns, shouldn't we look to the Word of God to understand what Yeshua has in mind when he tells us to love God and love people?

In Matthew 4:4, Yeshua quotes Deuteronomy 8:3 when being tempted by the devil:

> But He answering, said, "It has been written, 'Man shall not live by bread alone, but by every word that comes from the mouth of יהוה.'"

The books of the Bible contain the words of יהוה, from Genesis to Revelation. We don't get to decide who God is or what it means to love Him based on our own reasoning. We are called to go by His words.

Yeshua gives us the gift of righteousness and calls us to obey him (John 14:15). We obey him by loving God with all our being and loving people as Yeshua loved us (Matthew 22:36–40, John 13:34). If we don't care enough to spend time looking into who God is based on what He says about Himself, we are not even trying to love Him with all our being. If we don't care enough to spend time looking into what it means to love people as Yeshua loved us, then we are not even trying to love people as Yeshua loved us. All it takes is the tiniest concern, faith no larger than a mustard seed, to put forth some effort to understand these matters. God knows that we won't be perfect in this, but He lovingly expects us to at the very least give it a shot.

We've been given the gift of righteousness and called to obey. If we really want to answer the call to obey, we must read the Word of God, and that includes the Torah, which Yeshua lived out perfectly.

Loving Expectation

MUCH OF CHRISTIANITY today can't stand the idea that God actually expects us to do something. I see this as very childlike: "Wait a minute, you actually expect me to do my own laundry?" Yeah, it's your laundry. God provided the washing machine and the detergent. He provided the very clothes that you got dirty. He even provided the body you need in order to put the clothes into the washing machine, pour in the detergent, and push the little button to start it.

You see, those who are repulsed at the idea of being expected to do anything are the same ones who wouldn't really enjoy eternal life with Yeshua, anyway. Life means having a role in existence. It means putting forth effort. It is a gift from God. He didn't need us in order to create a beautiful world. But He gifted us with life, and now we get to have an actual role in the world. We're not expected to lift an elephant over our head, but if someone falls down, is it too much to be expected to lend them a hand in getting back up?

Churches today may have good intentions, but many are pumping out a hollow gospel: claim Jesus, go tell others to claim Jesus, and don't let anyone tell you that you need to do anything else. Many people then become Christians and charge forward before gaining a real understanding of who God is and what true love looks like. As a result, much of Christianity now looks like a pyramid scheme—the only thing some Christians seemed concerned about (other than certain political topics) is recruiting others to recruit others to recruit others. Beneath all the recruiting, there doesn't appear to be a whole lot of substance.

Church culture has demonized the idea of people being expected to do anything. If someone says that you're supposed to do something, then they must be teaching a false gospel and murdering Yeshua all over again. This is the kind of tactic, though, that empowers a pyramid scheme to continue to exist even when it has nothing to offer. The scheme doesn't have to make sense. People just need to be fearful of anything that isn't the scheme.

Please don't be fearful of what I'm telling you. The gift of righteousness cost Yeshua his life, and he has given it freely with the instruction to obey. He did not tell us to obey so that we'll be worthy of the gift. He told us to obey so that we can preserve the gift he's already given us, which is our ticket to eternal life. He told us to obey because he loves us, and he knows that this gift is the only thing that can save us from the punishment of the wicked that is to come.

Yeshua's call to obey is a beautiful thing, because the obedience he is referring to is loving God and loving people. Why would we be resistant to this sort of obedience?

Of course, the problem today isn't the idea of obeying the command to love God and love people. The problem is defining what that means. Yeshua says in John 15:13:

> "No one has greater love than this: that one should lay down his life for his friends."

It's ironic that a million Christians could argue doctrine until they're blue in the face, and as long as they're arguing, not one of them has laid down their lives for the others, yet many would still claim they are arguing out of love. By the way, in the very next verse, John 15:14, Yeshua says:

> "You are My friends if you do whatever I command you."

Yeshua says in Matthew 5:46–48:

> "For if you love those loving you, what reward have you? Are the tax collectors not doing the same too? And if you greet your brothers only, what do you do more than others? Are the tax collectors not doing so too? Therefore, be perfect, as your Father in the heavens is perfect."

Yeshua commands us to be perfect. Now how in the world can he expect us to be perfect? This is an unreasonable expectation, unless he gives us help. That is exactly what he does. He gives us the righteousness that we cannot achieve on our own. He makes us perfect when we believe that he died on our behalf, and then he calls us to continue on in righteousness. We don't have to make up for lost time or fix every mistake we've made or rebuild everything we've broken. That is what forgiveness and repentance are all about. God forgives us because of Yeshua, and those who really, *truly* believe in this good news repent of the way they had been living their lives, making mistakes and destroying that which is good. We can now focus all our energies on moving forward in that righteousness that Yeshua gave us as a gift. What's more, he empowers us with the Holy Spirit, writing God's law on our hearts (Jeremiah 31:33), so that we have the desire and therefore the power to obey, moving forward in righteousness.

The command to be perfect is literally a loving expectation. It is an expectation to love. We can argue about the Torah, the law of God, but when it's all said and done, Yeshua said that all of the law hangs on the two commands of loving God and loving people. When it's all said and done, Yeshua obeyed the Torah.

I'm not going to let the people around me or myself be the authority on what Yeshua expects of me when he tells me to love God and love people. I'm going to let the Word of God be that authority, because that was the authority to which Yeshua submitted.

Part 5

The Law of God

Before You Feast on This Part

I FIND IT CURIOUS that two of the major themes of the Bible that much of Christianity has written off in one way or another are the Torah and the millennial reign of Yeshua. The millennial reign is laid out explicitly in Revelation, and I suppose that's why many Christians are eager to discount it as something literal and call it something figurative instead. But there are other places in Scripture that point to a literal reign of Yeshua on this earth.

For example, after Yeshua ascends into heaven, two messengers appear to the believers. Acts 1:10–11 says:

> And as they were gazing into the heaven as He went up, see, two men stood by them dressed in white, who also said, "Men of Galil, why do you stand looking up into the heaven? This same יהושע, who was taken up from you into the heaven, shall come in the same way as you saw Him go into the heaven."

These messengers tell the people that Yeshua will return in the same way he went up. If we follow the logic of this idea, it points to a literal reign of Yeshua on earth. He's going to come back to earth in the same way he left the earth. We would have to say that he didn't literally ascend into heaven if we want to maintain that he won't literally be returning.

When Yeshua literally returns to the earth, what do you think he's going to be doing? He's going to be ruling.

Zechariah 14:1–4 says:

> See, a day shall come for יהוה, and your spoil shall be divided in your midst. And I shall gather all the nations to battle against Yerushalayim. And the city shall be taken, the houses plundered, and the women ravished. Half of the city shall go into exile, but the remnant of the people shall not be cut off from

the city. And יהוה shall go forth, and He shall fight against those nations, as He fights in the day of battle. And in that day His feet shall stand upon the Mount of Olives, which faces Yerushalayim on the east. And the Mount of Olives shall be split in two, from east to west, a very great valley, and half of the mountain shall move toward the north and half of it toward the south.

Notice that Zechariah writes, "in that day His feet shall stand upon the Mount of Olives". When Yeshua ascended, he and his disciples were in Bethany, which was a village on the Mount of Olives. Those messengers weren't joking when they said he would return in the same way as they saw him go up. He left the Mount of Olives, and he will be returning to the Mount of Olives.

As a side note, I recently learned that there is a fault line that passes through the Mount of Olives. I find that fascinating in connection with Zechariah writing, "And the Mount of Olives shall be split in two".

There are many other Scriptures that point to a literal reign to come, when God's Chosen comes and defeats the sovereigns of the earth: Psalm 2, Isaiah 9:7, Jeremiah 23:5, Ezekiel 37:24, Daniel 2:44, Micah 5:2–4, and Luke 1:32–33. (It's not hard to find these—a Bible with references does most of the work for you.)

Notice what Yeshua tells the disciples before he ascends in Acts 1:6–7:

> So when they had come together, they asked Him, saying, "Master, would You at this time restore the reign to Yisraěl?" And He said to them, "It is not for you to know times or seasons which the Father has put in His own authority."

The disciples were expecting Yeshua to literally restore the reign to Israel. Yeshua tells them it is not for them to know the times or seasons. If the disciples were mistaken in thinking that Yeshua would literally restore the reign to Israel, Yeshua did not take the opportunity here to correct them.

When we read Scripture as it's written, it points to a literal reign to come. When we start getting comfortable interpreting Scripture to fit manmade doctrine, it doesn't matter what Scripture says—we'll find some way to twist it to fit the mold of our doctrine.

When we take Scripture at its word, we start seeing how it gives us much more information about the millennial reign than we originally thought. In addition to what the Scriptures tell us, there are some things we can come to understand on our own (without skewing the Scriptures) because we are thinking in terms of a literal reign.

For example, in a literal reign, there is a king who reigns. That king is the law—he holds sovereign power. That's a very interesting connection to make in terms of Scripture. When we read the Bible, we are reading God's Word. The first part of God's Word is God's law, the Torah. When we get to the book of John, we read about God's Word becoming flesh (John 1:14). This is Yeshua. Now, if God's law is God's Word and God's Word became flesh in the form of Yeshua, that means Yeshua is the embodiment of God's law. Yeshua is God's law. The king is the law.

If there is a literal reign, there is a literal law. We already know what that law is going to be. It's contained in the most popular book in the world, and you likely own a copy of it. And yet, sadly, so many people don't want to learn about it. We prefer law that is here and now, and not law that is to come.

If there is a literal reign to come, and we have access to its law now, we would do well to get on with learning it.

Legalism, Games, and Technicalities

THE IRONY OF RELIGION is that it tells us we don't need God's law because we're not supposed to be living under a law, and then it proceeds to give us its own law. It's a sleight-of-hand trick. It's true that we're not supposed to be living *under* the law. But the reality is that we are going to end up living *according* to *some* law. If it's not God's law, it's going to be some other law. It may be Christian law, it may be societal law, it may be self-law. Regardless, where there is a vacuum, some law will inhabit, because law is just a system of rules for operating by. If we're not living by some law, then we're just meandering around mindlessly.

This is the whole idea behind the new covenant. Jeremiah 31:31–33 says:

> "See, the days are coming," declares יהוה, "when I shall make a renewed covenant with the house of Yisraěl and with the house of Yehuḏah, not like the covenant I made with their fathers in the day when I strengthened their hand to bring them out of the land of Mitsrayim, My covenant which they broke, though I was a husband to them," declares יהוה. "For this is the covenant I shall make with the house of Yisraěl after those days, declares יהוה: I shall put My Torah in their inward parts, and write it on their hearts. And I shall be their Elohim, and they shall be My people."

The writer of Hebrews reiterates this in Hebrews 10:15–18:

> And the Set-apart Spirit also witnesses to us, for after having said before, "This is the covenant that I shall make with them after those days, says יהוה, giving My laws into their hearts, and in their minds I shall write them," and, "Their sins and their lawlessnesses I shall remember no more." Now where there is

forgiveness of these, there is no longer a slaughter offering for sin.

Again, we're not called to be living *under* God's law—being under a law means being subject to the punishment for breaking the law. As Hebrews states, where there is forgiveness, there is no longer a slaughter offering for sin. The punishment for breaking the law has been paid. Living *under* the law means living like we still must face the punishment for breaking the law, and that implies a rejection of what Yeshua did for us.

When we read the Bible for what it says, we cannot avoid this conclusion: even though we don't live under God's law, God's law never changed. Yes, Yeshua's death on the cross paid the penalty for the world's lawlessness. Yeshua's death on the cross also ushered in the new covenant, which, as we read in Hebrews 10:15–18 and Jeremiah 31:31–33, effectively transferred God's law from being written on stone tablets to being written on our hearts. We don't live under God's law, but God's law never changed. What changed was the fact that Yeshua paid the penalty for the world's lawlessness, as well as the location of God's law from that point forward. Within the old covenant, God's law was written on stone tablets. It was physically inscribed on stone. Likewise, God's people were expected to physically obey the commands of the law. Under the new covenant, the Holy Spirit writes God's law on our hearts. It is not a matter of simply obeying the things that are written on stone. It is a matter of fully embodying God's law within us, down to our basest desires. For example, Yeshua spoke of not holding anger against your brother and not lusting after a woman, because the law does not apply to external behavior only, but rather to our thinking and desiring, as well.

The Christian faith (the *faith*, not the *religion*) is not about abandoning the law of God—it is about embracing it fully. This truth is written within the law of God itself. Deuteronomy 6:5–8 says:

> "And you shall love יהוה your Elohim with all your heart, and with all your being, and with all your might. And these Words which I am commanding you today shall be in your heart, and you shall impress them upon your children, and shall speak of them when you sit in your house, and when you walk by the way, and when you lie down, and when you rise up, and shall bind them as a sign on your hand, and they shall be as frontlets between your eyes."

We misrepresent the Bible when we treat God's law as synonymous with the old covenant. The old covenant has passed away, but the law of God is still very much at play in the hearts of those who have received the Holy Spirit. The old covenant was an agreement God had with His people—He would be their God, and those who obeyed His law would be His people. But the people He called to obey His law (the Israelites) did not obey His law.

God created the new covenant through Yeshua. When Yeshua died, he satisfied the consequences for our transgressions of the law under the old covenant, allowing a new covenant to take place between God and His people—He would be their God, and those who had His law written on their hearts would be His people. This is supposed to be us, we who have placed our faith in Yeshua, accepting His sacrifice on behalf of our sins, and receiving the Holy Spirit, who writes God's law on our hearts, giving us the desire to obey Him. This new covenant is what restores humanity to the position God had intended for us originally, when He first created Adam and Eve and told them to have dominion over the earth.

When God created Adam and Eve, He gave them freedom. Freedom to eat of any tree except the one, and freedom to enjoy their lives. Freedom is a wonderful thing, but it is taken away when we are living *under* a law. Again, living under a law means living like we still have to face the punishment for breaking the law. This results in a lifestyle of legalism.

The problem never was the Torah itself. The Torah came from God, and it is good (1 Timothy 1:8). The problem was the human heart, which led us to a legalistic spirit towards the Torah (and the traditions of men). The Jews had developed a way of being in which they meticulously hyper focused on the details of the law and their traditions, and in doing that, they neglected the more important matters. Yeshua says in Matthew 23:23:

> "Woe to you, scribes and Pharisees, hypocrites! Because you tithe the mint and the anise and the cumin, and have neglected the weightier matters of the Torah: the right-ruling and the compassion and the belief. These need to have been done, without neglecting the others."

And, again, we see the great commandment in Matthew 22:36–40:

> "Teacher, which is the great command in the Torah?" And יהושע said to him, "'You shall love יהוה your Elohim with all your heart, and with all your being, and with all your mind.' This is the first and great command. And the second is like it, 'You shall

LEGALISM, GAMES, AND TECHNICALITIES

love your neighbour as yourself.' On these two commands hang all the Torah and the Prophets."

Yeshua is telling the religious teachers that the whole point of the Torah is to guide us in loving God and loving people. If we try and obey the Torah without prioritizing love, then we're not actually obeying the Torah, because we are focused on justifying ourselves through our good works instead of focused on loving God and loving others. That is the issue Yeshua, Peter, and Paul keep confronting throughout the New Testament.

Notice how succinctly this account in Luke captures the situation. Luke 10:25-29 says:

> And see, a certain one learned in the Torah stood up, trying Him, and saying, "Teacher, what shall I do to inherit everlasting life?" And He said to him, "What has been written in the Torah? How do you read it?" And he answering, said, "'You shall love יהוה your Elohim with all your heart, and with all your being, and with all your strength, and with all your mind,' and 'your neighbour as yourself.'" And He said to him, "You have answered rightly. Do this and you shall live." But he, wishing to declare himself righteous, said to יהושע, "And who is my neighbour?"

This was a man "learned in the Torah", and yet, even when Yeshua told him he answered correctly regarding loving God and loving his neighbor, he still wanted to declare himself righteous. It's as if this was all an intellectual game to him. He knew the right answers, but he wasn't as concerned about doing the right thing as he was about outshining the other students.

Yeshua proceeds to tell the parable of the good Samaritan, and then Luke 10:36-37 says:

> "Who, then, of these three, do you think, was neighbour to him who fell among the robbers?" And he said, "He who showed compassion on him." Then יהושע said to him, "Go and do likewise."

Yeshua stays focused on the main idea—love, love, love. Love your neighbor.

Legalism is an easy thing for any person to fall into. It may not be legalism towards the law of God. It might be legalism around a religion, a school of thought or a certain philosophy, or even a specific form of social etiquette. Legalism simply describes an excessive adherence to law or formula.

I love board games. Nerdy, complex, rule-intensive board games. I enjoy knowing exactly what the rules are and abiding by the rules as they are written, because, for me, the challenge of excelling and winning within the parameters of the rules completely enhances the fun.

I think back to playing soccer at recess in elementary school. I hated it whenever some kid picked up the ball and started running with it, and then everyone devolved into throwing the ball around. In my eyes, the game was ruined. Sure, it might be fun to run around mindlessly throwing a ball, but for how long? There's no challenge when there are no parameters.

That's why I like nerdy, complex, rule-intensive board games. Mastering the complexity to be able to not just play correctly but win is fun and satisfying for me.

That said, I have to be mindful of whom I'm playing with, because the whole point of playing board games is to have fun. Most of the time, I'm playing with people who don't find as much joy as I do in strictly adhering to the rules. If I start getting super technical about the details of the rules with people who don't enjoy this sort of behavior, I ruin the fun, not just for them, but for myself, too, because nobody is interested in playing anymore, and the challenge is gone. I certainly have been guilty of doing this, and I have learned that it's not worth it. If the point is to have fun, then I have to let go of my neurotic desire to adhere to the rules in a microscopic manner. That's not to say I break the rules myself. I just don't get so caught up on enforcing the rules for others that it ruins the game for everyone else. If I am willing to ruin the overall fun for everyone in pursuit of satisfying a minor detail within the rules, then I am not actually pursuing the more important matter of having fun. If I am willing to ruin the fun for everyone, then I am being legalistic, *excessively* adhering to the rules. I am no longer adhering to the rules for the purpose of having fun, but rather for the purpose of justifying myself.

If I'm playing a board game with my friend Craig, however, the situation looks quite different. Our fun is exponentially multiplied when we go back to the rules, debate them, and play within the proper parameters, no matter how microscopic the detail. We are not being legalistic, because this is fun for us, and we do it *because* we enjoy it, not because we feel obligated to do so.

Adhering to the rules is the way I prefer to play board games. For me, it is the most fun way to play. But if I refuse to meet people where they're at, I am only limiting my own enjoyment.

This is how I see Yeshua presenting love in the context of the Torah. The Torah is a major component of the rulebook for the game of life (which is the Bible). The whole point of participating in this game is to love God and love people. The Torah gives the rules for how to go about loving correctly. The more we understand and abide by the rules, the more effective we love. But if the way we approach the rules causes us to neglect the matter of loving God and loving people, then we are missing the whole point, and we need to reassess.

In Matthew 23:3-4, Yeshua says regarding the scribes and the Pharisees:

> "Therefore, whatever they say to you to guard, guard and do. But do not do according to their works, for they say, and do not do. For they bind heavy burdens, hard to bear, and lay them on men's shoulders, but with their finger they do not wish to move them."

Notice that Yeshua says, "Whatever they say to you to guard, guard and do." The Pharisees adamantly told people to obey the law, to follow the rules. Their message wasn't wrong in itself. Yeshua tells the people to listen to their message and do it. Yeshua then says, "But do not do according to their works, for they say, and do not do." The Pharisees were telling the people the right message—obey the law—but they weren't actually obeying the law themselves, because they weren't loving God and loving people, according to the law. They were more concerned about justifying themselves than they were about loving others.

Law, in general, is meant to give order to a multitude. This is why it doesn't work when individuals get caught up in obeying the law for the purpose of justifying themselves. We see this when criminals are declared innocent in court because of some technicality. Their lawyers play the system for the purpose of justifying the individual. When this happens, the defendant *technically* didn't break the law in the way they may have been accused. But they end up violating the spirit of the matter. They justify themselves through technicalities and legalism rather than obedience to the spirit of the law.

Law is not about serving the individual, but rather the whole. When we choose to approach the law for the purpose of justifying ourselves, we are no longer seeking after the primary goal of the law, because we are prioritizing ourselves over the whole.

Sabbath Legalism

MATTHEW 12:10–14 SAYS:

> And see, there was a man having a withered hand. And they asked Him, saying, "Is it right to heal on the Sabbath?" – so as to accuse Him. And He said to them, "What man is there among you who has one sheep, and if it falls into a pit on the Sabbath, shall not take hold of it and lift it out? How much more worth is a man than a sheep! So it is right to do good on the Sabbath." Then He said to the man, "Stretch out your hand." And he stretched it out, and it was restored, as healthy as the other. But the Pharisees went out and took counsel against Him, so as to destroy Him.

I've heard people argue that Yeshua broke the law in this passage by not honoring the Sabbath. That argument, however, assumes he was not honoring the Sabbath based on a very legalistic understanding of the Sabbath. It requires a perspective that is so focused on the microscopic details, particularly those pertaining to the traditions of men, that it forgets the larger, more important matters of loving God and loving people. Again, all of the law is about loving God and loving people. The Sabbath is a piece of the law, so we must consider it from the perspective of how it plays into this picture of loving God and loving people.

God sanctified the seventh day during creation, and He set it apart. Deuteronomy 5:15 says:

> And you shall remember that you were a slave in the land of Mitsrayim, and that יהוה your Elohim brought you out from there by a strong hand and by an outstretched arm. Therefore יהוה your Elohim commanded you to perform the Sabbath day.

Exodus 31:13 says:

> "And you, speak to the children of Yisraěl, saying, 'My Sabbaths you are to guard, by all means, for it is a sign between Me and you throughout your generations, to know that I, יהוה, am setting you apart.'"

And again, Exodus 31:17 says:

> "'Between Me and the children of Yisraěl it is a sign forever. For in six days יהוה made the heavens and the earth, and on the seventh day He rested and was refreshed.'"

God established the Sabbath as a sign between Him and His people. I know many Christians believe that the Sabbath was explicitly for the Israelites and not for Christians to observe. If we are brought into the family of God through Yeshua, though, we are Israelites, not by blood, but by adoption (Romans 8:15). We are grafted in (Romans 11:11–24), and we see throughout Scripture that God expects the foreigner who joins His people to observe the same law as the native-born (Exodus 12:49). While it is true that the *process* for accepting a foreigner as a native changed from the old covenant to the new covenant (circumcision of flesh to circumcision of heart), the framework still applies—when a foreigner desires to become part of God's people, they go through the proper initiation (circumcision of heart, i.e., broken-hearted repentance), and from that point forward, they are called to obey God's law first and foremost, and not the law of the nation from which they have come.

God's law isn't abolished (Matthew 5:17), but we are no longer *under* it in the way of receiving the penalty for breaking it.

Galatians 3:23–25 says:

> But before belief came, we were being guarded under Torah, having been shut up for the belief being about to be revealed. Therefore the Torah became our trainer unto Messiah, in order to be declared right by belief. And after belief has come, we are no longer under a trainer.

Colossians 2:13–14 says:

> And you, being dead in your trespasses and the uncircumcision of your flesh, He has made alive together with Him, having forgiven you all trespasses, having blotted out that which was written by hand against us – by the dogmas – which stood against us. And He has taken it out of the way, having nailed it to the stake.

When we understand this, we can see that the Sabbath is intended to be a sign between God and us (as opposed to some legal obligation). It is a sign that God brought us out of slavery. We are no longer *under* the yoke of slavery, just like we are no longer *under* the law. Just like the Israelites were no longer slaves to Egypt, we are no longer slaves to sin. When we work for six days and rest on the seventh, we proclaim that truth. We display to the rest of the world that we have been freed from oppression by the grace of God. Our intentional rest on the seventh day is a sign that we don't belong to Egypt, we don't belong to sin, we don't belong to death. We belong to God, purchased through the blood of Yeshua.

If the intent of the Sabbath is to be a sign between God and His people, then honoring the Sabbath is part of loving God *and* loving people. We love God by respecting what He told His people to do, and we love people by resting and rejoicing in God with one another. Yeshua said, "It is right to do good on the Sabbath." So, then, what does "doing good" mean on the Sabbath? It means loving God and loving people. Yeshua had a perfect understanding of love, and so he knew exactly how to conduct himself on the Sabbath.

Consider these three scenarios:

Scenario A

A son and his father schedule a day to spend together. They meet up at the agreed upon time and place, and they enjoy their day together.

Scenario B

A son and his father schedule a day to spend together. They meet up at the agreed upon time and place, but only a couple minutes into their day, the son's brother calls him with a real emergency. The father tells the son, "Go, take care of your brother," and the son leaves their scheduled plans, because both he and his father love the brother.

Scenario C

A son and his father schedule a day to spend together, but before the day arrives, the son decides his father no longer wants to meet up on that day. His father never told him this explicitly, but the son feels pretty confident in his assessment, anyway. So the son doesn't show up to meet his father at all.

Out of these three scenarios, which one seems to indicate a lack of respect on behalf of the son for his father? Scenario C, where the son just decides he's not going to show up, and he doesn't even talk it over with his father.

Does the son in Scenario A love his father more than the son in Scenario B because he (Scenario A) spent the entire day with his father? For all we know, no. The son in Scenario B left because both he and his father realized it was right for him to do good on that day (i.e., take care of his brother).

Like the father in these examples, God sets the Sabbath to establish a weekly meeting with his children. Since Yeshua established that all the Torah hangs on loving God and loving others, and since God established the Sabbath in Torah (the Ten Commandments), this lets us know that observing the Sabbath is a good thing—it is something that shows we love God and love others. However, like the son in the above scenarios, we have the choice of whether or not we will keep the appointment with the Father. Unfortunately, many Christians today are being taught that it is absolutely acceptable to fall into Scenario C and to treat the Sabbath with disregard.

When we really lean into the understanding that the Torah is all about loving God and loving people, certain situations are no longer as confusing as they once seemed through a lens of legalism. When we lean into this understanding, we begin to see why pieces of the law are the way they are.

Sabbath Law

IF AN AMBULANCE is speeding down the highway to get someone to the hospital for emergency medical treatment, is the driver breaking the law? We could technically say that he is speeding, but the priority of the man in need of emergency medical attention creates an exception.

Now, if someone is driving to work and sees the ambulance speeding, is it okay for that person to speed?

It's not okay for that person to speed just because they see the ambulance speeding. We know this, and yet we've created all kinds of justifications for not observing the Sabbath based on what we read about Yeshua in the Gospels. We've taken advantage of Yeshua's compassion for people and used it to reinterpret the law of God.

I'm focusing on the Sabbath here because I believe this is where the modern Christian view of God's law being abolished began. The Sabbath is one of the *Ten* Commandments. Not just one of 613 laws, but one of ten. At the end of 2 Chronicles, when Jerusalem is being captured and the people are being exiled to Babylon, 2 Chronicles 36:20–21 says:

> And those who escaped from the sword he exiled to Ba<u>b</u>el, where they became servants to him and his sons until the reign of the reign of Persia, in order to fill the word of יהוה by the mouth of Yirmeyahu, until the land had enjoyed her Sabbaths. As long as she lay waste she kept Sabbath, until seventy years were completed.

The people of Jerusalem were exiled until the land enjoyed her Sabbaths—seventy years. In other words, the Sabbaths weren't taking place while the people were in the land because they weren't honoring the Sabbath, so God had them exiled so that the land could enjoy the Sabbaths. The Sabbaths took place without the people there.

God told the people this would happen beforehand. Jeremiah 17:27 says:

> """"But if you do not obey Me to set apart the Sabbath day, and not to bear a burden when entering the gates of Yerushalayim on the Sabbath day, then I shall kindle a fire in its gates, and it shall consume the palaces of Yerushalayim, and not be quenched.""""

When we read through the Bible, it is apparent that the Sabbath is a big deal to God. It may cause you to wonder, "What, exactly, is the big deal? Okay, it's supposed to be a sign or whatever, but it's not like I'm murdering people or cheating on my wife if I don't observe the Sabbath."

First of all, we're taking it upon ourselves to define morality when we start prioritizing God's laws based on human reasoning.

Second, it's presumptuous for us to think we fully understand every implication of obeying or breaking God's laws. We have limited understanding, in general. We don't know fully what the repercussions are for neglecting the Sabbath.

Which brings me to the third point, maybe dishonoring the Sabbath is like murdering people or cheating on my wife. Those three are all part of the same list of ten that God gave to Moses. Not only that, but the Sabbath command came before those other two.

I'm not just saying this suggestively or esoterically, as if there's some divine mystery around the Sabbath that one day God will reveal to us. I think this is a very practical command. If every person in the world rested on the seventh day, at the end of every week, in order to reconnect with God, how much better off would we be? I know that our current system isn't set up in a way that is conducive to this (particularly in the way of not buying or selling for a whole day every week, which, as we will see later, is Scripturally connected to the Sabbath), but if this was the norm for our world, think of the implications.

Perhaps a better way of thinking about this is to think of all our current realities that can be attributed, at least in part, to not having a day of rest and reconnection to God. Anxiety, depression, a nonstop pursuit of money, the stress of burnout. Also a tendency to depend on a church or pastor for spiritual growth as opposed to having a personal relationship with God that gets nurtured at least one day a week.

We live in a world that is increasingly telling us, "Go fast, go hard, go now." It shouldn't be surprising that depression, mental illness, suicide, and mass shootings are all on the rise. We can't stop, and if we're being honest with ourselves, we don't know how. How are we supposed to set aside a whole day for rest when we've got bills to pay, mouths to feed, and business to attend to?

Over the past year, I've talked with quite a few people on the topics I'm writing about here, and I often get the response, "I don't have enough time to really look into that stuff."

I usually don't point it out to them, but these same people have time for Netflix, vacations, going to bars or restaurants, reading books, and a plethora of other activities. I'm not intending to accuse here—I'm just like these people. I enjoy all that stuff, and I often feel like I don't have time for anything other than what I'm already doing. I only say this to make the point that the world we live in causes us to feel suffocated when it comes to time and commitments. We feel overloaded, overbooked, overstressed, and overwhelmed. But when we really look at the things that compose our weekly schedules, does the significance of those things match up with the stress we feel?

For me, the answer is no, and that makes me wonder why.

God is our creator. Being the creator of something means understanding how it works. In a certain sense, we are machines, and we require certain inputs to go on producing our outputs functionally. One of our needed inputs is rest. Not just going-to-sleep-at-night rest, but spiritual rest taking place within consciousness.

The Sabbath keeps us functioning properly. That's why it's a big deal on the practical level. Not only does it give us the rest we need, but it conditions us to be able to voluntarily set aside the stressors of life and reconnect with God in order to take care of ourselves. I believe many people feel so strapped for time and overloaded with obligations because they don't regularly practice setting aside their stress for the purpose of personal recovery.

We may not understand exactly how this works, but I have faith that neglecting the Sabbath results in a worn-out person who is then more vulnerable to temptation and sin. When the Sabbath is neglected on a worldwide scale, the ultimate result is a world that is more given to and trapped in sin.

I also believe this is why Yeshua found the Pharisees' legalism around the Sabbath particularly offensive. This was supposed to be a day given by God for the people to recover, recharge, and reconnect with Him. Instead, the Pharisees turned it into a day that was more laborious than all the others because of their staunch legalism and all the expectations that came as a result. They made the concept of not working into a chore. They were taking the people back to their slavery in Egypt, where the Israelites didn't have the freedom to set their work aside and rest.

When it comes to Yeshua and the Pharisees going back and forth on the Sabbath, we need to understand that, once again, the problem was the spirit of legalism, not the commandment of God. Christianity threw the baby out with the bathwater on this one—we got rid of Sabbath legalism by getting rid of the Sabbath. We tinkered with one of the Ten Commandments, a law given by God. And once there's a tear in the fabric, it doesn't take much to rip it.

The "New Sabbath" Argument

I'D LIKE TO address what I would guess many of you might be thinking right now: "Well, I do observe a Sabbath, of sorts. I go to church on Sunday." When you look into the history of the Sabbath and Sunday developing into the Christian day of worship, there is a lot to take in and consider. If you are willing to consider religious tradition on equal footing with the Scriptures, then there are numerous arguments that you could formulate for why it is acceptable to hold Sunday as the new Sabbath. But if you maintain that the Scriptures should take priority over religious tradition, it's more difficult to do this while staying true to what the Scriptures actually say.

Before moving forward, I want to encourage you to identify where your thinking lands on this topic, otherwise it quickly gets messy trying to sort through. Which of these statements best aligns with your thinking:

1. The Sabbath day is the seventh day of the week and should be observed each week according to the fourth commandment.
2. The Sabbath day was effectively changed to the first day of the week after Yeshua resurrected on the first day.
3. The Sabbath day can be whatever day you want to make it.
4. There is no longer a need to observe a Sabbath at all—we're no longer under the law and it doesn't make a difference to God whether we observe it or not.
5. I have no opinion on the matter.

I realize that you may not fully align with any of those, but hopefully there is one that comes closer to your thinking than the others.

The reason I encourage you to decide here where your thinking lands on the matter is because I have had conversations about the Sabbath with Christians who seemed to move from 2 to 3 to 4 to 5 like they were optional steppingstones based on how the conversation developed. They began with the mindset that the Sabbath was effectively changed to Sunday (number 2), but then when they were confronted with a challenge to that, their thinking evolved into either the belief that the Sabbath can be any day of the week as long as you rest (number 3) or the belief that there is no longer a need to observe the Sabbath (number 4). If that belief proceeded to be challenged, they then evolved into having less of an opinion on the matter altogether (number 5), as if the subject wasn't really important enough to demand an opinion anyway, effectively ending any kind of thoughtful conversation.

I hope you'll take a moment to seriously decide how you feel about this subject. I'm not trying to get you to commit to an opinion so that I can win an argument. I'm just trying to be clear about each position at play because I find it very tedious trying to discuss a position that is evolving right in the midst of the discussion.

I most closely align with number 1. I have already been sharing my thoughts about this and will continue to do so.

I will address number 2 in just a moment.

If you align with number 3, that the Sabbath day can be whatever day you want to make it as long as you're resting, I imagine you have a respect for the principle of rest, but perhaps not a respect for the Sabbath day as a time for meeting with God. I used to be aligned with perspective 3. What moved me away from it was seriously considering the question, "What authority is this view based on?" I realized that those who call the seventh day the Sabbath have the Scriptures as their authority, and those who call the first day the Sabbath have the church as their authority. But what authority is perspective 3 based on? I realized it was based on the authority of self: "*My* Sabbath day will be whatever day *I* want it to be."

The only authority informing the view of number 3 is the self, and when that's the authority, there's no real prioritization of the Sabbath. There's only prioritization of self. The Sabbath in that context just ends up defaulting to matters of convenience and opportunity. When I understood perspective number 3 in these terms, I realized I might as well be a part of perspective 4, believing that there's no longer a need to observe a Sabbath at all. I didn't really believe the Sabbath day could be whatever day I wanted it to be. I just believed that it was a good idea to regularly rest. It wasn't about honoring God. It was about taking care of myself.

But then I realized I also had problems with perspective number 4, that there's no longer a need to observe a Sabbath at all.

If you align with number 4, I encourage you to consider why the Sabbath was given as the fourth commandment, right after have no other gods, have no idols, and don't bring His name to naught. Scripture makes clear why it's given as a commandment. Do you know the reasons given? If not, I hope you'll look into it. If you do know the reasons given, then I believe you're misunderstanding the spirit of the matter around this commandment. It's not about legalistically obeying some arbitrary law. It's about God blessing His people with both existence and freedom. When we try to do away with this commandment, we are trying to do away with a strong piece of evidence and a weekly reminder that God is good and wants to bless us.

The Sabbath is a blessing from God, a day to rest, a day to reflect on our creation and our freedom, both of which were given to us freely by God. The perspective of number 4 views the Sabbath as a burden or a chore instead of a blessing or a gift, which is exactly what the Pharisees were promoting by applying a strict legalism to the day.

It's kind of like receiving a luxury car as a gift and your main sentiment is, "Great, now I have to fill it up with gas." Rather than focusing on the good and being grateful, you focus on the responsibility and end up bitter.

Those who align with number 4, like the Pharisees, consider the Sabbath a task to be done. The only difference is that the Pharisees addressed the task by checking off the "to-do" boxes associated with their perceived task, whereas those who align with number 4 address the task by saying it no longer needs to be done at all. The Pharisees filled the car up with gas and rode around in it, but they never had a love for the gift nor for the one who gave it to them. Today, those who align with number 4 simply return the gift each week and thank God for the refund money, calling it (ironically) "freedom".

Make no mistake, there is just as much legalistic perspective around the Sabbath within those who align with number 4 as there is within the Pharisees. That's why I don't want to spend more time than this addressing number 4, because those who land there for good often possess a false heart and not just a false teaching. Until they have eyes that see the spirit of the matter (that the Sabbath was a gift intended to bless the people) they will forever miss the truth.

If you align with number 5, I appreciate your honesty. I hope that reading this book helps you form an opinion of your own.

That leaves perspective number 2. If you maintain that the Sabbath day was effectively changed to the first day of the week after Yeshua resurrected on the first day, I just want us to try and get on the same page about what the Bible (particularly the New Testament) actually says about this. Again, if you are willing to consider religious tradition on equal footing with the Scriptures, then I understand why you would feel the way you do. But if you believe the Bible should take priority, then I really don't see a solid case being made explicitly through the Scriptures for this perspective.

The primary argument I've heard revolves around the idea that, after Yeshua resurrected, the believers met on the first day of the week. This idea is based on two verses, which we will look at shortly.

There are certainly other verses used to make other points, but those points tend to gravitate to perspective number 4 rather than number 2. I challenge you to find a verse anywhere in the New Testament *explicitly* instructing us to abandon the seventh-day Sabbath and keep the first day instead.

For example, Colossians 2:16–17 says:

> Let no one therefore judge you in eating or in drinking, or in respect of a festival or a new moon or Sabbaths – which are a shadow of what is to come – but the Body of the Messiah.

This verse is not making a point about an alteration of the Sabbath or any other command. When people use it in such a way, they are distorting its focus and superimposing inferences. Eating, drinking, festivals, new moons, and Sabbaths are being used here as examples to show the larger point Paul is making, which is that we are forgiven in Yeshua's death and no longer condemned by our shortcomings. This verse is making the point that we therefore should not let anyone other than the Body of the Messiah judge us on any matter. In other words, don't allow yourself to be judged by the world regarding what is right—Yeshua should be your only judge. That's it. Paul's not saying, "Don't remember the Sabbath anymore," or "Don't celebrate the feasts," and he's certainly not saying, "The first day of the week is the new Sabbath." Read it again for yourself.

He's not saying any of those things. He's saying, "Don't let others judge you if you are living in Yeshua. Their judgment is false."

This is one of many verses from the New Testament that gets misconstrued to fit the narrative that we should no longer keep the Sabbath. Again, it's not making a point about an end to or alteration of the Sabbath, and it's especially not endorsing a change from the seventh day to the first day. It's making a point that we have been freed from the condemnation we deserve for breaking the law.

This verse and others like it do not give justification for perspective number 2, that the Sabbath changed from the seventh day to the first day. Again, religious tradition does, but when you read these kinds of verses for what they say (and are honest about what they say), you find that there is no command in Scripture to move the Sabbath from the seventh day to the first day.

This brings me back to the two verses that talk about the first day of the week.

Acts 20:7 says:

> And on day one of the week, the taught ones having gathered together to break bread, Sha'ul, intending to depart the next day, was reasoning with them and was extending the word till midnight.

First Corinthians 16:2 says:

> Every day one of the week let each one of you set aside, storing up whatever he is prospered, so that there are no collections when I come.

We must keep in mind here that we are not discussing whether it is acceptable to meet together on the first day of the week. We are discussing whether Scripture tells us that the seventh-day Sabbath (as commanded by God in the Torah) changed to the first day of the week.

The argument to be made for perspective number 2 using these two verses holds that the first-century church met on the first day of the week, and therefore that (as opposed to keeping the seventh-day Sabbath) was the new precedent according to God's will for believers going forward.

We can make all sorts of judgments about that argument on our own:

- That makes sense.
- That doesn't make sense.

- I kind of see the logic.
- Etc.

But what do the Scriptures *actually* say? Do they say the Sabbath day changed from the seventh day to the first day?

They do not. The Sabbath is mentioned more than a hundred times throughout the Bible, with multiple instances in which God Himself explicitly calls it the seventh day. Acts 20:7 and 1 Corinthians 16:2 are the only two examples we're given of the believers meeting together on the first day. Neither of those verses give any sort of command instructing believers to stop remembering the Sabbath on the seventh day and to start treating the first day as the Sabbath instead. If the seventh-day Sabbath was commanded explicitly multiple times by God Himself throughout the Bible, is it not strange to think His will would be to change that command without giving a single explicit statement to do so? (Remember, we're talking about perspective number 2, the belief that the Sabbath changed from the seventh day to the first day. If we want to argue that we're not required to keep the Sabbath because we're no longer under the law, that is more aligned with perspective number 4 and is a different discussion altogether.)

This may cause us to wonder, "Well why were the believers meeting on the first day of the week in both of those examples? What are we supposed to do with that?"

Again, we're not discussing whether it is acceptable to meet together on other days of the week. We're discussing whether we've been *instructed by God's Word* to remember and keep set apart the first day instead of the seventh day. God's Word does not tell us to do that.

I hope my issue with perspective number 2 is clear. When you read the entire Bible, Scripture *explicitly* refers to the Sabbath as the seventh day and God's set-apart day. Also, Scripture *explicitly* commands God's people to remember it. Again, these things are *explicit* in Scripture. On the other hand, Scripture *never explicitly* tells us that the Sabbath has changed to the first day or that the first day is God's new set-apart day. Scripture *never explicitly* commands God's people to remember the first day as God's Sabbath. The argument that Sunday is the new Sabbath day seeks to justify the Christian religion more than honor the integrity of the Word of God. To justify this view using the Bible, we have to employ major inferences that did not originate in the actual Scriptures.

If you felt like you were aligned with perspective number 2, perhaps you are tempted here to do what I was describing earlier and move from perspective 2 to perspective 3 or 4.

You might say, "Well, yeah, I suppose the Bible doesn't explicitly tell us to change the Sabbath from the seventh day to the first day. But isn't the fact that the believers were meeting together on the first day of the week just evidence that we have the freedom to do that?"

I would simply ask in response, "How is the fact that the believers were meeting together on the first day of the week evidence that we're free to disobey one of the Ten Commandments?" It may be evidence that we're free to meet on the first day of the week if we choose to do so, but where in either of those verses does it say anything about neglecting or replacing God's Sabbath?

Do you see my point here? We're taking two verses that are simply describing a circumstance, applying major inferences, and using our conclusions to nullify a direct command of God.

If you're still convinced that those two verses about the disciples meeting together on the first day of the week are pointing to some new standard regarding the Sabbath, then let's look a little more closely at those verses, because they have more context going on than many people realize.

Those Two Verses

LET'S LOOK AT Acts 20:7 with a little more context. Acts 20:6–7 says:

> And we sailed away from Philippi after the Days of Unleavened Bread, and came to them at Troas in five days, where we stayed seven days. And on day one of the week, the taught ones having gathered together to break bread, Sha'ul, intending to depart the next day, was reasoning with them and was extending the word till midnight.

If we drop down a few verses from there, we read in Acts 20:16:

> For Sha'ul had decided to sail past Ephesos, so that he might lose no time in Asia, for he was hurrying to be at Yerushalayim, if possible, on the Day of the Festival of Sha<u>b</u>u'oth.

Acts 20:6 tells us that they came to Troas "after the Days of Unleavened Bread". Acts 20:7 says, "And on day one of the week..."

So what's significant about that? The Greek word for "week" there is "sabbaton". (You can verify this for yourself using blueletterbible.org.) This same Greek word is translated elsewhere as "sabbath day" and "sabbath". In fact, the King James Version translates this word as "sabbath day" thirty-seven times, "sabbath" twenty-two times, and "week" only nine times.

While it may seem obvious to translate this word as "week" in this context, what would happen if we considered this passage with one of the other translations of this word? Consider this:

> And on day one of the sabbath day, the taught ones having gathered together to break bread, Sha'ul, intending to depart the next day, was reasoning with them and was extending the word till midnight.

You may ask, "Why in the world would we translate it like that? That doesn't make sense."

If we look again at the Greek from which this is translated, we find that the word "day" is *assumed* when this verse is translated into English (meaning there is no explicit Greek word for "day" present in this verse; translators of the English Bible have inserted it here based on assumptions).

The Greek word "heis" in this verse, which means "one", is translated in the King James Version as "first".

Now, when the word "sabbaton" is translated as "week", it makes sense to assume the word "day" belongs there. Otherwise, we'd be reading, "And on one of the week," or, "And on the first of the week." It seems obvious to go ahead and add "day" in there to clarify for English readers.

But if we translate "sabbaton" as "sabbath day", then suddenly we have, "And on the first of the sabbath day".

You might think, "Okay. That still doesn't make sense."

It only doesn't make sense when we don't understand the feast days. If we're familiar with Leviticus 23, though, we can see what's going on here. At the end of this section in Acts, we see in Acts 20:16 that Paul was hurrying to make it to Jerusalem on the Day of the Festival of Shabuʻoth, which is the Feast of Weeks. Do you recall how the timing of the Feast of Weeks is calculated?

Leviticus 23:15–16 says, concerning the timing for the Feast of Weeks:

> "'And from the morrow after the Sabbath, from the day that you brought the sheaf of the wave offering, you shall count for yourselves: seven completed Sabbaths. Until the morrow after the seventh Sabbath you count fifty days, then you shall bring a new grain offering to יהוה.'"

The timing for the Feast of Weeks is calculated by counting seven sabbaths from the Feast of Firstfruits, and then it is the day following that seventh Sabbath.

Remember, Acts 20:6 tells us that they came to Troas "after the Days of Unleavened Bread". The Feast of Firstfruits takes place during the Days of Unleavened Bread.

This implies that the Feast of Firstfruits had recently taken place. Now if we look at the very next verse, Acts 20:7, with our updated translation, we read, "And on one [the first] of the sabbath day".

Given the timings provided in Acts 20:6, it is reasonable to consider Acts 20:7 as referring to the first of the seven sabbath days that needed to take place before the Feast of Weeks (Sha<u>b</u>uʻoth), for which Paul was hurrying to get to Jerusalem. In fact, this seems to be a more consistent way of viewing this portion of Acts given the explicit references to Unleavened Bread in Acts 20:6 and the Festival of Sha<u>b</u>uʻoth in Acts 20:16. Prior to this account, Scripture does not give us any indication that the believers were meeting on the first day of the week, but it does give us indication that the believers were honoring the feast days of Leviticus.

If we look at 1 Corinthians 16, we have a similar circumstance. First Corinthians 16:2 says:

> Every day one of the week let each one of you set aside, storing up whatever he is prospered, so that there are no collections when I come.

Then, if we drop down to 1 Corinthians 16:8, we read:

> And I shall remain in Ephesos until the Festival of Sha<u>b</u>uʻoth.

Again, we see the timing contextualized by the approach of the Festival of Sha<u>b</u>uʻoth.

The word "every" in 1 Corinthians 16:2 comes from the Greek preposition "kata". The King James Version translates that word into English as "upon".

Otherwise, it's the same verbiage for "day one of the week" ("heis sabbaton"), in which "day" is assumed and "sabbaton" could also be translated "sabbath day" or "sabbath".

I find it extremely curious that the only two instances of the believers gathering on the first day of the week are both connected to the Feast of Weeks within a few verses. It makes me wonder, "If the church is so eager to point to these two verses as reason for meeting on the first day of the week, why isn't it equally eager to point to the feasts mentioned in these same sections of Scripture as reason for keeping the feasts?"

If you are tracking with me at this point, and you see a reasonable argument that these two verses (traditionally translated as "first day of the week") are more biblically cohesive when translated as "first of the sabbath day" in reference to the countdown to the Feast of Weeks, you may be wondering at this point, "Well, how could a misunderstanding like this have happened?"

Once again, we must keep in mind the history of the church regarding Constantine, how the Roman Empire established the Roman Catholic Church. The Roman Catholic Church created edicts around what days to worship and what days to celebrate. Throughout the Dark Ages, literacy wasn't common. People had to rely on what the church told them. So by the time the Bible was being translated for wider spread distribution, church tradition would have been more familiar to much of the population than the Scriptures (as it still seems to be today). Translators would have been just as much removed from the biblical feasts as our current culture is. The translations of verses like Acts 20:7 and 1 Corinthians 16:2 would inevitably be influenced by cultural precedent. Put plainly, it makes sense to assume that these verses are talking about Sunday if we're already under the impression that Sunday is "the Lord's Day". But if we simply read the Bible for what it says, that's not the message it conveys holistically.

All of this may appear like I'm making a big deal out of a relatively small thing. But from my perspective, it's the exact opposite. The Christian religion accepted Sunday as "the Lord's Day", and since then it's been making a big deal out of these two verses. Objectively speaking, the Bible has much more to say about the seventh day being God's Sabbath than it does about believers gathering on the first day of the week. And yet, Christianity continues to anchor back to these two verses (verses that I believe have been misunderstood) for the sake of justifying a preexisting practice. There would be no need to make a big deal out of this now if religion had not made such a big deal out of two misunderstood verses in the first place. But since religion did make a big deal out of this issue, it needs to be addressed because so many people have been misinformed about the truth of God's Word.

I'm not trying to say that it's a sin for believers to get together on the first day of the week and worship God. I'm only trying to caution us away from thinking that the Scriptures tell us that we should no longer honor the seventh-day Sabbath. Church tradition has played a large role in presenting passages of Scripture as if they tell us not to honor the Sabbath. Nowhere does the Bible tell us *not to* honor the Sabbath, and especially not in as explicit terms as the Bible tells us that we *should* honor the Sabbath.

This has been one of the greatest deceptions coming out of the past two millennia, and I believe the consequences for buying into it are about to boil to the surface. I'll talk more on that in Part 7.

Is the Torah a Good Thing for Christians?

I COULDN'T FIND a purely biblical justification for no longer honoring the Sabbath when I read through the Scriptures. More than that, Christianity seemed to have a grudge against the entire Old Testament, and particularly the Torah, God's law, as if it were something bad. I understood there were certain historical events that contributed to this, like Christianity being embraced by the Roman Empire. But what was it within the actual Bible that led Christians to believe the Torah was outdated or something to be shunned? That hadn't been the vibe I got after actually reading the Bible.

So I went back to the Scriptures again, this time explicitly asking myself the question, "According to the Bible, is the Torah a good thing for Christians?"

Hopefully we're all agreed that, according to the Old Testament, the Torah is a good thing. The Old Testament contains the story of Israel, and God gave them His law through Moses for the Israelites to obey. The reason many Christians don't look at the Torah today with fondness as if it is good is because of what they claim the New Testament teaches about it.

For this reason, I want to look at the question, "According to the New Testament, is the Torah a good thing for Christians?"

To better understand holistically what the New Testament says about the Torah, I'm going to list every verse in the New Testament that is making reference to the Torah (based on a search in my Bible software using The Scriptures 2009 translation) along with surrounding verses as needed to help clarify context. That said, I will not be including the entire context of every verse I use, otherwise I might as well just copy and paste the entire New Testament.

IS THE TORAH A GOOD THING FOR CHRISTIANS?

I'm not an advocate of cherry-picking verses for the purpose of making a point. That's why I'm including every verse I found in the New Testament in The Scriptures 2009 translation that included "Torah", even if the verse isn't making an explicit point about the Torah. I don't want there to be suspicion that I've only selected verses that support my point, so I'm including them all. I know there are a lot, but I hope reading through them will help paint a better picture of what the New Testament has to say about the Torah, thereby helping to answer the question, "Is the Torah a good thing for Christians?"

New Testament Scriptures Containing "Torah"

Matthew

Matthew 5:17–18:

> "Do not think that I came to destroy the Torah or the Prophets. I did not come to destroy but to complete. For truly, I say to you, till the heaven and the earth pass away, one yod or one tittle shall by no means pass from the Torah till all be done."

Matthew 7:12:

> "Therefore, whatever you wish men to do to you, do also to them, for this is the Torah and the Prophets."

Matthew 11:13:

> "For all the prophets and the Torah prophesied till Yoḥanan."

Matthew 12:5:

> "Or did you not read in the Torah that on the Sabbath the priests in the Set-apart Place profane the Sabbath, and are blameless?"

Matthew 22:35–40:

> and one of them, one learned in the Torah, did question, trying Him, and saying, "Teacher, which is the great command in the Torah?" And יהושע said to him, "'You shall love יהוה your Elohim with all your heart, and with all your being, and with all your mind.' This is the first and great command. And the second is like it, 'You shall love your neighbour as yourself.' On these two commands hang all the Torah and the Prophets."

Matthew 23:23:

"Woe to you, scribes and Pharisees, hypocrites! Because you tithe the mint and the anise and the cumin, and have neglected the weightier matters of the Torah: the right-ruling and the compassion and the belief. These need to have been done, without neglecting the others."

Luke

Luke 2:22–24:

And when the days of her cleansing according to the Torah of Mosheh were completed, they brought Him to Yerushalayim to present Him to יהוה – as it has been written in the Torah of יהוה, "Every male who opens the womb shall be called set-apart to יהוה" and to give an offering according to what is said in the Torah of יהוה, "A pair of turtledoves or two young pigeons."

Luke 2:27:

And he came in the Spirit into the Set-apart Place. And as the parents brought in the Child יהושע, to do for Him according to the usual practice of the Torah,

Luke 2:39:

And when they had accomplished all matters according to the Torah of יהוה, they returned to Galil, to their city Natsareth.

Luke 5:17:

And on a certain day it came to be, as He was teaching, that there were Pharisees and teachers of the Torah sitting by, who had come out of every village of Galil, Yehudah, and Yerushalayim. And the power of יהוה was there to heal them.

Luke 7:30:

But the Pharisees and those learned in the Torah rejected the counsel of Elohim for themselves, not having been immersed by him.

Luke 10:25–28:

And see, a certain one learned in the Torah stood up, trying Him, and saying, "Teacher, what shall I do to inherit everlasting life?" And He said to him, "What has been written in the

Torah? How do you read it?" And he answering, said, "'You shall love יהוה your Elohim with all your heart, and with all your being, and with all your strength, and with all your mind,' and 'your neighbour as yourself.'" And He said to him, "You have answered rightly. Do this and you shall live."

Luke 11:45–46:

And one of those learned in the Torah, answering, said to Him, "Teacher, when You say this You insult us too." And He said, "Woe to you also, you learned in the Torah, because you load men with burdens hard to bear, and you yourselves do not touch the burdens with one of your fingers."

Luke 11:52:

"Woe to you learned in the Torah, because you took away the key of knowledge. You did not enter in yourselves, and those who were entering in you hindered."

Luke 14:3:

And יהושע responding, spoke to those learned in the Torah and the Pharisees, saying, "Is it right to heal on the Sabbath?"

Luke 16:16–17:

"The Torah and the prophets are until Yoḥanan. Since then the reign of Elohim is being announced, and everyone is doing violence upon it. And it is easier for the heaven and the earth to pass away than for one tittle of the Torah to fall."

Luke 24:44:

And He said to them, "These are the words which I spoke to you while I was still with you, that all have to be filled that were written in the Torah of Mosheh and the Prophets and the Tehillim concerning Me."

John

John 1:16–17:

And out of His completeness we all did receive, and favour upon favour, for the Torah was given through Mosheh – the favour and the truth came through יהושע Messiah.

John 1:45:

Philip found Nethanĕl and said to him, "We have found Him whom Mosheh wrote of in the Torah, and the prophets: יהושע of Natsareth – the son of Yosĕph."

John 7:19:

"Did not Mosheh give you the Torah? Yet not one of you does the Torah! Why do you seek to kill Me?"

John 7:23:

"If a man receives circumcision on the Sabbath, so that the Torah of Mosheh should not be broken, are you wroth with Me because I made a man entirely well on the Sabbath?"

John 7:47–51:

The Pharisees, therefore, answered them, "Have you also been led astray? Has anyone of the rulers or of the Pharisees believed in Him? But this crowd that does not know the Torah is accursed." Nakdimon – he who came to יהושע by night, being one of them – said to them, "Does our Torah judge the man unless it hears first from him and knows what he is doing?"

John 8:5–7:

"And in the Torah Mosheh commanded us that such should be stoned. What then do You say?" And this they said, trying Him, so that they might accuse Him. But יהושע, bending down, wrote on the ground with the finger, as though He did not hear. But as they kept on questioning Him, He straightened up and said to them, "He who is without sin among you, let him be the first to throw a stone at her."

John 8:17:

"And in your Torah also, it has been written that the witness of two men is true."

John 10:34:

יהושע answered them, "Is it not written in your own Torah, 'I said, "You are elohim"'?"

John 12:34:

The crowd answered Him, "We have heard out of the Torah that the Messiah remains forever. And how do You say, 'The Son of Aḏam has to be lifted up'? Who is this Son of Aḏam?"

John 15:24–25:

"If I did not do among them the works which no one else did, they would have no sin. But now they have both seen and have hated both Me and My Father, but...that the word might be filled which was written in their Torah, 'They hated Me without a cause.'"

Acts

Acts 5:34:

But a certain one in the council stood up, a Pharisee named Gamliʼěl, a teacher of the Torah, respected by all the people, and ordered them to put the emissaries outside for a little while,

Acts 6:13:

And they set up false witnesses who said, "This man does not cease to speak blasphemous words against this set-apart place and the Torah,"

Acts 7:52–53:

"Which of the prophets did your fathers not persecute? And they killed those who before announced the coming of the Righteous One, of whom you now have become the betrayers and murderers, who received the Torah as it was ordained by messengers, but did not watch over it."

Acts 13:15:

And after the reading of the Torah and the Prophets, the rulers of the congregation sent to them, saying, "Men, brothers, if you have any word of encouragement for the people, speak."

Acts 13:38–39:

"Let it therefore be known to you, brothers, that through this One forgiveness of sins is proclaimed to you, and by Him everyone who believes is declared right from all sins from which you were not able to be declared right by the Torah of Mosheh."

Acts 15:5:

And some of the believers who belonged to the sect of the Pharisees, rose up, saying, "It is necessary to circumcise them, and to command them to keep the Torah of Mosheh."

Acts 18:12–13:

And when Gallion was proconsul of Achaia, the Yehuḏim with one mind rose up against Sha'ul and brought him to the judgment seat, saying, "This one does seduce men to worship Elohim contrary to the Torah."

Acts 21:20–24:

And when they heard it, they praised the Master. And they said to him, "You see, brother, how many thousands of Yehuḏim there are who have believed, and all are ardent for the Torah, But they have been informed about you that you teach all the Yehuḏim who are among the nations to forsake Mosheh, saying not to circumcise the children nor to walk according to the practices. What then is it? They shall certainly hear that you have come. So do this, what we say to you: We have four men who have taken a vow. Take them and be cleansed with them, and pay their expenses so that they shave their heads. And all shall know that what they have been informed about you is not so, but that you yourself also walk orderly, keeping the Torah."

Acts 21:27–28:

And when the seven days were almost ended, the Yehuḏim from Asia, seeing him in the Set-apart Place, were stirring up all the crowd, and they laid hands on him, crying out, "Men of Yisra'ěl, help! This is the man who is teaching all men everywhere against the people, and the Torah, and this place. And besides, he also brought Greeks into the Set-apart Place and has profaned this Set-apart Place."

Acts 22:3:

"I am indeed a Yehuḏi, having been born in Tarsos of Kilikia, but brought up in this city at the feet of Gamli'ěl, having been instructed according to the exactness of the Torah of our fathers, being ardent for Elohim, as you all are today,"

Acts 22:12–13:

"And a certain Ḥananyah, a dedicated man according to the Torah, being well spoken of by all the Yehuḏim dwelling there, came to me, and stood by and said to me, 'Brother Sha'ul, look up.' And at that same hour I looked up at him."

Acts 23:3:

Then Sha'ul said to him, "Elohim is going to strike you, whitewashed wall! And do you sit judging me according to the Torah, and do you command me to be struck contrary to the Torah?"

Acts 23:29:

I found out that he was accused concerning questions of their Torah, but there was no charge against him deserving death or chains.

Acts 24:14–15:

"And this I confess to you, that according to the Way which they call a sect, so I worship the Elohim of my fathers, believing all that has been written in the Torah and in the Prophets, having an expectation in Elohim, which they themselves also wait for, that there is to be a resurrection of the dead, both of the righteous and the unrighteous."

Acts 25:7–8:

And when he had come, the Yehuḏim who had come down from Yerushalayim stood about, bringing many and heavy charges against Sha'ul, which they were unable to prove, while Sha'ul said in his own defence, "Neither against the Torah of the Yehuḏim, nor against the Set-apart Place, nor against Caesar did I commit any sin."

Acts 28:23:

And having appointed him a day, many came to him where he was staying, to whom he was explaining, earnestly witnessing about the reign of Elohim, and persuading them concerning יהושע from both the Torah of Mosheh and the Prophets, from morning until evening.

Romans

Romans 2:12–29:

For as many as sinned without Torah shall also perish without Torah, and as many as sinned in the Torah shall be judged by the Torah. For not the hearers of the Torah are righteous in the sight of Elohim, but the doers of the Torah shall be declared right. For when nations, who do not have the Torah, by nature do what is in the Torah, although not having the Torah, they are a torah to themselves, who show the work of the Torah written in their hearts, their conscience also bearing witness, and between themselves their thoughts accusing or even excusing, in the day when Elohim shall judge the secrets of men through יהושע Messiah, according to my Good News. See, you are called a Yehuḏi, and rest on the Torah, and make your boast in Elohim, and know the desire of Elohim, and approve what is superior, being instructed out of the Torah, and are trusting that you yourself are a guide to the blind, a light to those who are in darkness, an instructor of foolish ones, a teacher of babes, having the form of knowledge and of the truth in the Torah. You, then, who teach another, do you not teach yourself? You who proclaim that a man should not steal, do you steal? You who say, "Do not commit adultery," do you commit adultery? You who abominate idols, do you rob temples? You who make your boast in the Torah, through the transgression of the Torah do you disrespect Elohim? For "The Name of Elohim is blasphemed among the nations because of you," as it has been written. For circumcision indeed profits if you practise the Torah, but if you are a transgressor of the Torah, your circumcision has become uncircumcision. So, if an uncircumcised one watches over the righteousnesses of the Torah, shall not his uncircumcision be reckoned as circumcision? And the uncircumcised by nature, who perfects the Torah, shall judge you who notwithstanding letter and circumcision are a transgressor of the Torah! For he is not a Yehuḏi who is so outwardly, neither is circumcision that which is outward in the flesh. But a Yehuḏi is he who is so inwardly, and circumcision is that of the heart, in Spirit, not literally, whose praise is not from men but from Elohim.

Romans 3:19–31:

And we know that whatever the Torah says, it says to those who are in the Torah, so that every mouth might be stopped, and all the world come under judgment before Elohim. Therefore by works of Torah no flesh shall be declared right before Him, for by the Torah is the knowledge of sin. But now, apart from the Torah, a righteousness of Elohim has been revealed, being witnessed by the Torah and the Prophets, and the righteousness of Elohim is through belief in יהושע Messiah to all and on all who believe. For there is no difference, for all have sinned and fall short of the esteem of Elohim, being declared right, without paying, by His favour through the redemption which is in Messiah יהושע, whom Elohim set forth as an atonement, through belief in His blood, to demonstrate His righteousness, because in His tolerance Elohim had passed over the sins that had taken place before, to demonstrate at the present time His righteousness, that He is righteous and declares righteous the one who has belief in יהושע. Where, then, is the boasting? It is shut out. By what torah? Of works? No, but by the torah of belief. For we reckon that a man is declared right by belief without works of Torah. Or is He the Elohim of the Yehuḏim only, and not also of the nations? Yes, of the nations also, since it is one Elohim who shall declare right the circumcised by belief and the uncircumcised through belief. Do we then nullify the Torah through the belief? Let it not be! On the contrary, we establish the Torah.

Romans 4:13–16:

For the promise that he should be the heir of the world, was not to Aḇraham or to his seed through the Torah, but through a righteousness of belief. For if those who are of the Torah are heirs, belief has been made useless, and the promise has been nullified, for the Torah works out wrath, for where there is no Torah there is no transgression. On account of this it is of belief, that it be according to favour, for the promise to be made certain to all the seed, not only to those who are of the Torah, but also to those who are of the belief of Aḇraham, who is father of us all –

Romans 5:12–13:

For this reason, even as through one man sin did enter into the world, and death through sin, and thus death spread to all men, because all sinned – for until the Torah, sin was in the world, but sin is not reckoned when there is no Torah.

Romans 5:20–21:

And the Torah came in beside, so that the trespass would increase. But where sin increased, favour increased still more, so that as sin did reign in death, even so favour might reign through righteousness to everlasting life through יהושע Messiah our Master.

Romans 6:15:

What then? Shall we sin because we are not under Torah but under favour? Let it not be!

Romans 7:1–25:

Or do you not know, brothers – for I speak to those knowing the Torah – that the Torah rules over a man as long as he lives? For the married woman has been bound by Torah to the living husband, but if the husband dies, she is released from the Torah concerning her husband. So then, while her husband lives, she shall be called an adulteress if she becomes another man's. But if her husband dies, she is free from that part of the Torah, so that she is not an adulteress, having become another man's. So my brothers, you also were put to death to the Torah through the body of Messiah, for you to become another's, the One who was raised from the dead, that we should bear fruit to Elohim. For when we were in the flesh, the passions of sins, through the Torah, were working in our members to bear fruit to death. But now we have been released from the Torah, having died to what we were held by, so that we should serve in newness of Spirit and not in oldness of letter. What, then, shall we say? Is the Torah sin? Let it not be! However, I did not know sin except through the Torah. For also the covetousness I knew not if the Torah had not said, "You shall not covet." But sin, having taken the occasion through the command, did work in me all sorts of covetousness. For apart from Torah sin is dead. And I was alive apart from the Torah once, but when the command came, the sin revived, and I died. And the command which was to result in life, this I found to result in death. For sin, having taken the occasion through the command, deceived me, and through it killed me. So that the Torah truly is set-apart, and the command set-apart, and righteous, and good. Therefore, has that which is good become death to me? Let it not be! But the sin, that sin might be manifest, was working death in me through what is good, so that sin through the command might become an exceedingly great sinner. For we know that the Torah is Spiritual, but I am fleshly, sold under sin. For what I work, I know not. For what I wish, that I do not practise, but what I hate, that I do. But if I do what I do not wish, I agree with the Torah that it is good. And now, it is no longer I that work it, but the sin dwelling in me. For I know that in me, that is in my flesh, dwells no good. For to wish is present with me, but to work the good I do not find. For the good that I wish to do, I do not do; but the evil I do not wish to do, this I practise. And if I do that which I do not wish, it is no longer I who work it, but the sin dwelling in me. I find therefore this law, that when I wish to do the good, that the evil is present with me. For I delight in the Torah of Elohim according to the inward man, but I see another torah in my members, battling against the torah of my mind, and bringing me into captivity to the torah of sin which is in my members. Wretched man that I am! Who shall deliver me from this body of death? Thanks to Elohim, through יהושע Messiah our Master! So then, with the mind I myself truly serve the Torah of Elohim, but with the flesh the torah of sin.

Romans 8:2–8:

For the torah of the Spirit of the life in Messiah יהושע has set me free from the torah of sin and of death. For the Torah being powerless, in that it was weak through the flesh, Elohim, having sent His own Son in the likeness of flesh of sin, and concerning sin, condemned sin in the flesh, so that the righteousness of the Torah should be completed in us who do not walk according to the flesh but according to the Spirit. For those who live according to the flesh set their minds on the matters of the flesh, but those who live according to the Spirit, the matters of the Spirit. For the mind of the flesh is death, but the mind of the Spirit is life and peace. Because the mind of the flesh is enmity towards Elohim, for it does not subject itself to the Torah of Elohim, neither indeed is it able, and those who are in the flesh are unable to please Elohim.

Romans 9:3–5:

For I myself could have wished to be banished from Messiah for the sake of my brothers, my relatives according to the flesh, who are the children of Yisra'ěl, to whom is the adoption, and the esteem, and the covenants, and the giving of the Torah, and the worship, and the promises, whose are the fathers, and from whom is the Messiah according to the flesh, who is over all, Elohim-blessed forever. Aměn.

Romans 9:30–32:

What shall we say then? That nations not following after righteousness, have obtained righteousness, even the righteousness of belief, but Yisra'ěl following after the Torah of righteousness, has not arrived at the Torah of righteousness. Why? Because it was not of belief, but as by works of Torah. For they stumbled at the Stone of stumbling.

Romans 10:4–5:

For Messiah is the goal of the 'Torah unto righteousness' to everyone who believes. For Mosheh writes about the righteousness which is of the Torah, "The man who does these shall live by them."

Romans 13:8–10:

Owe no one any matter except to love one another, for he who loves another has filled the Torah. For this, "You shall not commit adultery," "You shall not murder," "You shall not steal," "You shall not bear false witness," "You shall not covet," and if there is any other command, it is summed up in this word, "You shall love your neighbour as yourself." Love does no evil to a neighbour. Therefore, love is completion of the Torah.

1 Corinthians

1 Corinthians 7:39:

A wife is bound by Torah as long as her husband lives, and if her husband dies, she is free to be married to whom she desires, only in the Master.

1 Corinthians 9:8–10:

Do I say this as a man? Or does not the Torah say the same too? For it has been written in the Torah of Mosheh, "You shall not muzzle an ox while it treads out the grain." Is it about oxen Elohim is concerned? Or does He say it because of us all? For this was written because of us, that he who ploughs should plough in expectation, and the thresher in expectation of sharing.

1 Corinthians 9:19–21:

For though I am free from all, I made myself a servant to all, in order to win more, and to the Yehuḏim I became as a Yehuḏi, that I might win Yehuḏim; to those who are under Torah, as under Torah, so as to win those who are under Torah; to those without Torah, as without Torah – not being without Torah toward Elohim, but under Torah of Messiah – so as to win those who are without Torah.

1 Corinthians 14:21:

In the Torah it has been written, "With men of other tongues and other lips I shall speak to this people. And even so, they shall not hear Me, says יהוה."

1 Corinthians 14:34:

Let your women be silent in the assemblies, for they are not allowed to speak, but let them subject themselves, as the Torah also says.

1 Corinthians 15:56:

And the sting of death is the sin, and the power of the sin is the Torah.

Galatians

Galatians 2:15–21:

"We, Yehuḏim by nature, and not of the nations, sinners, knowing that a man is not declared right by works of Torah, but through belief in יהושע Messiah, even we have believed in Messiah יהושע, in order to be declared right by belief in Messiah and not by works of Torah, because by works of Torah no flesh shall be declared right. And if, while seeking to be declared right by Messiah, we ourselves also are found sinners, is Messiah then a servant of sin? Let it not be! For if I rebuild what I once overthrew, I establish myself a transgressor. For through Torah I died to Torah, in order to live to Elohim. I have been impaled with Messiah, and I no longer live, but Messiah lives in me. And that which I now live in the flesh I live by belief in the Son of Elohim, who loved me and gave Himself for me. I do not set aside the favour of Elohim, for if righteousness is through Torah, then Messiah died for naught."

Galatians 3:1–24:

O senseless Galatians! Who has put you under a spell, not to obey the truth – before whose eyes יהושע Messiah was clearly portrayed among you as impaled? This only I wish to learn from you: Did you receive the Spirit by works of Torah, or by the hearing of belief? Are you so senseless? Having begun in the Spirit, do you now end in the flesh? Have you suffered so much in vain – if indeed in vain? Is He, then, who is supplying the Spirit to you and working miracles among you, doing it by works of Torah, or by hearing of belief? Even so Aḇraham "did believe Elohim, and it was reckoned unto him as righteousness." Know, then, that those who are of belief are sons of Aḇraham. And the Scripture, having foreseen that Elohim would declare right the nations by belief, announced the Good News to Aḇraham beforehand, saying, "All the nations shall be blessed in you," so that those who are of belief are blessed with Aḇraham, the believer. For as many as are of works of Torah are under the curse, for it has been written, "Cursed is everyone who does not continue in all that has been written in the Book of the Torah, to do them." And that no one is declared right by Torah before Elohim is clear, for "The righteous shall live by belief." And the Torah is not of belief, but "The man who does them shall live by them." Messiah redeemed us from the curse of the Torah, having become a curse for us – for it has been written, "Cursed is everyone who hangs upon a tree." in order that the blessing of Aḇraham might come upon the nations in Messiah יהושע, to receive the promise of the Spirit through belief. Brothers, as a man I say it: a covenant, even though it is man's, yet if it is confirmed, no one sets it aside, or adds to it. But the promises were spoken to Aḇraham, and to his Seed. He does not say, "And to seeds," as of many, but as of one, "And to your Seed," who is Messiah. Now this I say, Torah, that came four hundred and thirty years later, does not annul a covenant previously confirmed by Elohim in Messiah, so as to do away with the promise. For if the inheritance is by Torah, it is no longer by promise, but Elohim gave it to Aḇraham through a promise. Why, then, the Torah? It was added because of transgressions, until the Seed should come to whom the promise was made. And it was ordained through messengers in the hand of a mediator. The Mediator, however, is not of one, but Elohim is one. Is the Torah then against the promises of Elohim? Let it not be! For if a torah had been given that was able to make alive, truly righteousness would have been by Torah. But the Scripture has shut up all mankind under sin, that the promise by belief in יהושע Messiah might be given to those who believe. But before belief came, we were being guarded under Torah, having been shut up for the belief being about to be revealed. Therefore the Torah became our trainer unto Messiah, in order to be declared right by belief.

Galatians 4:4-5:

But when the completion of the time came, Elohim sent forth His Son, born of a woman, born under Torah, to redeem those who were under Torah, in order to receive the adoption as sons.

Galatians 4:21:

Say to me, you who wish to be under Torah, do you not hear the Torah?

Galatians 5:3-4:

And I witness again to every man being circumcised that he is a debtor to do the entire Torah. You who are declared right by Torah have severed yourselves from Messiah, you have fallen from favour.

Galatians 5:14:

For the entire Torah is completed in one word, in this, "You shall love your neighbour as yourself."

Galatians 5:18-23:

But if you are led by the Spirit, you are not under Torah. And the works of the flesh are well-known, which are these: adultery, whoring, uncleanness, indecency, idolatry, drug sorcery, hatred, quarrels, jealousies, fits of rage, selfish ambitions, dissensions, factions, envy, murders, drunkenness, wild parties, and the like – of which I forewarn you, even as I also said before, that those who practise such as these shall not inherit the reign of Elohim. But the fruit of the Spirit is love, joy, peace, patience, kindness, goodness, trustworthiness, gentleness, self-control. Against such there is no Torah.

Galatians 6:2:

Bear one another's burdens, and so complete the Torah of Messiah.

Galatians 6:13:

For those who are circumcised do not even watch over the Torah, but they wish to have you circumcised so that they might boast in your flesh.

Ephesians

Ephesians 2:14–16:

> For He is our peace, who has made both one, and having broken down the partition of the barrier, having abolished in His flesh the enmity – the torah of the commands in dogma – so as to create in Himself one renewed man from the two, thus making peace, and to completely restore to favour both of them unto Elohim in one body through the stake, having destroyed the enmity by it.

Philippians

Philippians 3:4–5:

> though I too might have trust in the flesh. If anyone else thinks to trust in the flesh, I more – circumcised the eighth day, of the race of Yisraěl, of the tribe of Binyamin, a Hebrew of Hebrews, according to Torah a Pharisee,

1 Timothy

1 Timothy 1:5–11:

> Now the goal of this command is love from a clean heart, from a good conscience and a sincere belief, which some, having missed the goal, turned aside to senseless talk, wishing to be teachers of Torah, understanding neither what they say nor concerning what they strongly affirm. And we know that the Torah is good if one uses it legitimately, knowing this: that Torah is not laid down for a righteous being, but for the lawless and unruly, for the wicked and for sinners, for the wrong-doers and profane, for those who kill their fathers or mothers, for murderers, or those who whore, for sodomites, for kidnappers, for liars, for perjurers, and for whatever else that is contrary to sound teaching, according to the esteemed Good News of the blessed Elohim which was entrusted to me.

Titus

Titus 3:9:

> But keep away from foolish questions, and genealogies, and strife and quarrels about the Torah, for they are unprofitable and useless.

Hebrews

Hebrews 7:5–6:

> And truly, those who are of the sons of Lĕwi, who receive the priesthood, have a command to receive tithes from the people according to the Torah, that is, from their brothers, though they have come from the loins of Aḇraham, however, the one whose genealogy is not derived from them received tithes from Aḇraham, and blessed the one who held the promises.

Hebrews 7:11:

> Truly, then, if perfection were through the Lĕwitical priesthood – for under it the people were given the Torah – why was there still need for another priest to arise according to the order of Malkitseḏeq, and not be called according to the order of Aharon?

Hebrews 7:14–19:

> For it is perfectly clear that our Master arose from Yehuḏah, a tribe about which Mosheh never spoke of concerning priesthood, and this is clearer still, if another priest arises in the likeness of Malkitseḏeq, who has become, not according to the torah of fleshly command, but according to the power of an endless life, or He does witness, "You are a priest forever according to the order of Malkitseḏeq." For there is indeed a setting aside of the former command because of its weakness and unprofitableness, for the Torah perfected naught, but the bringing in of a better expectation, through which we draw near to Elohim.

Hebrews 7:28:

> For the Torah appoints as high priests men who have weakness, but the word of the oath which came after the Torah, appoints the Son having been perfected forever.

Hebrews 8:4–5:

> For if indeed He were on earth, He would not be a priest, since there are priests who offer the gifts according to the Torah, who serve a copy and shadow of the heavenly, as Mosheh was warned when he was about to make the Tent. For He said, "See that you make all according to the pattern shown you on the mountain."

Hebrews 9:19–22:

> For when, according to Torah, every command had been spoken by Mosheh to all the people, he took the blood of calves and goats, with water, and scarlet wool, and hyssop, and sprinkled both the book itself and all the people, saying, "This is the blood of the covenant which Elohim commanded you." And in the same way he sprinkled with blood both the Tent and all the vessels of the service. And, according to the Torah, almost all is cleansed with blood, and without shedding of blood there is no forgiveness.

Hebrews 10:1:

> For the Torah, having a shadow of the good matters to come, and not the image itself of the matters, was never able to make perfect those who draw near with the same slaughter offerings which they offer continually year by year.

Hebrews 10:8:

> Saying above, "Slaughter and meal offering, and ascending offerings, and offerings for sin You did not desire, nor delighted in," which are offered according to the Torah, then He said, "See, I come to do Your desire, O Elohim." He takes away the first to establish the second.

Hebrews 10:28–29:

> Anyone who has disregarded the Torah of Mosheh dies without compassion on the witness of two or three witnesses. How much worse punishment do you think shall he deserve who has trampled the Son of Elohim underfoot, counted the blood of the covenant by which he was set apart as common, and insulted the Spirit of favour?

James

James 1:25:

> But he that looked into the perfect Torah, that of freedom, and continues in it, not becoming a hearer that forgets, but a doer of work, this one shall be blessed in his doing of the Torah.

James 2:8–12:

> If you truly accomplish the sovereign law according to the Scripture, "You shall love your neighbour as yourself," you do well, but if you show partiality, you commit sin, being found guilty by the Torah as transgressors. For whoever shall guard all the Torah, and yet stumble in one point, he is guilty of all. For He who said, "Do not commit adultery," also said, "Do not murder." Now if you do not commit adultery, but you do murder, you have become a transgressor of Torah. So speak and so do as those who are to be judged by a Torah of freedom.

James 4:11:

> Brothers, do not speak against one another. He that speaks against a brother and judges his brother, speaks against Torah and judges Torah. And if you judge Torah, you are not a doer of Torah but a judge.

So... Is It Good?

IF YOU HAVEN'T already done so, read through the entire Bible so you can make your own assessment here. There are numerous "Bible in a Year" reading plans that you can find online or through phone apps. It may take a while, but I assure you it is well worth the time. If you have read through the entire Bible before, then I encourage you to do it again with another translation (perhaps The Scriptures 2009) and take note of the different conclusions you take away.

After reading the whole Bible and then considering all those verses from the New Testament that include the Torah, I believe that, according to the Bible, the Torah is a good thing for the Christian if one uses it legitimately (1 Timothy 1:8). Perhaps many Christians would agree with me on that, and the real question is, *Should* the Christian use the Torah, or does it even matter? To answer this question, we have to understand what we're talking about categorically.

Should the Christian use the Torah to call themselves righteous before God? No.

Should the Christian use the Torah to carry out their belief in God? Yes.

The doctrine of justification through faith in Yeshua is hugely important, because it is *belief* that God attributes to man as righteousness. This is what we see all through Hebrews 11, and this is the basis for Abraham being the father of all believers. God wants to see that we believe Him. When we believe that Yeshua took the punishment for our sins, we are telling God, "I believe You!" But this is the point at which I see Christianity making a mess of things. We've tried to translate "faith" and "belief" to mean "thought" (as in, mental acknowledgement of Yeshua's atoning sacrifice), and that's just not how the Bible presents these concepts. Rather, the Bible shows us that true faith necessarily leads to actions that correspond to whatever ideas we have faith in.

Here's a simple illustration: if you have faith that your house is on fire, you get out. It is the faith that leads to the action. Abraham was counted righteous because of his faith, but the reason we know he had faith is because of his actions. He actually left his home and went to the place God told him to go to, he trusted in God's promise to bless him with many descendants, and he was willing to give up his son if that's what God wanted from him. The things he did aligned with his belief in God.

Now, if you really, *truly* believe that someone who lived a perfect life willingly suffered and died for you so that you could have access to an eternal life that you deservedly lost, how would that really, *truly* affect the way you live your life? Would you love that man? Would you consider him your friend?

Yeshua says in John 15:14:

> "You are My friends if you do whatever I command you."

What did he command us to do? Matthew 22:37–40 says:

> And יהושע said to him, "'You shall love יהוה your Elohim with all your heart, and with all your being, and with all your mind.' This is the first and great command. And the second is like it, 'You shall love your neighbour as yourself.' On these two commands hang all the Torah and the Prophets."

We have become quick to say, "Love God and love people," and yet slow to explain what loving God and loving people really means. This is dangerous when we live in a culture that says, "I love God," in one breath and, "I love pizza," in the next. What does loving God with all your heart, being, and mind mean? This is why God gave us the Torah, so that we could understand what it means to love Him and love people from His point of view.

We might say, "Well, God gave us the New Testament, and through Yeshua we know what it means to love God and love people." That's true. But Yeshua based his life on perfect obedience to the Torah, so if we want to understand what Yeshua's life looked like to understand love, we must understand what the Torah teaches.

Yeshua lived a Torah-observant life. He observed the Sabbath and the biblical feasts, among other things. Christianity is quick to acknowledge that Yeshua said, "Follow me." The problem is that Christianity subsequently takes great liberties in identifying what parts of Yeshua's life we are to "follow Him" in. For example, even though Yeshua observed the Sabbath, observed the biblical feasts, and (like the rest of the Jewish society he lived in) only ate biblically clean foods, Christianity has taught that we are not to follow Yeshua in these ways, which has led to much confusion.

There are certain verses in the New Testament that may appear to be justification for not following Yeshua in matters like those listed above. For example, Acts 15:5–10 says:

> And some of the believers who belonged to the sect of the Pharisees, rose up, saying, "It is necessary to circumcise them, and to command them to keep the Torah of Mosheh." And the emissaries and elders came together to look into this matter. And when there had been much dispute, Kěpha [Peter] rose up and said to them, "Men, brothers, you know that a good while ago Elohim chose among us, that by my mouth the nations should hear the word of the Good News and believe. And Elohim, who knows the heart, bore witness to them, by giving them the Set-apart Spirit, as also to us, and made no distinction between us and them, cleansing their hearts by belief. Now then, why do you try Elohim by putting a yoke on the neck of the taught ones which neither our fathers nor we were able to bear? But through the favour of the Master יהושע Messiah we trust to be saved, in the same way as they."

And then James says in verses 19–20:

> "Therefore I judge that we should not trouble those from among the nations who are turning to Elohim, but that we write to them to abstain from the defilements of idols, and from whoring, and from what is strangled, and from blood."

It is easy to say here, "See, even Peter said don't put a yoke on people by telling them to observe the Torah." But pay attention to what's really going on here. This is a spirit of the matter conversation. Through their demanding, the Pharisees were prioritizing external conformity over nurturing the new believers' heart change. Peter and James weren't commenting on whether it is good to follow Torah. They were responding to the implications being made about being righteous.

The modern day equivalent of this might look like a person coming to church, believing in Yeshua for the first time, and the elders of the church immediately listing out all the requirements for church membership, demanding the new believer get on board in order for their faith to be valid.

Peter and James were clarifying what was truly necessary as a response to the spirit of the Pharisees. They weren't saying, "We should abandon the Torah." They were saying, "Stop trying to make this journey more difficult for these new believers."

Look at the very next thing James says in verse 21:

> "For from ancient generations Mosheh has, in every city, those proclaiming him – being read in the congregations every Sabbath."

Why would James say this as a follow-up? He was indicating that these new believers can learn all about these laws in time by hearing the Torah taught every Sabbath, the same way church leaders today might say new believers can learn about church membership, small groups, and whatever else in time by coming to church each Sunday. Peter and James were not making a case against obeying the Torah. They were making a case against a spirit of oppression within the faith. The assumption was that these new believers would grow in Torah over time.

Christianity, however, moved in the opposite direction, neglecting Torah, and ultimately totally rejecting it. It's no wonder that we're seeing so many divisions within Christianity today. Everybody wants to love, but nobody wants to agree on how that should be done. We then dissolve into this mode of "You love the way you want to love and I'll love the way I want to love." From that we see this philosophy abounding, "Your truth isn't my truth," and at that point we're left with a bunch of foolish religiosity. Manmade doctrine.

When we allow ourselves to get into a spot like that, it's difficult to get out. I imagine a deep pit with slippery, muddy walls that are really hard to climb. It's so difficult to get out of a spot like that because we've abandoned foundational truths to build upon. Without those truths, we can't climb up the muddy walls, and so pretty soon we just give up on trying to get out. Someone might come along to offer a helpful tip for getting out, and we think, "Well, that's your truth. I'll stick with my truth, thank you very much," and we content ourselves with sitting in our muddy hole.

We need to correct the spirit of the matter here. Living in an age of instant communication, in a population of billions, with shameless marketing everywhere we look, it's easy to get jaded. It's also easy to get really tired. In this way, the appeal of living with a "Your truth isn't my truth" perspective is obvious—it's easy, because you don't have to compromise anything you find pleasurable with convicting beliefs. This is why Christians have skewed the "grace through faith alone" doctrine so heavily that we don't have an appropriate understanding of faith anymore. If faith is simply a matter of thought or opinion, then I can just say I believe in Yeshua, claim my mansion up in heaven, and otherwise go on defining truth for myself. This way of being may offer a lot of worldly pleasure, but it has created a crisis in the way of meaning, purpose, and Truth.

The Torah can help us here.

We are not called to be *under* the Torah. What does that mean? Well, what does it mean when someone is not under the law, in general? It means they're not subject to the consequences given for breaking the law. It means they are above the law. It means they are not living in a spirit of oppression, fearing that if they slip up once they're forever damned. It means they are living in a *spirit* of freedom, love, and joy. When we have faith in Yeshua, that is us.

We are not subject to the consequences given for breaking the Torah. Does that mean that we should disregard the Torah? Paul writes in Romans 3:31:

> Do we then nullify the Torah through the belief? Let it not be! On the contrary, we establish the Torah.

No, we don't disregard the Torah. We regard it, not because we're fearful of some consequence we'll be given if we don't, but because we *love* Yeshua. This is spelled out logically in Scripture: if we love Yeshua, then we obey him (this is according to his words), and if we obey him, we love God and we love one another. Paul writes in Romans 13:8–10:

> Owe no one any matter except to love one another, for he who loves another has filled the Torah. For this, "You shall not commit adultery," "You shall not murder," "You shall not steal," "You shall not bear false witness," "You shall not covet," and if there is any other command, it is summed up in this word, "You shall love your neighbour as yourself." Love does no evil to a neighbour. Therefore, love is completion of the Torah.

When we obey the Torah in the context of having faith in Yeshua as the one who makes us righteous, the Torah gives us specific instructions on how to love God and love people. We have no other gods, we do not make idols, we do not bring God's name to naught, we remember the

Sabbath, we do not murder, we do not commit adultery, we do not steal, we do not lie, and we do not covet our neighbor.

Once again, following the commands of Torah is not what leads to salvation, because we have already fallen to sin. Yeshua is the one who provides salvation. That is why we refer to *Yeshua* as our Savior.

We do not obey to *get* something. We obey to *show* something.

Is the Torah any replacement for Yeshua? Absolutely not.

Is the Torah good? Well, Yeshua lived his life by it and commanded us to follow Him.

So what do you think?

The Torah Sets Up the Gospel

THESE WERE MY thoughts as I listened to more messages simultaneously proclaiming Yeshua as Messiah and the goodness of God's law (Torah). I began seeing how verses in the New Testament, often used by Christians to argue that we no longer need to concern ourselves with the Torah, weren't actually meaning that.

For example, many Christians look at the story of Peter's vision in Acts 10 as indication that God abolished the dietary laws presented in Leviticus 12. Acts 10:15 says:

> And a voice came to him again the second time, "What Elohim has cleansed you do not consider common."

On the surface, this may seem like God is commenting on the dietary laws, because Peter's vision involved animals. But when we keep reading the account, we see that Peter has doubts about what the vision means (Acts 10:17). And then, in Acts 10:28, Peter explains to Cornelius and his household what he realized the vision meant:

> And he said to them, "You know that a Yehudi man is not allowed to associate with, or go to one of another race. But Elohim has shown me that I should not call any man common or unclean."

Peter never says that the dietary laws of the Torah are no longer relevant. He explains that his vision was about people.

There are other verses in the New Testament that may appear to be abolishing the dietary laws, such as Romans 14:2–3, which we looked at earlier:

> One indeed believes to eat all food, but he who is weak eats only vegetables. He that eats, let him not despise him who does not

eat, and he that does not eat, let him not judge him who eats, for Elohim received him.

Other versions say "meat" in place of "food". Either way, this verse is not a commentary on the dietary laws. Look at the comparison. All food (or all meat) versus only vegetables. If God had already established what was suitable to be eaten within the dietary laws and hadn't clearly changed His expectations around this, then the phrase "all food" would be referring to that which was food according to God (as laid out in the dietary laws of the Torah), not man. Paul was comparing food according to the Torah with food that was appropriate according to man's custom—some people believed that they should only eat vegetables, and Paul was saying, "If some want to eat only vegetables, let them, but do not judge those who determine not to obey man's traditions." The Torah does not command that we should only eat vegetables.

When we look at these Scriptures through our 21st-century lenses, we don't have the same mindset as Paul, because we have long since abandoned those dietary laws. We consider pork to be food, but Paul did not. And so when Paul writes "all food", the category he is referring to is different from the category we think of.

Pretend I wrote, "Some eat all food, and others are vegan. Whoever eats all food, don't despise the vegans. Vegans, don't judge those who eat all food." Now pretend that two thousand years in the future, someone reads what I wrote and says, "Awesome. He just said that it's okay to eat feces." You see, in this scenario, it is commonplace for people in the future to eat feces. From my 21st-century perspective, I didn't see the need to clarify that I wasn't talking about anything and everything under the sun when I said "food". However, the people of this future scenario decided that I must be talking about whatever *they* considered to be food as opposed to whatever *I* considered to be food. If I had the chance to tell those people, "No, that's not fit for food. It's dirty. Don't eat it," I would. I think that's what Paul would say, too, about some of the things that we consider to be food today.

There are numerous verses in the New Testament that Christianity applies with a retroactive mindset to justify culture being the way it is today. When these verses get pulled out in isolation and tagged to a specific topic (whether or not they are truly referring to that topic), it seems pretty compelling to the ones who don't read the Bible for themselves. If you consider the Bible holistically, you have more context with which you can understand what the Scriptures are truly talking about.

When we read the New Testament without understanding what's written in the law and the prophets, we end up making stuff up.

For example, I have heard the argument that the only commands from the Old Testament that we are still expected to obey are those that are reiterated in the New Testament. I believe the basis for this view comes from the understanding that the Old *Testament* is synonymous with the old *covenant*. With this in mind, we can go to Hebrews 8 and read about the old covenant passing away and a new, better covenant taking its place. If we accept that the Old Testament and the old covenant are one in the same, then this seems like reasonable logic.

But if we take a step back, we can see that the terms "Old Testament" and "New Testament" were applied retroactively to the Bible to categorize the books. In other words, the writers of the Bible didn't consider their books to be part of the Old Testament or the New Testament. They were just inspired by God to write what they wrote. Though we refer to it today as the Old Testament, Yeshua and his followers would have referred to these Scriptures as the law, the prophets, and the writings. These Scriptures tell us about the old covenant, but is it correct to say that the Scriptures themselves are the old covenant?

If we go back to Hebrews 8, we see that the writer of Hebrews explains the transition from the old covenant to the new covenant by quoting from the book of Jeremiah, which Christians today consider to be part of the Old Testament. Now if the Old Testament and the old covenant are one in the same, isn't it a bit strange that the writer of Hebrews quotes from the Old Testament in making the case that the Old Testament is no more? It's as if the writer is simultaneously establishing and rejecting the authority of those Scriptures.

This is where the argument comes in that anything included in the New Testament remains valid. In other words, the writer of Hebrews quoted the book of Jeremiah there, so that portion of Scripture is still valid. Therefore, we don't consider it to be obsolete. If you spend just a little bit of time really thinking through this view, though, it quickly gets out of hand. Are we only talking about direct quotes here, or do general references count? If only half a verse is quoted, do we disregard the other half? Does it have to express the command in the form of a command, or is it sufficient to just mention the idea of the command?

With roughly a third of the New Testament being quotes from and references to the Old Testament, this view presents a wildly complicated reality for Christians that I believe many Christians are willing to look past, even though it has created much confusion within Christianity. It is a far more complicated and arbitrary system than the view that the entire Bible remains the established Word of God, and within its pages we can learn about the old covenant and the new covenant.

So what are the old covenant and the new covenant, then, if not the Old Testament and the New Testament? First, just consider what a covenant is, in general. It's an agreement between two parties. So, the old covenant was an agreement between God and His people, and the new covenant is a new agreement between God and His people, one that took the place of the first agreement.

With this in mind, we read in Genesis 17:9–10:

> And Elohim said to Aḇraham, "As for you, guard My covenant, you and your seed after you throughout their generations. This is My covenant which you guard between Me and you, and your seed after you: Every male child among you is to be circumcised."

The old covenant centered around *physical* circumcision. The agreement was that God would bless Abraham and his offspring, making them fruitful and giving them land as an everlasting possession, and Abraham and his offspring would be circumcised.

We read in Jeremiah 31:31–34:

> "See, the days are coming," declares יהוה, "when I shall make a renewed covenant with the house of Yisraěl and with the house of Yehuḏah, not like the covenant I made with their fathers in the day when I strengthened their hand to bring them out of the land of Mitsrayim, My covenant which they broke, though I was a husband to them," declares יהוה. "For this is the covenant I shall make with the house of Yisraěl after those days, declares יהוה: I shall put My Torah in their inward parts, and write it on their hearts. And I shall be their Elohim, and they shall be My people. And no longer shall they teach, each one his neighbour, and each one his brother, saying, 'Know יהוה,' for they shall all know Me, from the least of them to the greatest of them," declares יהוה. "For I shall forgive their crookedness, and remember their sin no more."

The new covenant centers around *heart* circumcision (see Deuteronomy 30:6, Jeremiah 4:4, Ezekiel 36:26, and Romans 2:29). The agreement is that God writes His Torah on our hearts, forgives us of our crookedness, and remembers our sin no more. As for our part within the covenant, we (from having His Torah written on our hearts) have our hearts circumcised, giving us the desire to walk in obedience to God's commands.

Why are these covenants centered around the concept of circumcision? Circumcision points to sensitivity. Physical circumcision introduces higher sensitivity in the flesh, and heart circumcision introduces higher sensitivity in the spirit. It's not that God doesn't want us to physically obey His law. It's simply that the more important matter is the spiritual one. God doesn't want us to grudgingly obey Him. He wants us to have a heart that knows Him, loves Him, and *desires* to please Him. The new covenant doesn't abolish God's law. It moves His law from tablets of stone into our hearts. It is a *spiritual* transaction.

This is why, when we read through the New Testament, we find Paul adamantly arguing the topic of circumcision. We often make the mistake of thinking that Paul is just using circumcision as an example of God's law to make the point that the law has been abolished. But that's not what he's doing. He's not arguing the Torah. He's arguing the covenant, and how the old covenant caused us to be *under* the Torah. In other words, the agreement is no longer that we are God's people if we have been circumcised in the flesh. The agreement now is that we are God's people if our hearts have been circumcised (i.e., if we walk in love with the *desire* to obey Him).

As I started seeing some of these Scriptures throughout the Bible through new lenses, I found the idea of obeying the Torah more and more appealing. I didn't find the idea of being *under* the Torah more appealing, but the idea of *choosing* to obey it out of love. That is the essence of the new covenant.

This appeal created a much more cohesive understanding of the Bible within me than I had ever had before. I began seeing how Genesis through Revelation was consistent narrative as opposed to cryptic messaging.

A bird's-eye narrative of the Scriptures would be something like this:

After the fall of man, God chose Abraham because of his faith. God used physical circumcision as a covenant between Him and Abraham, to declare that Abraham and his offspring were His people. Through Abraham, God established a nation, called Israel, and gave them His law (Torah), which told them what righteousness looked like. Nobody in

Israel could achieve righteousness, however, because they all broke the law. Israel ended up splitting into two nations after one of their kings chased after other gods, not obeying God's law. These two nations were Judah and Israel. Both Judah and Israel ended up being so unfaithful to God (continuously breaking His law) that God allowed foreign nations to invade and capture them. The nation of Israel was ultimately scattered throughout the world, and the nation of Judah had the opportunity to return to Jerusalem and rebuild the temple. God promised through the prophets that he would one day restore Israel, those who had been scattered throughout the world. He also promised that He would one day create a new covenant between Him and His people. Meanwhile, the people of Judah (the Jews), grew more and more religious in ceremony and legalistic towards God's law, and so God stopped speaking to the people through His prophets.

There seemed to be a silence from God for 400 years, and then a virgin had a baby and named him Yeshua. He was a Jew. He grew up, and he obeyed the law of God perfectly. He had no other gods before God, he worshipped no idols, he didn't use God's name in vain, he remembered the Sabbath and kept it holy, he honored his parents, he didn't murder, he didn't commit adultery, he didn't steal, he didn't lie, and he didn't covet. He obeyed all the other laws in the Torah, as well, and he did it all within the context of loving God with all his heart, being, and mind and loving people as himself. Through his righteousness, he was empowered to heal the sick and cast out demons. He taught with great wisdom and avoided the traps of the religious. Eventually, he was sold out by one of his confidants, and he allowed himself to be executed. Three days later, he resurrected from the dead. He appeared to his friends over the course of forty days, and then he ascended to heaven to be with his Father, with the promise that he would one day return, gather all of his people from the corners of the earth, and reign as king. Some ten days later, the Spirit descended upon the believers, establishing the new covenant foretold by Jeremiah, writing God's Torah on their inward parts, empowering them with new hearts that desired to obey. From that point forward, this heart change has been the agreement between God and His people, an agreement in which God faithfully forgives us and remembers our sin no more.

God's law, the Torah, is a beautiful thing. When it was incomplete, or unfulfilled, we were lost. Now that it is complete, or fulfilled (Matthew 5:17), we are rescued. That is the Gospel, the good news that, through faith in Yeshua, we can enter into the new covenant, which offers us forgiveness of sin, and receive back the righteousness that will lead us into eternal life with our Maker, the blessing from which we had otherwise disqualified ourselves.

Those who belong to Yeshua are those who love him and obey him (John 14:15). If we love him, we will love God with all our heart, being, and mind, and we will love others as he loved us. If we love him and believe in him, we receive the gift of his righteousness, the Set-apart Spirit of God, and the desire to obey, and we continue to walk according to that gift of righteousness all our days, until he returns for us.

If we want to love others the way Yeshua loved us, there's really no legitimate alternative to considering what the Torah has to say.

Why So Much Torah?

YOU MAY BE THINKING, "Torah, Torah, Torah . . . why so much Torah? I understand why you would call it a good thing, but isn't the way you're focusing so heavily on it indication that you really do believe we're made righteous through obeying the law?"

Not at all. We are made righteous through belief in Yeshua. But like James writes in the second half of James 2:18, "Show me your belief without your works, and I shall show you my belief by my works."

I'm talking about the Torah so much here because this is the problem point for Christianity today. We have put so much energy into rejecting the idea that we are made righteous through obedience to the law (which is a good idea to reject in itself) that we have arrived at the false conclusion that the law has no purpose. That is the issue, and its effect in our world is obvious: many Christians today reject the law of God in favor of some other standard. In this way, they have become *lawless*.

Righteousness is given to us through faith in Yeshua. Our faith is made known through our works. What "works" do you think James is referring to? When we interpret this for ourselves, apart from the Word of God, we are being lawless.

Think about it like this. Pretend a police officer pulls you over because a vehicle like yours has been stolen. The police officer asks you for license and registration. You hand him a Polaroid picture of yourself with your name handwritten across the bottom along with a sticky note that reads, "This car belongs to me."

Do you honestly think the police officer would look at those "documents" and say, "Well, everything looks in order here. Carry on."? Why would he not do that? Because *there is a law* that determines what is acceptable in the way of proof. The car may really be yours. Maybe it was a gift. But after you received it, rather than moving forward *lawfully*, you decided to make up your own system of proof.

That is what Christians are doing today. They are receiving righteousness as a gift through faith in Yeshua, but then rather than moving forward as prescribed by the Bible, they are determining what is good for them to do based on church culture or on what they personally feel. They are trying to substitute Polaroid pictures and sticky notes for license and registration. It is literal lawlessness, in that there is no regard for God's law.

When I look around at Christian culture, I see this all over the place. This is why I find 2 Thessalonians 2 quite sobering. I hope this is a wake-up call if you haven't already had one. Paul writes in 2 Thessalonians 2:1–12:

> As to the coming of our Master יהושע Messiah and our gathering together to Him, we ask you, brothers, not to become easily unsettled in mind or troubled, either by spirit or by word or by letter, as if from us, as if the day of יהוה has come. Let no one deceive you in any way, because the falling away is to come first, and the man of lawlessness is to be revealed, the son of destruction, who opposes and exalts himself above all that is called Elohim or that is worshipped, so that he sits as Elohim in the Dwelling Place of Elohim, showing himself that he is Elohim. Do you not remember that I told you this while I was still with you? And now you know what restrains, for him to be revealed in his time. For the secret of lawlessness is already at work – only until he who now restrains comes out of the midst. And then the lawless one shall be revealed, whom the Master shall consume with the Spirit of His mouth and bring to naught with the manifestation of His coming. The coming of the lawless one is according to the working of Satan, with all power and signs and wonders of falsehood, and with all deceit of unrighteousness in those perishing, because they did not receive the love of the truth, in order for them to be saved. And for this reason Elohim sends them a working of delusion, for them to believe the falsehood, in order that all should be judged who did not believe the truth, but have delighted in the unrighteousness.

Paul is telling the Thessalonians in the first century not to be unsettled or troubled about the second coming of Yeshua, because the falling away had to come first. What is he talking about here? The next thing he says is, "... and the man of lawlessness is to be revealed...", so perhaps there is a connection between the falling away and the man of lawlessness.

The more I consider the Torah and the way that Christianity has come to reject God's law, the more I believe these ideas expressed by Paul in 2 Thessalonians are pointing to the time we're in now. We are not seeing a falling away in terms of proclamations of faith. We are seeing a falling away in terms of obedience. Everybody is doing their own thing rather than obeying the commands of God as spelled out in His law.

Notice what else Paul writes concerning the man of lawlessness: " . . . so that he sits as Elohim in the Dwelling Place of Elohim, showing himself that he is Elohim." What is the dwelling place of Elohim? Before Yeshua died, God's dwelling place was the temple. After Yeshua's death, God's dwelling place became man's heart. The Holy Spirit dwells within us. So what does it mean for the man of lawlessness to sit in the dwelling place of God? It means that he loves and reveres himself above God. That is why he is the man of lawlessness—he doesn't respect the law of God and prefers living by his own rules.

How does something like this happen in a faith that claims their king is God's son (understanding that "king" is a lawful title) and that this king obeyed God's law? Paul writes, "The coming of the lawless one is according to the working of Satan . . . with all deceit of unrighteousness in those perishing, because they did not receive the love of the truth . . . " Not loving the truth makes us vulnerable to Satan's deceptions, and that leads to lawlessness. This is exactly what Satan wants, because when we reject God's law, we are rejecting the very commands that can lead us back to the truth. When we reject God's law, we are lost, exalting ourselves in the place of Elohim.

So again, why so much Torah? Why have I been so focused on God's law? Because, while it does not restore our righteousness, it still has a purpose, and we have been neglecting that purpose. The more we neglect it, the harder it becomes to find our way back to God's truth. God gave us His law so that we might know truth as it pertains to righteousness. Real Truth, as He determines it to be.

If Yeshua is the completion of the Torah, and all the law and prophets point to Yeshua, then we should not be taking it upon ourselves to isolate the two. Yeshua and the law go hand in hand. The distinction comes in understanding where we receive our righteousness from. Our righteousness does not come from our efforts to obey the law. If it did, we would have no righteousness to speak of. It comes from belief in Yeshua's obedience to the law of God. When we reject the law of God, we are rejecting the full truth of the Gospel.

When Paul speaks of the man of lawlessness in 2 Thessalonians 2, what "law" do you think he is referring to? The laws of nature? American law? No. He is talking about God's law. According to the Bible, that is the Torah.

So the next question is this: when Paul speaks of the man of lawlessness in 2 Thessalonians 2, whom do you think he is referring to? Perhaps he has someone specific in mind. Or perhaps he is referring to anyone who rejects the law of God, thereby being lawless. Do you see how anyone who has decided not to obey God's law is, by definition, the man of lawlessness?

This is my concern, and this is why I am stressing the Torah here. I read Paul's words in 2 Thessalonians 2, and I see the man of lawlessness as a type. It's like saying the criminal serves the time. It works as a concept, and "the criminal" refers to whomever the shoe fits.

The man of lawlessness isn't the man of lawlessness simply because he decides he wants to be lawless. Paul tells us, "The coming of the lawless one is according to the working of Satan . . . with all deceit . . . " The coming of the lawless one involves deception.

This deception didn't spring up overnight. It has been the working of Satan for some time now. We can see how it's taken its gradual course throughout history via the Christian religion teaching that the Torah has been abolished. To see the deception for what it is, we must choose God's Word over the manmade doctrines of religion.

The Galatian Situation

I love the book of Galatians. I am constantly returning to Galatians 5:22–23 to remind myself of the fruit of the Spirit, and that against such there is no Torah.

That said, I want to acknowledge what may appear to be an irony, that this book is titled *The Spirit of the Matter*, and yet it encourages obedience to God's law. This may appear ironic due to a belief that there is a fundamental opposition between living according to the law and living according to the Spirit.

I want to clarify my belief with one small tweak: there is a fundamental opposition between living *under* the law and living according to the Spirit.

Think of sunscreen. Sunscreen protects your skin from the sun. The right amount of exposure to the sun can result in skin cancer, and skin cancer has the capability to kill you. Is it therefore good to worship sunscreen as your savior? No, it isn't. However, just because sunscreen isn't our savior, should we completely do away with it? No, we shouldn't. It is still wise to wear sunscreen in situations of intense sun exposure.

The law tells us what sin is so we can avoid it. Sin can destroy us. Is it therefore good to worship the law as our savior? No, it isn't. However, just because the law isn't our savior, should we completely do away with it? No, we shouldn't. It is still wise to look to the law in situations of intense sin exposure.

It's funny how humanity embraces so many things in life as good even though those things still fall short of being our savior. There are so many people, principles, and products that offer wisdom even though they are not Yeshua. We embrace those people, principles, and products as wisdom, and then we snarl at the Torah like it's threatening our children.

This is where the true irony lies. Just think about it for a moment. If we're truly living according to the Spirit, and not under the law, we are not living in a spirit of fear. And yet we have an impulsively fearful reaction to the law. Kind of ironic, right?

I love the book of Galatians, but this letter may be the most used epistle of Paul to attack the law of God. It's easy to use it this way when we don't consider context and hastily jump to simplistic conclusions based on Paul's words.

Consider, for example, Galatians 5:1-4:

> In the freedom with which Messiah has made us free, stand firm, then, and do not again be held with a yoke of slavery. See, I, Sha'ul, say to you that if you become circumcised, Messiah shall be of no use to you. And I witness again to every man being circumcised that he is a debtor to do the entire Torah. You who are declared right by Torah have severed yourselves from Messiah, you have fallen from favour.

It is so easy to walk away from these verses chanting, "Do not again be held with a yoke of slavery!" But do we really understand what Paul is saying here when we do that?

I could just as easily walk away chanting, "Don't circumcise your babies!" After all, Paul does say, "And I witness again to every man being circumcised that he is a debtor to do the entire Torah." So is every man on earth who has ever been circumcised a debtor to the Torah because of his circumcision? Certainly not. But then how do we make sense of Paul's words?

Paul makes sense of his own words in the very next verse: "You who are declared right by the Torah have severed yourselves from Messiah". Paul isn't talking to people who are *following* the Torah. Paul is talking to people who are *declaring themselves right (i.e., righteous) by* the Torah. This is, once again, a spirit of the matter issue.

If we want to make the claim that Paul is talking about literal, physical obedience to the Torah, then we also ought to take away that any man who has literally, physically been circumcised is under the Torah. But that's not his message. His message pertains to their hearts. If you believe that your circumcision saves you, then you are responsible for obeying the law perfectly. Likewise, if you believe you've achieved righteousness because you've done such a great job in obeying the Torah, then you've separated yourself from the grace of Yeshua.

Put another way, if you don't consider Yeshua's death to be the payment for your sin, then you will be held accountable for each and every wicked deed you have ever committed, regardless of how well you observed the Torah otherwise. It doesn't matter how good of a person you are in every other moment, if the cop pulls you over for speeding, that means you broke the law. He's entitled to give you a ticket.

Galatians 5:18 says:

> But if you are led by the Spirit, you are not under Torah.

There is a certain, technical truth to the idea that, if we are pulled over by the cop for speeding, we can say, "Okay, send the bill to Yeshua." But that sort of focus inevitably distorts the spirit of the matter. Yeshua's sacrifice shouldn't be causing us to say, "Alright, I can speed now and not have to pay tickets!" It should be causing us to not speed.

If we are led by the Spirit, we are not under Torah. Just think through that for a moment. Why are we not under Torah if we are led by the Spirit?

If we are led by the Spirit, the Torah has nothing to charge against us. If we are led by the Spirit (the same Spirit that was in Yeshua), we walk in love (John 15:12), we walk in obedience (John 15:14), and, in so doing, we fulfill the Torah's requirements (Galatians 5:14).

The logical implication here is this: being under the Torah has nothing to do with following the Torah and everything to do with not loving one another. The call of Yeshua is to prioritize love, and we put ourselves back under the Torah when we abandon love and grace in pursuit of trying to legalistically adhere to law. When we prioritize love, we don't speed down the highway unless it's an emergency that merits such an action, because the law says, "Don't speed," and it says that for a reason (i.e., we could hurt or kill somebody).

Galatians is a powerful book with a bounty of wisdom. But we can't just take Paul's words and use them to attack any mention of the Torah. We must understand the situation of the Galatians. Apparently, there was some notion among them that they would be counted righteous by obeying the Torah as opposed to having faith in Yeshua. If that is a spirit with which we are tempted, then we should absolutely focus on Paul's words here to apply their wisdom.

However, most American Christians don't seem to fit that profile. If you are an American Christian, do you honestly believe that your main problem is a spirit that seeks salvation through obeying the Torah? Perhaps it's a spirit that seeks salvation through going to church, but

American Christian culture is so detached from observing the Torah that the Galatian situation is likely not your situation.

Again, if you're being honest with yourself, do you think your primary spiritual issue is the mentality that excessively adhering to the first five books of the Bible will lead to your salvation? I can make this real clear for a lot of Christians by asking, "How do you feel about Genesis 1, the very first chapter of the Torah?" Our culture does not excessively adhere to these books. The book of Galatians holds much wisdom, but the Galatian situation is not exactly our situation.

So what is our situation? I'd suggest that our situation is the exact inverse of the Galatians'. We don't excessively adhere to the Torah in the name of righteousness. We excessively abandon it in the name of righteousness.

Part 6

The End and the Beginning

Before You Feast on This Part

I WAS A CREATIVE WRITING and philosophy major. Since middle school, and maybe even before, I knew I wanted to be a writer. It has always been a weird thought. I say that because I have never understood exactly why I've been so convinced of that thought through the years. I've never been a great writer or anything like that. I do pretty well with poetry (at least in my own mind). Otherwise, I have a lot of creative ideas and stories always churning in my head, but I'm a pretty mediocre writer when it comes to the technical discipline of writing. So I've never fully understood why I put so much emphasis on writing throughout my life.

When James and I had the same work shift at the rescue mission, about once a week, he and I would meet up for lunch beforehand. We went to The Big Easy, a restaurant in downtown Raleigh, then we walked around Moore Square Park for a while, talking, before going into work. On one of these walks, James told me that he had prayed for God to send him a writer some time ago. Now, here I was.

I thought this was funny. Kendra and I moved to Raleigh in what felt to be prompting from the Holy Spirit, coming out of everything that happened at our church in Manhattan. We felt compelled to leave the city, and the only practical motive for choosing Raleigh was its placement—four hours from each of our parents.

Furthermore, I had this conviction on my heart to write a book. I had the title and everything. I determined that I was going to knock it out. And then I didn't.

And then I met James, COVID happened, and 2020 ended up being the only year weird enough to parallel all these topics I ended up contemplating. And then James told me he had prayed for God to send him a writer.

It was all a bit silly to me, and I loved it.

Cents and Sensibility

My favorite poem by Shel Silverstein is called "Smart". In the poem, a boy trades a dollar bill given to him by his father for two quarters, because two is more than one. He then proceeds to trade the quarters for three dimes, because three is more than two. He does this until he ends up with five pennies. At the end of the poem, he believes himself to be clever and his father to be proud.

The boy's logic isn't wrong—five truly is more than one. But all it takes is one piece of critical information (that the different pieces of money have different values) to undermine his entire system of logic and reasoning.

People are eagerly trading away the one Word of God for five cents' worth of human reasoning, and they are feeling pretty smart about the whole thing.

If you make the decision that you are smart enough about something to deviate your thinking from the Bible on one point, you'd better be ready to go the distance. The Bible either is God's Word or it isn't. If you want to believe what the Bible says, except for the Genesis account, then you're trading a dollar for two quarters. Next it will be the Bible minus Genesis and Revelation (two quarters for three dimes). Then it's considering most of the Bible to be figurative (three dimes for four nickels). And finally, human reasoning has determined that the Bible is just wrong (five pennies).

Consider the values being offered by the starting point and the finishing point. The value offered by the Bible as God's Word is eternal and abundant life. The value offered by five cents' worth of human reasoning is finite life and eternal meaninglessness.

This is why I believe people are not being genuine if they say they are ninety-nine percent confident there is no God or life after death. I do not believe they are genuine in saying they are ninety-nine percent confident. I think deep down, they feel one hundred percent confident, but they say ninety-nine percent to avoid looking arrogant.

If they really did have one percent of true doubt, that would be sufficient reason to place their bet on faith.

For anyone who is mostly confident that there is no life after this one but less than one hundred percent certain of it, I believe this is the position you are in:

You are stuck in a room with two doors and no other way out. Each door has a sign on it, and the signs are telling you the truth.

Door A

This door most likely will get you out of here. If it is the correct door, you will forget about all of this and cease to be. However, there is a chance it is the wrong door. If it is the wrong door, it will lead you to a lot of pain and suffering.

Door B

This door most likely will not get you out of here. If it is the correct door, you will have succeeded in this challenge and receive unending joy. However, if it is the wrong door, you will forget about all of this and cease to be.

Now why would anyone choose Door A? The best-case scenario for Door A is the worst-case scenario for Door B.

People say they have no choice in the matter. Sure, they'd love to believe that there is a God and a life after this one, but they just can't bring themselves to the point of belief. And if they don't truly believe it, then they consider it a violation of their integrity to say they do. All in all, they simply can't believe it.

If this is you, I implore you to recognize the way in which you are being held hostage. This is spiritual warfare, influencing you to think that you have no choice in the matter. You are trapped because you believe in a bleak reality, and part of this reality is the belief that you can't change what you believe. You are trapped by circular thinking. Don't accept that. You are the only one who can control what you believe. Sure, you might not wake up tomorrow feeling totally convinced, but you can choose to work towards it. Consider the man speaking to Yeshua in Mark 9:24:

> And immediately the father of the child cried out and said with tears, "I believe Master, help my unbelief!"

Also consider Yeshua's words in John 8:31–32:

> So יהושע said to those Yehuḏim who believed Him, "If you stay in My Word, you are truly My taught ones, and you shall know the truth, and the truth shall make you free."

I don't doubt that people feel trapped in their belief, like they can't choose to change it. But I don't feel trapped in my belief. I feel free, and I feel that I could change my belief if I wanted to. But why would I want to? The opposing belief has nothing to offer me.

When you actually have a choice in the matter, it doesn't make any sense to choose the door of human understanding instead of the door of faith. It's just not a smart bet.

Now I'm not saying that determining a smart bet can or should lead someone into having a genuine faith in God. I am saying that it should give some reason for at least looking into the matter further. I appeal on these grounds because I am appealing to those who believe they prioritize human reasoning.

If you say that you don't believe in God, but you have even the tiniest doubt within you about that belief, why would you waste your time doing anything else other than understanding why you have that doubt and putting it to rest? After all, if it turns out that that doubt has any truth behind it, the implications are huge.

One might say, "Well you can never know for sure." Yes, but that's my point here. If you can never know for sure, then whatever side you defer to is a deferring of faith. So why would you defer to the side that prioritizes human understanding above faith if you can never know for sure?

Furthermore, why would you defer to the side that is saying, "There is no objective meaning in this existence, so use your understanding to figure things out"? What are you really figuring out in this existence?

Lastly, why would you defer to the side that says, "The primary reason you should work for progress now is so that future generations can experience a better world"? That sort of altruism is either disingenuous or naïve. The majority of people in this life suffer terribly. We may have come across some brilliant scientific advances in the last couple centuries, but we've also seen the population rise from millions to billions within those same centuries, thereby increasing the amount of suffering in the world. Our advances have allowed a minority of the human population to experience great comfort, luxury, and enjoyment, but what about the billions of people who are being born into a life of suffering and torment? If there really is no objective moral standard transcending human understanding, then wouldn't the best thing we can do be euthanizing a large portion of the population? If you are one hundred percent convinced that there is no God and no life after this one, then it is cruel to work towards the propagation of humanity in the midst of a world like ours.

This leads us to a fundamental divide. Do you prioritize life or pleasure? The only reason we would be appalled at euthanizing a large portion of the population would be because we value and prioritize life. Otherwise, it makes sense to "put to sleep" those who are suffering and are in pain, those who are consuming valuable resources that could otherwise be enjoyed by those who are receiving much pleasure in life. Putting those people out of their misery would be the most noble action for a mindset that prioritizes pleasure.

When you don't believe in a life after this one, why *would* you prioritize life over pleasure? When this life is all there is, it can only be appraised in terms of its pleasure, because anything beyond pleasure will inevitably melt into meaninglessness. When there is more to the picture, life can be appraised in terms of love. Love is the reason we prioritize life over pleasure. We press on through circumstances that are undesirable, painful, and not pleasurable because we believe there is a higher purpose in doing so, one that will endure beyond this lifetime. That higher purpose is bringing more people into God's family while we still can.

Whether you don't believe in God or you don't believe God's Word means what it says, it doesn't make sense to live this way and feel happy about our existence. The best parts of this world are nothing more than a chronically sick person who has put on makeup and gotten all dressed up in hopes of fooling everyone else. We're all sick and dying. Compared with the beauty of the life to come, the worldly pleasures of this life are like scratching mosquito bites—they're only pleasurable because they help us address something irritating and wrong.

I've watched and participated in enough philosophical arguments and debates to know that the argument never ends. To every point that I've made here, there are easily ten counterarguments, and to every one of those, there are ten more counterarguments. It takes intelligence to participate in a debate and wisdom to step out of one. The real value of any debate is in understanding the larger picture, what is at stake, and what are the practical implications of each perspective. I encourage everyone to really think practically about the reasoning behind choosing Door A instead of Door B.

Again, I appeal on the grounds of reason because I am appealing to those who prioritize their reasoning over God's Word. But it is not my reasoning that ultimately gives my spirit peace and joy in these matters. It is my faith. Reasoning is fun and enjoyable, but it is inferior, and I believe sound reasoning can help us understand that. Everything we do operates on a system of faith. We've been given the blessing of reasoning so that we can understand the world around us, but as soon as we start thinking we know better than the one who gave us that reasoning, we're making a mistake. We're trading in our very souls for five cents.

Science, Creationism, and the Spirit of the Matter

REMEMBER HOW JACOB wrestled with God? Out of all the topics covered in this book, this may be the most difficult one for you to wrestle with God over. I want to say up front that what I am *not* trying to do here is scientifically combat some of the mainstream narratives existing today. I am not a scientist, and I don't claim to be one. That said, I also am not stupid, and I am capable of thinking for myself. I believe the same is true for you. There will always be people who are smarter, more experienced, and better articulated than we are in any given subject. It is good to listen to what these people have to say about their field of expertise, but no other person owns your mind. It is yours. Use it, engage it, sharpen it.

I am not trying to scientifically combat some of the mainstream narratives existing today, but I also am not proposing you accept or reject anything without good reason. Science is helpful, valuable, and good, and I will be mentioning some resources that I hope you'll look into for yourself if you are seeking answers that are more scientifically oriented.

What I am trying to do here is help you wrestle with God on this topic. It's not an easy one, and I understand that. The world around us has made us feel insecure about even approaching this topic with real consideration. Many well-meaning people are no longer willing to wrestle with God over it because they're afraid of looking foolish. I just want to help you and others see that it's not foolish. It's part of God's Word. So let's look at it.

Okay. Are you ready to wrestle?

Second Peter 3:1–9 says:

> This is now, beloved ones, the second letter I write to you, in which I stir up your sincere mind, to remember the words

> previously spoken by the set-apart prophets, and of the command of the Master and Saviour, spoken by your emissaries, knowing this first: that mockers shall come in the last days with mocking, walking according to their own lusts, and saying, "Where is the promise of His coming? For since the fathers fell asleep, all continues as from the beginning of creation." For they choose to have this hidden from them: that the heavens were of old, and the earth standing out of water and in the water, by the Word of Elohim, through which the world at that time was destroyed, being flooded with water. And the present heavens and the earth are treasured up by the same Word, being kept for fire, to a day of judgment and destruction of wicked men. But, beloved ones, let not this one matter be hidden from you: that with יהוה one day is as a thousand years, and a thousand years as one day. יהוה is not slow in regard to the promise, as some count slowness, but is patient toward us, not wishing that any should perish but that all should come to repentance.

I had become a Christian who said, "Yeah, it seems like the earth is billions of years old. The creation account in Genesis must be figurative."

I also had adamantly insisted that either way, it wasn't what my faith was based on, so I wasn't too concerned about it.

I had discovered and developed my own way of addressing the apparent discrepancy and dealing with it in a way in which I felt the rest of the world would still consider me to be a credible human being.

What I hadn't done is actually taken it upon myself to look into the evidence and arguments that formed the foundation of an old-earth view. Sure, I could throw out phrases like "carbon dating" and "fossil evidence", but I didn't really know what I was talking about.

Of course, at the time I could carelessly justify it away by saying, "For some things you just have to rely on the expertise of others." That's what I was doing. I was relying on the expertise of scientists, because I couldn't hope to understand all the complexities involved in forming a viable model for earth's history. That wasn't my thing, so I chose to defer to others.

The reason that was problematic is because my ignorance was a result of a discrepancy between what current culture said and what the Bible said, and rather than look into the issue while maintaining what the Bible said *or* simply defer to the Bible (either of which would have been faithfully appropriate choices), I chose to defer to what current culture was saying.

Now hear me out on this point. I am not saying that the problem at hand was that I took on a view that the earth is billions of years old. The problem was that I first absolved myself of responsibility for looking into the matter and then deferred to the side of current culture rather than the Bible. I say "current" culture because that is what it is. The view that the earth is billions of years old is a development of the last couple centuries.

I hope you can see the point I'm making here. I'm not even arguing the theories involved. I am making a point about the spirit of the matter, as it pertained to me. My spirit was more concerned with maintaining some silly notion of credibility than it was concerned with understanding actual truth. More importantly, though, the way in which I went about trying to maintain that notion of credibility revealed an ugly truth about myself: I was completely comfortable with the world having more influence than God's Word over my thinking. Put another way, I had more faith in the world than I had in God's Word, and that didn't bother me.

The Bible told me that God created the world in six days and rested on the seventh. The world told me that that was impossible. Even though I had every resource at my fingertips—books and libraries, teachers, and even the Internet—I didn't bother spending a second looking into it seriously. "Yep, sounds good to me," I told myself. I let the world tell me that the Bible is wrong with a shrug of my shoulders.

I didn't even bother recognizing all the ways in which I had mindlessly accepted an inconsistent mentality. I didn't pause to consider the fact that science had also proven that Mary couldn't have been a virgin when she had Jesus. Science had proven that Jesus couldn't have resurrected from the dead or ascended into heaven. Science had proven that nearly all the Bible was either figurative or garbage.

But that didn't bother me. I felt okay about maintaining those other scientifically ridiculous beliefs. It was just the whole creation account that I had a problem with. I guess in my eyes, God was big enough to miraculously impregnate a woman, miraculously bring people back from the dead, and miraculously bring them into heaven, but He wasn't quite big enough to miraculously create the world in six days despite our understanding of the data we have today.

These arbitrary distinctions had me feeling like quite the credible human being.

I'm laying into this point so thickly because I know that it is no use moving forward if this foundational piece isn't understood. We now live in a time in which professing to believe the very beginning of the Bible as it is written is grounds for being mocked and ridiculed. How sad is that?

Again, I haven't even touched on the theories involved here. I've only described our situation today. If someone wants to present a case for the earth being roughly six thousand years old, we scoff and write them off as stupid, even if we don't have a thorough knowledge of the evidence and reasoning composing the competing point of view. We have become effectively blinded to the dominating spirit involved, which is arrogance.

I find it a problem to maintain a spirit *that is eager* to say, "Well, whether or not the earth was created in six days doesn't really shake my faith." That used to be my spirit. It sounds very noble, but its eagerness betrays a real fear within us. We fear being mocked and ridiculed. We fear being discredited and considered stupid. We fear that the world is right and the Bible is wrong, and rather than seeking truth within the context of having faith in the Bible, we take it upon ourselves to interpret the Scriptures in ways that not even Yeshua interpreted them in order to reconcile what the Bible says with what the world says.

When we eagerly say, "Well, either way, it doesn't shake my faith," we have already chosen a side, because it already has shaken our faith. We forfeit the integrity of being able to say, "My faith is based on the Bible," because we're living according to the exact inverse, as if the Bible is based on our faith. When we claim that the Bible means something other than what it says, we strip it of its authority. In lieu of its authority, we empower ourselves to determine truth.

Here you may say, "Well you're one to talk. What do you call all that business with the days of creation being prophetic?"

There is a distinct difference between 1) claiming words are prophetic while meaning what they say and 2) claiming words don't mean what they say. The Bible is beautiful in that it is full of real accounts that are saturated with prophetic meaning. We tarnish its beauty and breed confusion when we see fable and fantasy in place of history and prophecy.

The Bible does hold deep meaning, but the Holy Spirit reveals it to us *when we have faith in what it says*. We do not discover its meaning by trying to understand the world on our own and then layering that understanding on top of what is already written. That is exactly what we have done with the earth's history.

The real disconnect at play is not a matter of rational versus irrational or reasonable versus unreasonable. The real disconnect is a matter of value system. One value system prioritizes faith, and the other prioritizes understanding. Both are wonderful things, but when we prioritize understanding above faith, we become arrogant. When we prioritize faith above understanding, we become grateful.

Every moment of our being is founded upon some faith within us, whether we recognize it or not. I have faith when I get out of bed in the morning that the layout of my home is the same as it was yesterday. I have faith that my eyes are feeding my brain an accurate depiction of the things I am seeing. I have faith that the sun will set and that it will rise the next morning. I don't have to think about these things constantly in order to feel comfortable or assured. That is the beauty of faith. It allows us to have joy in an otherwise precarious reality, and it allows us to trust upon certain foundational truths in order to move forward with innovation.

When we prioritize understanding above faith, we neglect these truths about faith, and we attribute the benefits of grace and faith to our own achievement. I did nothing last night to ensure that I would still be breathing this morning, and yet if I am not careful, I will slip into the arrogant illusion that I am entitled to certain things within this life, this life which I did nothing to merit in the first place.

This is why I consider the "belief in science" as a foundational or core belief to be much more naïve and juvenile than the belief in God. Believing in God freely recognizes and admits to the roles of grace and faith in life. Believing in science, as the phrase is often used today, claims to only trust in what is perceivable while utilizing trust in what is imperceivable every step of the way to develop any theory or idea.

To be clear, I am not saying that science is without merit. It has very strong merit in certain situations. I believe that a broad range of scientific and medical advances—everything from antibiotics to coronary artery bypasses—have offered much good to society over the years. The issue is when we become comfortable prioritizing "belief in science" above what is stated in God's Word.

We have to understand the role of value system before we can move forward in the discussion, otherwise there are two different discussions taking place.

Earlier I spoke facetiously of science proving that the Bible was either figurative or garbage. Many people genuinely believe this. I do not. The disconnect is in the value system. Because many people prioritize their understanding above all, they are unwilling to consider the reality of certain phenomena that they have not personally witnessed or that eludes their understanding. Their faith is in human understanding, whether it's their own or that of others. I consider this outlook to be arrogant. It is completely self-assured by definition, because the thing it is assured in and of is itself. It's a cycle of patting oneself on the back for having the ability to pat oneself on the back.

This outlook is problematic in that it stunts discovery, because it is not as open-minded as it pretends to be. It is only open-minded to the extent that others agree that if something exists, it must fit within the parameters of our understanding. Otherwise, that something should be eliminated from the equation.

That creates a real problem with a book that explicitly teaches belief as a virtue.

Luke 7:50 says:

> And He said to the woman, "Your belief has saved you. Go in peace."

Luke 8:48 says:

> And He said to her, "Take courage, daughter, your belief has healed you. Go in peace."

Luke 17:19 says:

> And He said to him, "Rise, go your way. Your belief has made you well."

Luke 18:42 says:

> And יהושע said to him, "Receive your sight! Your belief has saved you."

Luke, the writer of this Gospel, was a physician, and he included many instances of Yeshua telling people they were made well because of their belief.

Romans 3:27–28 says:

> Where is boasting then? It is excluded. By what law? Of works? No, but by the law of faith. Therefore we conclude that a man is justified by faith apart from the deeds of the law.

Notice how these verses in Romans contrast faith with boasting, which is being proud. These verses are referring to the works of the Torah and faith in Yeshua, but I see conceptual connections to what is happening today in the arena of science. There is an arrogance around the scientific process. Again, the scientific process is a good thing. The Torah,

SCIENCE, CREATIONISM, AND THE SPIRIT OF THE MATTER

also, is a good thing. But the spirit with which we are feeling justified by the scientific process is corrupted. The evidence for that is in how quickly Christians have given up on the first few chapters of God's Word because of claims that the scientific process has inarguably proven them to be wrong. In other words, we have given up on God's Word because human understanding claims to have proven it wrong.

Pay close attention to another piece of Scripture within the first three chapters of God's Word. Genesis 3:1 says:

> And the naḥash was more crafty than all the lives of the field which יהוה Elohim had made, and he said to the woman, "Is it true that Elohim has said, 'Do not eat of every tree of the garden'?"

Later in Genesis 3:4, we read:

> And the naḥash said to the woman, "You shall certainly not die."

The serpent's words are filled with lies, though they don't seem outlandish. This scene evolves into the fall of man, and it starts with a misleading question.

I have heard people wonder why the age of the earth would appear different from what it actually is. In other words, why would our testing processes date the earth to be billions of years old if it's only thousands of years old? Is it possible that God created matter in a state of already being aged, or that He effected some change over the rate of radioactive decay throughout history?

Many Christians say they cannot see why God would do something like that. It would just breed confusion, and that seems cruel. I challenge those Christians to answer (with the same honesty) this question, "If the Bible is God's Word, why would He have given us a creation narrative that is not true?" That seems far crueler and more confusing.

I would suggest clarifying the possible scenarios within this thought experiment. Either God did something to alter the appearance of the age of the earth, some other force did something to alter the appearance of the age of the earth, or we are missing something vital in our understanding of the whole matter. Personally, I am inclined to believe that the third option is inevitably at play here. If God did something to alter the appearance of the age of the earth, we are missing something in our understanding of why. If some other force had a role in it, we are missing something in our recognition of that. And if nothing has altered the appearance of the age of the earth, then we are missing something vital in our understanding of earth's aging process generally.

This is the position of faith in God's Word, believing that *we* are missing something when there is a discrepancy between our understanding and what His Word says.

Of course, we can avoid all of that by saying that we do have it right, we are certain that the earth is more than four billion years old, and Genesis is just a figurative piece of poetry. This is the position of human understanding.

Or, we can attempt to cleverly insert millions and billions of years in between certain verses to account for lost time. I consider this to be desperate engineering.

I am no longer willing to take on either of those last two positions because I decided that my faith is based on the Bible, and the Bible is not based on my faith. I must mean that differently from someone who says that their faith is based on the Bible even though they don't accept the Genesis creation account as it is written.

If that is you, then I ask, what does your faith even mean? You do know that science has proven in the same manner that Mary couldn't have been a virgin and that Yeshua couldn't have resurrected and ascended into heaven, right?

I realize there are many who are willing to make the claim that the first few chapters of Genesis aren't meant to be taken as literal accounts, but rather they are figurative. If that is the case, then we are left with the question of why Yeshua used these Scriptures in his teachings as if they were literal accounts (Matthew 19:4–5, Matthew 23:35, Luke 11:49–51).

Also, Moses, who is generally credited with writing the first five books of the Bible, wrote in Exodus 20:11:

> "For in six days יהוה made the heavens and the earth, the sea, and all that is in them, and rested the seventh day. Therefore יהוה blessed the Sabbath day and set it apart."

Now if Moses wrote Genesis 1 not intending it to be taken literally, then why would he have written Exodus 20:11, which simply confirms the *literal* account of creation in Genesis 1? If you believe that God inspired these books so it wasn't really Moses intending anything, then why would God confirm the literal account in Genesis 1 with Exodus 20:11? Exodus 20:11 falls right in the middle of the Ten Commandments. One of the Ten Commandments is "Do not lie". So why would God, in the

SCIENCE, CREATIONISM, AND THE SPIRIT OF THE MATTER

middle of calling out ten particularly critical laws, include a lie? If you don't want to call it a lie, then why would He interrupt a set of literal commands with a figurative history?

When we try to make the account of creation in Genesis figurative, we are doing something that nobody in the Bible did. If you think it is okay for us to consider it figurative because of the time period we live in, I suggest you are being duped by some spiritual deception.

I don't have all the answers to every question. That is exactly why I am of the position I am—I prioritize my faith in the Bible above my understanding.

Those who prioritize their understanding above faith are the ones who should be accountable for answering every question. And yet they can't. Even so, they are deceived into thinking that their understanding has made them like God.

Can we not see the irony in the fact that we are trying to discount the same portion of Scripture that gives us the account of the original deception, that which caused humanity to trust in its own understanding rather than God?

"Is it true that Elohim has said, 'Do not eat of every tree of the garden'? . . . You shall certainly not die."

"Did God really say that He created the heavens and the earth in six days? . . . You don't really have to believe that."

Prioritizing our own understanding over faith in God is what put us in this mess in the first place.

The Astronaut, the Aliens, and the Politics

PRETEND A 35-YEAR-OLD human male astronaut journeys to a new planet where there exist intelligent aliens. These aliens spawn spontaneously, fully grown, and their average life span is one year. None of them have ever witnessed a living creature forming in a womb and being born from another organism.

When the astronaut arrives, he gives them a letter written in their language that tells them that he is 35 years old, that he was conceived by a man and a woman, that he was formed in the womb of the woman, and that he was born as a baby after nine months. The letter tells them how much he weighed and how long he was when he was born.

The aliens accept what the letter says, even though they're unfamiliar with the processes described.

The astronaut lives among the aliens, but after five years, five whole generations of aliens have come and gone since the astronaut arrived.

Now imagine the aliens decide to run tests on the human astronaut. They find that his human body creates new cells. They document his height and weight, and they even take pictures of him.

After five more years pass and five more generations of aliens have come and gone, the new generation of aliens collects new data on the astronaut. At this point, the astronaut is 45 years old. When this new generation compares their new data to the data collected when he was 40 years old, they become confused.

They return to the letter he arrived with, explaining that he was born a baby, some five feet shorter and 180 pounds lighter than he is now, and that he was 35 years old when he arrived. They quickly run the numbers using the data taken when he was 40 and the new data, and they determine that the letter must be in error. They determine that, due to the almost nonexistent change in certain data points taken throughout the past ten years of the man's life, if this astronaut was truly born as a baby with the measurements provided, he would have to have been born much, much earlier than 45 years ago.

The aliens' logic is sound, but because they are unwilling to have faith in the letter the astronaut arrived with, they prevent themselves from thinking through any possible models that could reconcile the discrepancy they perceive. Of course, the letter is correct, but the aliens have never seen an organism be born and grow rapidly into an adult, and so they choose to rely on that which they have observed and that which they can understand.

That is what is happening now with the institution of science and the age of the earth. There are real scientists who believe in a young earth and feel that there is more investigating to be done with regard to the conclusions that have been drawn based on the dating methods and geological discoveries. They are not discounting the evidence. They are raising the question of whether we have *interpreted* the evidence correctly. Sadly, they are being shamed for raising their questions, and, as a result, fewer speak out about it than actually exist. There are therefore less energy and resources being spent in formulating potentially viable models representing other interpretations of the data at hand.

Why is there shame being dished out within the world of science for people who are raising questions? I think the common answer given would be that "science has proven something, and now there are religious fanatics trying to undermine the integrity of these conclusions simply because these conclusions do not align with their religious texts".

But that is a gross misrepresentation of the spirit of the matter. And if you take the time to look into it, I believe you can see it for yourself.

The reality is that there are two competing religions within the field of science, and it is their *values* that define them, not their academia or intelligence.

One of the particular problems engrained in this issue is the fact that intelligence is a key factor in good science. As a result, the majority of the population is willing to quickly acquiesce to whatever narrative is published by mainstream science to avoid looking stupid.

That's what I did. I didn't want to look stupid, so when I heard that science had determined that the earth was billions of years old, I acted like that guy looking at his car engine with his mechanic: "Oh, yeah, for sure, for sure. That's what I thought, as well."

The only reason I revisited the topic was because I was intrigued by Ansley's model and the thought that the seven-day creation story was prophetic of a seven-thousand-year total history of earth. Even then, it wasn't that intentional of a revisit. I thought about it in terms of what I still held to be true, and how it did seem like an arbitrary distinction to discredit the creation account while maintaining everything else in my faith. But I didn't really go looking for answers.

Then, one Sunday afternoon, Kendra was scrolling through YouTube and said, "I'm curious what this is about."

I walked over and saw a video called *Is Genesis History?* It was an hour and forty-four minutes, and we decided to sit down and watch it.

I highly recommend watching this for yourself. Del Tackett interviews creationist scientists who provide testimonies related to their respective fields.

I am not going to attempt to go into each area discussed, because I would inevitably do it a disservice. That is why I recommend watching it for yourself.

After watching this, I continued looking into the area of creationism within science, and I found that there are many more scientists who are creationists than the current narrative led me to believe.

Now here's the holdup. This debate within science has become as political as American politics, and we can no longer rely on simple statements from individuals telling us unadulterated truth.

For example, you may have seen *Bill Nye Debates Ken Ham* on YouTube. If you look up the reviews, here is the opening line from one of the top search results:

> Bill Nye and creationist Ken Ham have this debate about creationism, and, obviously, the facts were on Bill Nye's side, so Ken Ham, uh, just basically seemed like a crazy person, [laughter from colleague] in my eyes . . . for anyone who believes in logic and reasoning. He just, anything that he put out there, it was obviously part of his political agenda.

This statement is not an objective review. In fact, I would say this very review is part of a political agenda. Why else would this reporter say " . . . obviously, the facts were on Bill Nye's side," as opposed to " . . . the facts were on Bill Nye's side"?

This is what I mean when I say people don't want to appear stupid. The word "obviously" there is one tiny example of the simultaneous arrogance and insecurity at play within this debate. This arrogance presents itself as completely self-assured, and viewers eagerly acquiesce to these kinds of statements to avoid appearing stupid.

I watched the debate before I watched this review, and I didn't feel like Ken Ham seemed like a crazy person. I also didn't feel like Bill Nye was a crazy person. Furthermore, I place a lot of value on logic and reasoning. But this reporter told me that the facts were obviously on Bill Nye's side and Ken Ham seemed like a crazy person for anyone who believes in logic and reasoning.

This is an issue in our world today—we are surrounded by so many voices telling us what to think and what to believe, and it is so easy to just go with it. We prefer snappy one-liners to real critical thinking, and we prefer being on the team that appears to be winning as opposed to the underdog. Those preferences, however, have nothing to do with being on the side of truth, and we can see this throughout history.

Many people want to believe that things are different now than they were throughout history because of the scientific process and what we now know. We would never shame somebody today for claiming that the earth is not the center of the solar system. No, we've gotten things figured out.

That confidence is the arrogance with which past generations shamed individuals for claiming truths that were not aligned with the currently accepted belief systems.

I'm sure a lot of people would scoff at the alien analogy I presented. But notice how that scoffing puts one in the same boat with the aliens. Yes, the aliens observed correctly and employed sound logic. But they were still wrong.

And notice how I didn't even use a fantasy creature for them to be wrong about. He was a real human being, whose rate of growth and development changed throughout the course of his life. The aliens couldn't understand this because they were not able to observe *all* his growth, and they therefore had to rely on the rate of growth they had collected.

I realize there are major differences between that analogy and our reality, and I also freely admit that I am out of my league here in the way of science. But I am not going to be badgered or pressured into feeling stupid if I don't compromise my core beliefs about the Bible. I am out of my league here in the way of science, but I am fully capable of comprehending the larger, overarching concepts at play, and I will not feel like the stupid one if any other human being chooses to call me stupid.

People accuse creationism of deviating from science because creationists are imposing assumptions within the interpretation of observable data. But when we reach the point of drawing conclusions about ancient history, we have inevitably imposed numerous assumptions along the way. People then want to claim that science must employ reasonability when using assumptions to draw conclusions.

And here arises that issue of value system once again. Creationists believe that the Bible is enough of a reason to investigate things further. Those opposed believe otherwise. That's the bottom-line difference, and the debate has grown to be more political than academic.

It has become very easy to scoff at the notion that the Bible is enough of a reason to investigate a scientific matter further. I challenge you to refrain from scoffing and first consider the reasoning.

The Scriptures of the Bible have existed for thousands of years. The scientific method, as we know it today, has been around for a few hundred years.

I have no issue with the scientific method in itself. I think it is a very good thing, and I am grateful for the blessing of modern science. My issue is with a humanity that believes a set of Scriptures that has been accepted and believed upon for thousands of years as divinely inspired suddenly and "obviously" no longer has a legitimate role in helping us understand the world.

It is once again an issue with the spirit of the matter. It would be one thing if the world disagreed with creationism but allowed creationists to pursue creating a viable model without mocking them every step of the way. But that's not what's happening. As soon as someone presents a theory related to creationism, it is written off as "crazy". Perhaps that assessment would be merited if the scientists involved truly were incoherent. But that's the thing—when you look into this stuff, you find Ph.D. holders coherently offering their points of view. You may disagree with them, but don't call them crazy because you have a different opinion.

Many say that it is a danger for creationists to continue because they undermine progress. I propose that it is much more dangerous to have a spirit of arrogance and mockery within the realm of science. If you're on the side of the truth, then the truth will justify you, and you won't need to employ political tactics of shaming your opponent to prove yourself right.

I've also heard the argument that we can't throw away the efforts and progress of previous generations to cling to a religious text. This argument is hollow, though, in that the Bible has been guiding humanity much longer than the scientific process. In other words, discounting the Bible is a much more major way of throwing away the efforts and progress of previous generations than allowing it to continue having a role in our understanding of the world.

Again, I don't have a problem with the scientific process. I have a problem with the spirit that says, "Thanks, Bible, for your service to humanity these last couple millennia. We, humanity, have got it from here."

And before you go and try to point out all the instances in which the Bible has been used for evil purposes, consider the use of modern weaponry and chemical warfare, as well, results of scientific achievement. People throughout history have used both religion and science for evil purposes and good purposes.

I challenge you to look into these matters without an air of arrogance or mocking. If you feel like you're not going to look into these matters, either because you don't feel like you have the time or you don't care to, then I encourage you to defer to the Bible. If you defer to what people are telling you is true, you are more likely to defer to a political position than you are to defer to truth.

The scene is now steeped with so much pride, arrogance, and mocking that it is not a truly academic debate. We see this in politics, we see this in religion, and we see this in the scientific community.

Two assumptions that are central to the old-earth theory are 1) that the aging processes of earth's organic materials that we have been observing in the last hundred years have remained constant throughout the entirety of earth's history and 2) that these processes have been in effect for as long as they possibly could be. In contrast to this, scientists who believe in a young earth (about 6,000 years old) hold the assumption that the aging processes we have been observing may have looked different throughout history or that they have not been in effect for as long as they possibly could be. It is fundamentally a question of whether the rate of the earth's aging can definitely be determined to be a constant rate existing for as long as it possibly could have. And when we consider that, the assumptions of the young-earth theory are not such a wild idea in light of the fact that lifeforms around us exhibit such behavior. Human beings grow rapidly during the first twenty to thirty years of life, and then the rate and process of aging changes. The confidence of the old-earth view that the processes of the earth exist in a more linear and constant fashion is not a result of those processes actually being observed over time—such confidence is a result of assumption.

The old-earth argument to this would be that there is no evidence or reason for believing that the earth's aging processes would have changed throughout time. Once again, this is a difference in values. There are scientists who believe that the Bible is enough of a reason to at the very least look into the matter deeper and see if further evidence for that claim can be found. Why is it that Christians in general are not more eager to be supportive of these individuals who are trying to do right by God's Word? I have heard many Christians mock creationists in the same way the world does. Even if we disagree, why would we mock those who have a faith in the Bible that transcends an opposing narrative given to them by the world?

I believe there is heavy spiritual warfare at play in this. Otherwise, why would the sentiment on this issue not be, "We disagree, but they have a hypothesis based on what they believe to be legitimate cause for belief. Let's see what they can come up with."?

Instead, the sentiment is, "Creationism? That's crazy. They need to stop." It is no longer an objective quest for truth. It is a war of pride and arrogance.

I want to revisit 2 Peter 3. Please read this portion of Scripture closely, bearing in mind everything being discussed here. Second Peter 3:1–9 says:

> This is now, beloved ones, the second letter I write to you, in which I stir up your sincere mind, to remember the words previously spoken by the set-apart prophets, and of the command of the Master and Saviour, spoken by your emissaries, knowing this first: that mockers shall come in the last days with mocking, walking according to their own lusts, and saying, "Where is the promise of His coming? For since the fathers fell asleep, all continues as from the beginning of creation." For they choose to have this hidden from them: that the heavens were of old, and the earth standing out of water and in the water, by the Word of Elohim, through which the world at that time was destroyed, being flooded with water. And the present heavens and the earth are treasured up by the same Word, being kept for fire, to a day of judgment and destruction of wicked men. But, beloved ones, let not this one matter be hidden from you: that with יהוה one day is as a thousand years, and a thousand years as one day. יהוה

is not slow in regard to the promise, as some count slowness, but is patient toward us, not wishing that any should perish but that all should come to repentance.

In verse 1, Peter writes, "I stir up your sincere mind, to remember".

Let us put aside mockery and arrogance in order to have sincere minds.

In verse 2, he says, "the words previously spoken by the set-apart prophets . . . "

What are the words spoken of by the prophets? The Bible.

In verse 3, he says, "knowing this first: that mockers shall come in the last days with mocking . . . "

What are the last days? If we consider the seven-day/seven-millennia framework, then the last days would be Days 5, 6, and 7. If we are in Day 6, then we are right in the midst of the last days. Who are the mockers? Those who mock believers of the Bible.

In verse 4, he writes that the mockers are saying, "Where is the promise of His coming? For since the fathers fell asleep, all continues as from the beginning of creation."

The mockers believe that all things continue as they were from the beginning of creation. Creationists are saying that perhaps some things (e.g., the rate of decay within radioactive dating) have somehow changed throughout history. Mockers are mocking, calling that ridiculous, and asserting that "all continues as from the beginning".

In verse 5, he says, "For they choose to have this hidden from them: that the heavens were of old, and the earth standing out of water and in the water, by the Word of Elohim".

They *choose* to have this hidden from them, that the heavens and the earth were created by the word of God, as recorded in Genesis.

In verse 6, he says, "through which the world at that time was destroyed, being flooded with water."

They willfully forget about the global flood as recorded in Genesis, which would have tremendous implications on the physical earth.

In verse 7, he says, "And the present heavens and the earth are treasured up by the same Word, being kept for fire, to a day of judgment and destruction of wicked men."

Who are the "wicked men"? Those who do not have faith in God and, by extension, God's Word. Remember, we are given the gift of righteousness through *faith*.

In verse 8, he says, "But, beloved ones, let not this one matter be hidden from you: that with יהוה one day is as a thousand years, and a thousand years as one day."

Why would he pointedly say "let not this one matter be hidden from you" only to follow up with a figurative generality? As we've already covered earlier in this book, the rest of verse 8 seems to point towards a literal seven-day/prophetic seven-millennia framework of the Genesis creation account.

In verse 9, he says, "יהוה is not slow in regard to the promise, as some count slowness, but is patient toward us, not wishing that any should perish but that all should come to repentance."

God doesn't want any of us to perish. He wants us to repent of our unfaithfulness.

You may not believe that Genesis 1 is a literal creation account, but I strongly recommend you refrain from mocking those who do.

Voluntary Humiliation

I HAVE ALWAYS ENJOYED reading Christian apologetics. It used to be a dream of mine to be an apologist, defending faith through systematic argument and reasoning. Perhaps that desire still exists in me, but something changed along the way.

When I take time to reflect, I realize the thing that changed was my direction, specifically the direction I was facing. For the longest time, I was facing the world, trying to understand and appeal to it, and I had faith that God was behind me in this. Not knowing exactly when, I see now that something sparked in me, catching my attention, causing me to turn around. I had to reorient myself so that I was facing God instead, with the world behind me. I had to trust God to watch my back.

That's where I am now, and that's where I intend to remain. Facing God is like wrestling with Him. It's intense, difficult, and scary. Not just from the consideration that it's God, but from the consideration of the world watching.

Do you think I'm unaware that I look like an idiot in the eyes of many "esteemed" human beings? Do you think I'm oblivious to the tone of our culture? Do you not think I've had the thought, "Once I put this book out there, I'm a target of mocking for the world?"

The feeling within me makes me think of Isaiah. We read in Isaiah 20:2–4:

> at that same time יהוה spoke by means of Yeshayahu [Isaiah] son of Amots, saying, "Go, and remove the sackcloth from your body, and take your sandals off your feet." And he did so, walking naked and barefoot. And יהוה said, "As My servant Yeshayahu has walked naked and barefoot three years for a sign and a wonder against Mitsrayim and Kush, so does the sovereign of Ashshur lead away the captives of Mitsrayim and the exiles of

Kush, young and old, naked and barefoot, with their buttocks uncovered – the shame of Mitsrayim.

God instructed Isaiah to walk around naked for three years as a sign and wonder against Egypt and Ethiopia. I can't imagine how humiliating and ostracizing that must have been for Isaiah. I feel like, in writing these things about the creation account, I'm just barely scratching the surface of the vulnerability Isaiah felt in front of the world.

We may ask, "Why would a loving God tell people to do this sort of thing? It's degrading and humiliating."

Maybe a better question would be, "Why would anyone actually listen to and obey this sort of instruction?"

I'm coming to understand why for myself.

I've asked God, "Why would You want me to make a fool of myself in the eyes of the world by talking about creationism? It's just going to result in the world thinking I'm stupid."

I found that I could answer that question on my own: "I don't know what it's going to result in."

When I asked, "But why me?" I found that I could answer that one for myself, also: "Because I have faced God, and now I can endure whatever lies ahead."

It took me a long time to get to this point (my whole life), but I'm here now. I made the choice to face God, and so, in a way, I volunteered for this. Once again, it makes me think of Isaiah. We read in Isaiah 6:8:

> And I heard the voice of יהוה, saying, "Whom do I send, and who would go for Us?" And I said, "Here am I! Send me."

Isaiah voluntarily responded to God's call that ultimately told him to walk around naked as a sign to the world.

So again, why would a loving God tell people to do this sort of thing? It's because He's trying to get through to the world. Time and time again, God uses humility and lowliness to demonstrate His glory and greatness. This is spelled out explicitly with Gideon in Judges 7:4 when God says, "The people are still too many," regarding Gideon's men before Gideon goes into battle. He didn't want anyone to think their victory was a result of Gideon's impressive army. This idea is reiterated over and over again throughout the stories of the Bible.

God doesn't want the world to make the mistake of thinking there's a more "natural" or "reasonable" explanation accounting for His role in our universe. If we willingly humble and allow ourselves to be mocked by the world for the purpose of pointing to God, it inevitably draws out the question, "What could possibly cause a person to do this voluntarily?" There are only two legitimate answers—insanity, or something great and glorious enough to convince the individual that the humility and discomfort will be well worth it in the end.

Noah would have looked like a crazy person, building a huge boat, claiming a flood was on the way. But the flood came, and Noah and his family were saved. God proved Himself through Noah.

Imagine that account had gone differently: Noah worked out extensive calculations to prove the flood was on the way, a large majority of the population accepted his theory, and they all lived safely through the flood. Who is responsible for the salvation there? We could say God, for giving Noah the capacity to work it all out, but certainly much of the population would remain convinced that God had nothing to do with it. They would claim that it was Noah's genius that saved them. The account of Noah and the flood sounds like lunacy to so many people today because that's exactly how God intended it—it had to be an act of God or lunacy. It was lunacy in the eyes of the world from the first moment Noah set to work on the ark. In this way, there were never grounds for the claim that human achievement pulled it off.

How about the account of Joseph rising to power in Egypt and saving his family from the drought? The milestones in that story leading to the climax are so farfetched, once again, it must be the hand of God or fairy tale.

Moses and the ten plagues, the exodus from Egypt, the parting of the Red Sea? Absurd, if not for the role of God.

Then there's David and Goliath, a shepherd boy taking on a giant warrior with his slingshot. It's either a story for children or orchestrated by God.

Daniel in the lion's den? Shadrach, Meshach, and Abednego in the furnace? Jonah in the big fish? Tall tale or big God.

Don't even get me started on Yeshua—virgin conception, water to wine, walking on water, resurrecting from the dead? Seriously?!

The Bible is *ridiculous*... unless it's the truth. There's no room for humanity's achievement accounting for the events written in the Bible, and that's exactly how God intended it. The call to faith necessarily involves looking foolish in the eyes of the world, because the world is fallen to sin. Sin causes us to think we can be like God. God gave us His Word to remind us that we can't be like Him because we aren't like Him, not in this way—we are the creation, and He is the creator.

Faith is the decision to use His Word as context for developing our understanding. When we begin categorizing the accounts of the Bible as either literal or figurative, we're just fooling ourselves. All of it is absurd if you're being honest with yourself. The only real difference between the absurdity we're willing to embrace and the absurdity we can't accept is where the world puts pressure. If we lived in a culture that holistically put the same amount of condescension and shaming on Yeshua's resurrection as it currently puts on the creation account in Genesis, I wonder what the current state of Christianity in our culture would look like.

The Realized but Unknown Creator

LIKE I SAID, I have always enjoyed Christian apologetics. I also used to enjoy books by scientists using their expertise to argue a reconciliation between old-earth views and faith in God. Eventually, though, I realized a very important distinction that I had been overlooking.

Here's the distinction: there is a difference between using science in the context of faith and using science to create faith.

I realized that many of the books I had read were written by brilliant individuals who started out as atheists but came to have faith in God through their scientific and philosophical pursuits. Now I don't think there's a problem with that in itself, but I've come to understand there is a problem if that is where the story ends. Why? Because that's not the kind of faith we are ultimately being called to.

Consider James 2:19:

> You believe that Elohim is one. You do well. The demons also believe – and shudder!

If scientific or philosophical undertakings lead an individual to believing that there is a creator of the universe, that's great. But that is not the extent to which we are called to go with our faith. I think the story of Abraham and Isaac demonstrates this. God told Abraham that he would have offspring through Sarah. Abraham believed God, which was all well and good, but if we're being honest, there wasn't a whole lot of risk involved in believing God in this situation, other than maybe looking and feeling a bit foolish. But once Sarah had Isaac and God asked Abraham to give him up, suddenly there was something real and tangible on the line. It wasn't enough that Abraham had theoretical belief. God wanted to demonstrate Abraham's belief to the world by showing that Abraham had true faith in God, even when it cost him his own flesh and blood. This is the kind of faith God is asking of us.

A faith that is born from logic, reasoning, evidence, proof, and human understanding is not the kind of faith God is asking of us. If you have that kind of faith, that's great, but that's not the faith God is calling us to.

Think of it in terms of a marriage. A husband and wife can have faith that their marriage exists, that it is legally binding, and that they are living together. That's not the kind of faith we mean, though, when we say we want a "faithful" spouse. We want a faithful spouse in the way of love, commitment, trust, and respect.

If we are waiting for our scientific studies and philosophical reasonings to convince us of God's existence, even when we get to that point, we still have not demonstrated the kind of faith He's looking for in us.

When I read books by brilliant minds who came to believe in God due to science, mathematics, philosophy, or any other mode of human reasoning, I am struck by the contrast between the complexity of their thinking around their academic area of expertise and the simplicity of their reasoning for connecting their expertise to the conclusion that God exists. They might go on for pages gushing over the complexity of DNA, the foundational order revealed through numbers, or the universality of the moral law. But ultimately, in order to get to their conclusion of belief in God, they always resort to some conjunction that is neither terribly complicated nor explicitly within the realm of their expertise. It is always some form of reaction to their expertise and not the expertise itself that leads them to their belief.

For example, one might nerd out extensively over DNA acting like a software program in the development of its organism, but their resulting conclusion that there is a God doesn't come from some tiny script written on the double helix that says, "There is a God." Their conclusion comes from the reaction, "Wow, this is incredible. Surely there is a mind behind this."

They may be a genius in their respective field, but the thought that gets them from their expertise to believing in God is necessarily a departure from their field and an embracing of their spirit. They cannot connect their data to their conclusion without a degree of faith or belief.

The same idea applies as it relates to history for which we weren't alive. This is why I take issue with the modern narrative regarding the history of the universe. There is no longer an honest admission of the role of belief within the conclusions being drawn. Even if we agree that no human walking this earth today was alive billions of years ago as a witness, certain experts still claim to "know" what happened billions of years ago. We "know" that the Big Bang took place 13.8 billion years ago, we "know" that the earth formed about 4.5 billion years ago, and we "know" that our first human ancestors evolved sometime around 6 million years ago. We don't *believe* these things based on the data we've observed and the principles upon which we've extrapolated. We *know* them.

I'm astounded that I'm culturally perceived to be the crazy party in this matter. Is it really foolish for me to request the admission of belief in this discussion? How did scientific thinking evolve from open-minded consideration to judgmental condescension? This is yet another "spirit of the matter" issue.

The real issue I have here is not with atheists, agnostics, or even those who believe in God while rejecting the Bible. I expect them to think I'm crazy because I believe in the Bible as God's Word. The real issue I have is with those who simultaneously call the Bible "the Word of God" while taking on a condescending perspective towards those who believe in the creation narrative of Genesis 1. If you choose to believe in an earth that is billions of years old while maintaining the Bible is the Word of God, so be it, but do not look down on or scoff at those who choose a belief that is more aligned and consistent with what the Bible actually says.

The Bible, by worldly standards, is a foolish book. God is seeking people who are willing to be foolish in the eyes of the world for the sake of being faithful to Him. Those who say they believe in the Bible but write off certain pieces as figurative seem to be reaching for the blessings while trying to avoid the foolish image. For me, this conjures up the image of a girl dating a guy because he buys her stuff, but as soon as she sees her friends coming their way, she pushes him into the bushes because she's embarrassed to be seen with him. That is the game this particular perspective is playing with God.

Many Christians nowadays would be quick to argue against that by saying we don't have to believe in the Bible's creation account as literal to be faithful to God.

Acts 17:22–24 says:

> And having stood in the midst of the Areopagus Sha'ul said, "Men of Athens, I see that you are very religious in every matter. For passing through and observing the objects of your worship, I even found a slaughter-place with this inscription: TO THE

UNKNOWN MIGHTY ONE. Not knowing then whom you worship, I make Him known to you: יהוה, who made the world and all that is in it, this One being Master of heaven and earth, does not dwell in dwellings made with hands."

Paul explains who God is to the Athenians by starting with God's role as our creator. Abandoning the creation account in Genesis inevitably brings us closer to the position of the Athenians, worshipping a God whom we don't really know.

That's what I often see now when I read books on apologetics and attempts to reconcile science and faith—intelligent, well-meaning people who don't know the God they're worshipping because they are unwilling to seek truth in the context of His Word. They choose to hold their own reasoning in higher regard than grace and faith, insisting upon being fully convinced through their own reasoning before accepting anything. In operating this way, they get glimpses of this alleged creator and cry out, "He's real! He's real!" They believe He exists, but they don't really know who He is because they reject what He has said about Himself, which is the full, imperceivable truth of who He is. They know they have a Father, but they don't have a relationship with Him. They have a relationship with an idea about Him. They don't know Him because they don't want to listen to Him. They only want to listen to the facts perceivable by their own reasoning.

The Final Chapter

IF YOU'RE READING this book, it seems obvious that this is not the final chapter. However, as the writer of this book, I can assure you that it is. As I am writing this chapter, I attest to the reality that I have already written every other chapter in this book. I am simply returning to this section now, after having written all the rest of the book, to finish.

The point to be made is this: as the author, I can easily have a different perspective on the final chapter from that of the reader.

Allow that thought to settle for a moment before I present this next thought.

If you're a participator in this life, it seems obvious that Genesis 1 is not the beginning. However, if you're the *author* of life, it really doesn't matter what any life form thinks, believes, or figures out. The beginning is whatever you say it is.

I believe that the Bible is God's Word. Many Christians will say the same thing, but we are not on the same page in what we mean by that. When I say I believe in the Bible as God's Word, I don't mean that I think it's a book filled with wise teachings, warm fuzzies, and good suggestions. I believe it is a script to our very existence. It begins at the beginning of our existence, when God created it all, and it ends at the end of this existence, when Yeshua turns everything back over to the Father at the end of the millennial reign, ushering in a new heaven and a new earth. The Bible records this existence from the beginning to the end, and it includes the parts in the middle that God chooses to include for the purpose of seeing this plot of existence come to fruition.

We make a categorical mistake in thinking this is a purely scientific discussion, as if science is the ultimate trump card, and there remains no other hierarch that can either rise above or undermine the conclusions drawn by scientific discoveries. We accuse certain faithful views of being arrogant for believing there's something "special" about humanity in the midst of this cold, dark universe. Yet we remain arrogant enough to believe—nay, *know* that we, part of a humanity that is supposedly millions of years old, in a universe that is billions of years old, are the generation that figured everything out. We've witnessed the twists and turns and complete one-eighties within scientific thinking throughout history, but now we've got the right science, that good science, and there's zero percent chance we're mistaken about things this time.

Perhaps I need to make my view a bit clearer and more straightforward. You may not fully appreciate the extent to how insane my view actually sounds to the ears of this world, so I'd like to make it plain.

Again, we make a categorical mistake in thinking this is a purely scientific discussion. It's like we're trying to purchase truth from the universe, and everyone has been convinced that science is the only currency that the universe will accept in exchange for its truth.

If you're an atheist, that makes sense. The universe is the highest power. It therefore is the most well-established truth vendor to go to. It operates according to physical principles, and science reliably informs us about these principles. Therefore, science is the currency we need in order to purchase truth from the universe.

As soon as you embrace a belief in a creator God, however, you compromise the integrity of that rationale. There are certain truths that remain the same, yes, but the physical universe is no longer the highest power. The one who created the universe is higher than the universe itself. In transcending the very universe, the creator by nature points to a truth that transcends what is embedded in the context of our universe.

We don't give due diligence to the vast and major implications that come from the seemingly simple belief that our universe has a creator. If our universe has a creator, then all our intelligence, discoveries, innovations, and accomplishments are categorically secondary to and trumped by the primary truth concerning our creator. We are created within the creation that is our universe, inevitably confined to its laws and parameters, whereas our creator necessarily transcends those same laws and parameters.

If God is the author of life, then we must think of existence in terms of an author and the book that author is writing.

If Sir Arthur Conan Doyle wrote a book and started it with Holmes and Watson walking the streets of London, we wouldn't say, "No, no, no, that's not right. That's obviously not where the story started. Holmes and

Watson must have woken up that morning, so we know it had to start before they were on the streets. Also, they must have been children at one time, with parents who raised them. No this story clearly doesn't start with Holmes and Watson walking the streets of London."

We wouldn't say that because we're thinking in categorically correct terms—not in terms of human biology, but in terms of author and book. The story *does* start with Holmes and Watson walking the streets of London because Doyle made the decision to start it there. We can imagine Holmes and Watson having childhoods as a natural extension of the plot, but the reality holds that their childhoods are not included in the book.

Why would Doyle start a book with Holmes and Watson walking the streets of London, even though the laws of reasoning within his very story would inevitably demand that they were once children? Why wouldn't he have started the story when they were children? Answer: because that's not the story he wanted to tell.

Furthermore, because Doyle is the author, he has the power, authority, right, and privilege to start his story right there on the streets of London with fully grown versions of Holmes and Watson.

If we can accept this logic from a literary perspective, then why would we do anything else with our God who authored the Bible?

For example, why would God start the story of existence at the seven-day creation account, only to embed in that very existence the deeply disturbing indication of a much more extensive history? This sounds like conspiracy theory until you correct the categorical thinking.

I've heard Christians admit that they believe God *could* create everything in a state of already appearing aged, but they just don't see why He would do that. I see a false sense of reasonability in this claim. Let me break down this assertion to show you what I mean.

If you're a Christian, then I assume you believe that humans are created in God's image. I also assume that you believe Yeshua/Jesus is the only begotten son of God. Now the real question is, do you believe Colossians 1:16:

> Because in Him were created all that are in the heavens and that are on earth, visible and invisible, whether thrones or rulerships or principalities or authorities – all have been created through Him and for Him.

Now, if you do believe that everything in the heavens and on the earth are created for Yeshua, then the answer for why God would create everything as stated in Genesis 1 is abundantly clear, if we're maintaining categorically correct thinking (i.e., not in terms of science, but in terms of an author and the book that author is writing). God created everything according to the Genesis account because this is the story He is interested in telling.

The story's about Yeshua and how he rescued the one creation that is made in God's image (humanity) from sin. So why would God create and entertain billions of years of lifelessness and emptiness if He could just as easily start at the exact place where the story (in His view) gets interesting?

If Doyle wants to write about a specific case that Sherlock Holmes solved, and the whole ordeal started that day when Holmes and Watson were walking through the streets of London, why would he bother writing volumes upon volumes of back story that are technically connected but not exactly relevant to the case, which is the very story he wants to tell? You see, it's not that Holmes's and Watson's childhoods aren't reasonable extensions of the laws and principles embedded in the story's plot, it's just that their childhoods are literally not included in the book. Perhaps they investigate a flat with a broken window. Doyle doesn't have to write out the account of the window being broken for the resulting broken window to appear in the story.

This is where people get up in arms about how preposterous this view is. They demand to know why God would create something that *appears* to have a history without *actually* having a history. It seems cruel and deceptive. That sentiment, however, is not a response to this belief about our universe. It is a response to the belief about a creator.

Think of it this way: try and write a story that starts at the very beginning of *everything*. Nothing in your story is allowed to indicate any sort of history prior to what you explain and show. How do you start from the *very* beginning?

That sort of reasoning simply doesn't work in our universe. We've established a number line that continues with negative integers after we reach zero. In other words, there's always cause for asking, "And what happened before that?"

It reminds me of that annoying child asking, "Why?" to every response given to them by the parent.

"We're going to the store."

"Why?"

"To pick up groceries."

"Why?"
"So we can eat."
"Why?"
"So we don't starve."
"Why?"
"Because starving is bad."
"Why?"
"Because it hurts."
"Why?"
"Because we have brains."
"Why?"
"Shut up."

The problem people have really isn't with the creation account in Genesis. The problem really lies with the creator. If the Bible started with, "In the beginning was the Big Bang," and it proceeded to account for billions of years of history, all initiated by a creator, that still wouldn't satisfy this humanity. We would still arrive at the conclusion that there *must* have been something prior to the Big Bang, and that the Bible is just ancient superstition.

This is why the Bible calls us to faith, not human reason. God knew this would happen from the very beginning: He would create, the creation would grow and learn, He would provide His creation with truth, but the creation would still become arrogant and reject His words. Therefore, His appeal is what it is: have faith. Believe. Abraham was considered righteous because he believed. And that's why God used Abraham's lineage to be a light and an appeal to the rest of the world. Believe. You're not able to fully understand using the faculties available to you. Therefore, for now, just believe in God's Word and develop your understanding in the context of His Word, not your own.

We must stay focused on the right category if we're going to realize the truth. This existence is no more about science than a child's soccer game is about physics. Science has a role in this existence, and physics has a role in the child's soccer game. But the dad doesn't show up to the soccer game because he's fascinated by the physics involved, and the Father doesn't marvel at billions of years' worth of evolutionary science that has nothing to do with His son.

Similarly, the dad doesn't show up to the soccer field months before his child's game to make sure everything's ready for the game ahead of time. He has no interest in the field itself, and its existence prior to his child's game is of no value to him. All that matters is that the field is present for his child's game, because that's what he really cares about watching.

If you believe Colossians 1:16, it shouldn't strike you as farfetched to hear that this whole universe is nothing more than a soccer field to showcase the Father's son. His son is awesome at the game. We all suck compared to him, but the Father invites *all* his son's friends out to pizza afterwards. I know this analogy is silly, but I believe it to be representative. You can get caught up on the nature of the field, the order and the precision governing its setup. But all that pales in comparison to the grandeur of the Father and the son, through whom and for whom the field was created in the first place.

So many people are quick to suggest that God is cruel if the Genesis 1 creation account is literal. We wonder why the history of His creation would be contrary to what it appears to be according to scientific evaluation. Scientific evaluation leads us to the conclusion that the dad is present because he's fascinated with the physics of the game. But if we just listen to the dad for a moment, his explanation isn't complicated: "Nah, I'm just here to watch my kid's soccer game. That's why I made this field in the first place."

You see, if the earth suggests a history that isn't real, it's only cruel if God withholds that information from us. As it is, we have a significant portion of the population calling a specific book "the Word of God". In that book, the very first verse of the very first chapter tells us, "In the beginning Elohim created the heavens and the earth." It then goes on to say that He created everything in seven days. If we keep on reading, we read that God tells us to have faith.

Can we agree that, so far, these ideas aren't too complicated? If so, then it's not really God who is being cruel. It's as if He has given His testimony, saying, "Here it is if you want it." He's not going to get down on His knees and beg you to believe Him on these matters, no more than the dad is going to get down on his knees and plead, "Please, believe me! I'm not here because I'm fascinated with physics. I'm here to watch my kid's soccer game!"

God loves us. We're the ones being cruel, not Him. He gives us life/existence and free will, even when we give Him nothing. If we decide to object to the narrative contained in the book that is more often referred to as God's Word than any other, that's on us, not on Him.

Do you really believe in a creator who could create everything in a state of already appearing aged? Do you really believe Yeshua is His son? If so, do you believe Colossians 1:16, that everything is created for him?

If so, then what's the holdup? When you listen to any dad proudly telling a story about their child, do you expect 99.99% of the story to be background setting the scene for whatever it is the child did? Do you interrupt him at the start of the story to say, "Surely this isn't the beginning of the story? There must have been events prior to this point."?

I think about my brother and my niece. My brother is a strait-laced, corporate kind of guy. Even so, he loves his daughter, and he shows up to programs, events, and recitals simply because she has a role in them. He doesn't care about the programs, events, or recitals. I've been to a few of them, and I can attest to the fact that it's not like showing up to a Broadway performance or Carnegie Hall.

That said, his child has a role in these programs, and they are therefore worth showing up for, because my brother loves his daughter.

Now, if that sort of sentiment exists between my brother and his daughter, how much more so does it apply between the creator of the universe and the one for whom He created the universe? It doesn't seem strange to me that God would start existence right before the creation of humanity because I've seen how any dad (including my brother) will show up to an elementary school auditorium right before his child's program starts. If he's truly able to show up exactly when he wants to (just before the show gets started), then it's nonsense to think he'd show up days, months, or years early. The elementary school auditorium may be larger, older, and more impressive than the child in the eyes of others. But when it comes to the dad, he's there for the kid.

I've come to understand that the Bible makes sense as a narrative, and, for that reason, I don't have an issue with the creation account. If we choose to accept that the Bible doesn't mean what it says, then, yes, suddenly we're forced to admit that the creation account doesn't make much sense in light of our scientific discoveries. But if we are living in an existence written by an author transcending our physical laws, our physical laws are not the most reliable source of truth. The words of our author transcend the laws of our story.

That's the real difference. I think science is a great thing. My perspective isn't a result of *misunderstanding* science. It's a result of *not prioritizing* science as an explanation for our existence. For those who don't have faith in a creator who can create such a world for the purpose of telling the story He wants to tell, I understand how this all seems like lunacy. But for those who claim to believe in such a creator, this shouldn't sound ridiculous. If you believe in the Bible, then it clearly says that everything in our existence was created through and for Yeshua. The Bible establishes a seven-day/seven-millennia timeframe, and Yeshua explicitly shows up in the flesh on the fourth day (the exact middle of the story), as well as the end of the sixth day and the entirety of the seventh day.

That's the story the Father wants to tell. It's the story of His son scoring the winning goal and their team coming out on top, despite all the odds.

If this notion sounds too absurd for you to digest, it's not because you're too smart. It's because you're too faithless. I don't mean that as an insult. It's just the literal truth. You don't have the faith required to believe that this universe was written into existence by an author who transcends the very laws He established within our creation. That's what it means to have faith in a creator—believing in a being who can do whatever He wants with our existence, including starting it all at whatever point He chooses.

If you want to disagree, fine. But don't try and make this an issue of intelligence versus stupidity. That's just a symptom of arrogance.

Some hear this view and say, "Well you just can't rationally argue with a mind like that." I sometimes feel similarly in the other direction. It's like I'm having a conversation with someone who is insisting *The Great Gatsby* starts with the Age of Exploration. I keep saying that it's a book that takes place in the 1920s, but the person I'm arguing with keeps saying it takes place in America, therefore it must start with the Age of Exploration. I hand them the book and say, "Start reading the book, and you tell me where it starts."

The person I'm arguing with then tosses the book over their shoulder and says, "Give me a break. We're talking logic here, not literature."

To which I say, "No, we are talking literature. I don't disagree with your logic, but if we're talking about *The Great Gatsby*, then the literature takes precedence over your logic on this point. The book doesn't start with the Age of Exploration. It starts with Nick Carraway in the 1920s telling us about how nonjudgmental he is."

The debate is not entirely and linearly scientific. It is categorical, making it a matter of faith and choice, not intelligence. Disagree with others, fine, but don't demean them. Perhaps they haven't had the same advantages you've had (such as a commitment to scientific study). Or perhaps you haven't had the same advantages they've had (such as a love that has led to faith). Whatever it is, don't be arrogant.

Trust the Lighthouse

A LOT OF CHRISTIANS today are saying that they don't see what the big deal is when it comes to this particular discussion. What's the big deal if Genesis 1 is literal or figurative? What's the big deal if some people take it to mean one thing and others take it to mean something else? What's the big deal since it's not an issue at the core of the faith?

That's the big deal, right there. The assumption that it's not an issue at the core of the faith.

The Bible is either God's Word, or it isn't. The most foolish perspective here is the one that says, "Well, kind of. Somewhere in between 'Yes' and 'No.'" If the Bible is *kind of* God's Word, then it's not.

This is an issue at the core of our faith, because the Word contains the beginning, and the beginning contains the Word.

John 1:1–5 says:

> In the beginning was the Word, and the Word was with Elohim, and the Word was Elohim. He was in the beginning with Elohim. All came to be through Him, and without Him not even one came to be that came to be. In Him was life, and the life was the light of men. And the light shines in the darkness, and the darkness has not overcome it.

The Word, the beginning, and Yeshua are all intimately connected. Yeshua is the Word, and he is the beginning. That's why this is an issue at the core of the faith. When we take what the Word of God says about the beginning and change its meaning, we are changing the identity of Yeshua. He is the beginning. When we accept that, we cannot say, "Well I'm going to interpret the beginning to mean XYZ, and it's really not a big deal because it has nothing to do with Yeshua." It has everything to do with Yeshua. It is Yeshua.

Revelation 22:13 says:

> "I am the 'Aleph' and the 'Taw', the Beginning and the End, the First and the Last."

Not only is Yeshua the beginning, but he is also the end. And now we see further what the big deal about this really is. The beginning points to the end, and the end points to the beginning. Yeshua is the beginning, and he was in the beginning. Yeshua is the end, and he will be in the end.

We have to understand that this life that we're living right now is not The People Show. It is The Yeshua Show. It is all about him, not us. The spiritual forces that are opposed to God are doing everything in their power to convince humanity otherwise because they hate God, and they hate us.

God gave humanity His Word as a lighthouse to guide us through this spiritual darkness. A lighthouse helps ships avoid crashing into land at night. A lighthouse needs to be bright, elevated, and clear. If sailors see a lighthouse and begin to think, "Well maybe this lighthouse isn't actually on land," they are reinterpreting the lighthouse for themselves. At that point, it no longer provides those sailors with its intended purpose.

The thought that a lighthouse isn't actually on land is not a big deal in itself. So what, that person doesn't believe that lighthouse is on land, big whoop. The implications that unfold because of that thought, however, lead to staggering consequences. It's the same thing with the creation account in Genesis. I agree that it doesn't *seem* like that big of a deal in itself if a person chooses to interpret the creation account in Genesis to fit some other narrative rather than take it at face value. But really think about the implications that unfold when we do that. We prioritize human understanding, human advising, and human science over trusting in God's Word. The bottom line is, we end up trusting people more than God.

Why would someone not think a lighthouse is on land? Maybe because they can't see the land. If all they can see is the light coming from the lighthouse, that means they can't see the land. And that's the whole point of the lighthouse. There will be times of darkness, and in those times, sailors will be able to see the light from the lighthouse and know the truth. By its light, they will be able to know more about the world around them than what the darkness is allowing them to see.

Why would God give humanity the Bible at all if we could just reason our way through every part of life? The Bible serves as a beacon of truth, giving us light in times of darkness. We should be all the more eager to run to the Bible's words when the world's narrative tells us something different. It means that we're in a patch of fog or darkness, and now more than ever we need to look out for the lighthouse to avoid crashing into rocks.

Reread what Revelation 22:13 says. The beginning is inextricably tied to the end. To put it more clearly, the creation narrative of the earth not only provides information on how the earth was formed, but also provides information on how the earth will end. It is serving as a lighthouse, indicating that we are coming up on something significant, potentially devastating. If we are coming up on something that has the potential to be devastating, we should be looking for direction from the lighthouse, not from the darkness.

I do not believe it is a coincidence that humanity in the last hundred years has discarded the creation account in Genesis like a used tissue. To be clear, the *timing* for this is no coincidence. It is significant, and we need to be looking to the Bible to guide us. Unfortunately, however, now more than ever, humanity has lost its faith in the Bible.

That faith is not going to be restored until it is restored from the very beginning. Either the Bible is God's Word, or it isn't. People aren't stupid. They know when they're hearing a load of garbage. It doesn't work to say that the Bible is the Word of God, but it doesn't really mean what it says. What kind of God is that? If someone's words don't mean what they say, then I don't want to hear them. They do me no good. Talk to me when you have something to say that you actually mean.

I believe God's Word means what it says, so I don't have an issue with trusting it. When we tell people the Bible doesn't mean what it says, we are creating trust issues between people and God. We can understand this easily with any human relationship. If I have a friend who sometimes means what he says and sometimes doesn't, I end up not trusting *all* the things he tells me. It is no different with God and His Word.

The Bible reveals to us that this life is a test of faith. Will we have faith in what God tells us, or will we not? When we believe someone *because* their words line up with what we already believe, that's not having faith in them. That's having faith in ourselves. When we believe someone *when* their words *don't* line up with what we already believe, that's having faith. That is the concept of the lighthouse—trust the lighthouse, *especially when* you can't see the land.

This is an issue at the core of our faith, because it reveals whether we really have faith or not. If we're only putting our faith in God when His Words already line up neatly with what we've already accepted and what makes sense to us, then we're not putting our faith in Him at all.

We are in an age of spiritual darkness. Truth is blurred, corruption is rampant, and science has displaced God in the hearts of man. This darkness will not last. The dawn of morning is on the way, but before it arrives, we will have to navigate through some dangerous waters. God's given a lighthouse to help us. We either trust in the light that we see in the distance, or we trust in the darkness that is all around us. There are severe implications for each choice.

Part 7

Set-apart Regathering

Before You Feast on This Part

MUCH OF WHAT I have written in the following part concerning mankind and the beast have been revelations of my own. I have tried to call out the pieces that have come from other teachers. I hope you'll read what I have to say but apply your own thinking and study to test my words for yourself. Don't accept the things I say here simply because they sound good (if they end up sounding good to you). Take these thoughts to Scripture and test them. Pray for the Spirit to guide you and reveal truth. Go on the adventure for yourself. I'm not trying to entice you with ideas so that you'll agree with me. I'm trying to nudge you into your own journey. I pray this is a blessing for you.

God's Pleasure Versus Man's Pleasure

IN THE LAST PART, I talked briefly about the prioritizations of life and pleasure. When there's nothing more to look forward to after this life, it makes sense to prioritize pleasure. When there is more life to come, however, we have reason to prioritize life itself.

I believe there is much more pleasure to be had in this life and in the life to come when we value life over pleasure rather than the other way around. God wants to give us pleasure, but it is pleasure that *He* calls good. As people who are infected with sin, we find certain pleasures to be appealing that are not good according to God. We can know what pleasures are good according to God by looking to Scripture.

Isaiah 58:13–14 says:

> "If you do turn back your foot from the Sabbath, from doing your pleasure on My set-apart day, and shall call the Sabbath 'a delight,' the set-apart day of יהוה 'esteemed,' and shall esteem it, not doing your own ways, nor finding your own pleasure, nor speaking your own words, then you shall delight yourself in יהוה. And I shall cause you to ride on the heights of the earth, and feed you with the inheritance of Ya'aqob your father. For the mouth of יהוה has spoken!"

God is telling the people through Isaiah that He wants to pour out pleasure upon them, but in order for Him to do that, they have to stop seeking their own pleasure apart from Him. They have to turn around from what they've been doing—they have to repent.

But God's not speaking about their lawlessness in general here. He's explicitly referring to the Sabbath. He tells them to turn back from doing their own pleasure on *His* set-apart day. It's not sufficient for us to say that the Sabbath was just a Jewish thing or an Israelite thing. Between this section and 2 Chronicles 36, in which we saw that the land would keep her Sabbaths even without the people living there, we can see how the Sabbath is larger than just the people. This is *God's* set-apart day, and God Himself says that this day serves as a sign between Him and His people.

Now we need to clarify here. This does not mean that observing the Sabbath justifies us or makes us righteous. Again, that is all Yeshua and nothing else. This is a *sign* of that justification. It is us proclaiming that we belong to God. I think of those stickers they hand out after you vote—"I VOTED." Wearing the sticker has no effect over who wins the election, but it represents a vote that gets counted. The sticker is just a sign that you went through the voting process.

I find it curious how difficult the Sabbath concept seems to be for humanity. Between reading the Bible and observing the past couple millennia, there doesn't seem to be a solid period of time in which people got it right. In Numbers 15:32–36, we read of a man breaking the Sabbath not long after the Israelites were led out of slavery. We read that the people of Jerusalem were exiled so that the land could keep her Sabbaths. We read that the Pharisees made the Sabbath a burdensome chore. And then we see Christianity abandoning or changing the Sabbath to fit what seems good to man.

Again, God tells the people through Isaiah to turn back from doing their own pleasure on His set-apart day. The one consistency I see throughout humanity's history of breaking the Sabbath is man doing man's own pleasure on God's set-apart day. Generation after generation has shown man choosing his own pleasure rather than faith in God's blessing.

We might claim to have faith in God's promised blessings. But if God is telling us through His Word that the seventh day is His set-apart day and that it is a sign between Him and His people, and if, after hearing that, we still arrive at a different conclusion based on the elaborate justifications of man and religion, we're still choosing our own pleasure over faith in God's blessing.

Instead of the voting sticker, think of team jerseys. If you're on a team that wears green jerseys, you're expected to wear a green jersey to the game. It's a sign that you're on the team. You're not on the team because you wear a green jersey. You're on the team because you tried out and got picked, and then you attended all of the practices. But then, when gametime rolled around, you showed up wearing the other team's color.

Maybe it was unintentional. Maybe someone gave you wrong information. The moment of truth comes when you get the correct info. Do you change jerseys, or do you refuse?

Perhaps you refuse because you don't like the color green and would rather wear the other team's color. You choose *your pleasure* over what has been established for the team. You don't get kicked off the team then and there, but you certainly don't play in the game. You're benched.

The next game rolls around, and the same thing happens. You show up wearing the other team's jersey and refuse to change. Again, you don't play.

There comes a point when the coach pulls you into his office. "You're a great player, but you've made it clear you don't want to be a part of this team. I've gotta let you go."

Earlier I talked about the millennial reign, how there will be a time when Yeshua literally returns and rules over the earth. That time is coming upon us quickly. When it comes, there will still be work to be done. There will be great need for teaching, rebuilding, governing, healing, and all sorts of things. Those who make it to the millennial reign will have jobs to do, but Yeshua will be reigning as king. As king, he will be ruling with perfect law and order. Now, when that time comes, which people will he probably delegate more authority to: those who took it upon themselves to interpret the commands of God as they saw fit, or those who proved themselves trustworthy in obeying and guarding the commands of God as they were spoken by God?

Those who take it upon themselves to interpret the Bible in their own ways will need to be taught the basics at that time to get up to speed. Lesson one: Elohim's Word is final, do not reinterpret. Lesson two: In the beginning, Elohim created the heavens and the earth. And so forth.

If we're eagerly awaiting the return of Yeshua but neglecting the Word of God, what, exactly, are we eagerly awaiting? Yeshua is the Word of God in the flesh.

If the idea of learning and obeying God's law feels overwhelming to you, anchor yourself to the two greatest commands—love God and love people. Everything else hangs upon those two. After you have internalized those two, go to the Ten Commandments. Go to Exodus 20, and read through them slowly, asking yourself if you are trying to be obedient to each one. (It's helpful to refer to Matthew 5–7 as you're doing this—Yeshua clarifies a lot of questions in these chapters.)

Then, when you start seeking to obey the Ten Commandments more seriously, you find that you have an entire day every week to meditate on and learn God's law—the Sabbath. How perfect of a setup is that? We get overwhelmed at the prospect of learning something because we feel we don't have the time. God structured His law to help us with this.

Love God and love people. That's the foundation for all of it. From there, go to the Ten Commandments. Pretty simple so far, right? Then it's just a question of whether or not you will actually obey. Will you honor the Sabbath each week, refraining from work and meditating on God and His law? If so, you will quickly grow in your knowledge and love of God's law. If not, then the coach might have to call you into his office. You're just making it clear you don't really want to be on the team. Maybe he doesn't kick you off the team, but he tells you you've got to go back and relearn the fundamentals of the game. Either way, you're not going to be a starting player.

You're not on the team because you wear the jersey. You wear the jersey because you're on the team. The Sabbath is like a jersey. It's a sign that we're on God's team. If we are prioritizing life in God, why are we fighting against this commandment which He laid out for us so clearly? If we are resisting honoring God's set-apart day, then perhaps we are prioritizing our own pleasure.

Beastly Pleasure Versus Godly Law

THIS "LIFE VERSUS PLEASURE" divide spans the entire Bible. We see it starting in Genesis, and we see it in Revelation.

Genesis 1:24–28 says:

> And Elohim said, "Let the earth bring forth the living being according to its kind: livestock and creeping creatures and beasts of the earth, according to its kind." And it came to be so. And Elohim made the beast of the earth according to its kind, livestock according to its kind, and all that creep on the earth according to its kind. And Elohim saw that it was good. And Elohim said, "Let Us make man in Our image, according to Our likeness, and let them rule over the fish of the sea, and over the birds of the heavens, and over the livestock, and over all the earth and over all the creeping creatures that creep on the ground." And Elohim created the man in His image, in the image of Elohim He created him – male and female He created them. And Elohim blessed them, and Elohim said to them, "Be fruitful and increase, and fill the earth and subdue it, and rule over the fish of the sea, and over the birds of the heavens, and over all creeping creatures on the earth."

We read that God created the beast of the earth, and then He created man in His image. God blessed man and gave him instructions, including having dominion over the earth and every living creature.

So what is it that distinguishes man from beast? This can be a broad philosophical conversation, but I just want to look at it through a biblical lens.

Man is distinct from beast because of law. It is true that man is distinct from beast because he is made in God's image, but in order to help us understand that more practically, I want to consider the subject of law.

Law implies a set of rules given by an authority to be followed. In this way, God gave man law from the very beginning. God gave man instructions, or rules ("Be fruitful and increase, and fill the earth and subdue it"), and he charged man with ruling over the rest of the world. In other words, God delegated authority to man in order that man would give law to the rest of the earth. God also gave man the rule of not eating from the Tree of the Knowledge of Good and Evil.

In this way, humanity violated law when Adam and Eve ate from the Tree of the Knowledge of Good and Evil. This is the point at which man went from being the authority distributing the law (having dominion over the earth) to being under the law and subject to it.

First Timothy 1:5–11 says:

> Now the goal of this command is love from a clean heart, from a good conscience and a sincere belief, which some, having missed the goal, turned aside to senseless talk, wishing to be teachers of Torah, understanding neither what they say nor concerning what they strongly affirm. And we know that the Torah is good if one uses it legitimately, knowing this: that Torah is not laid down for a righteous being, but for the lawless and unruly, for the wicked and for sinners, for the wrong-doers and profane, for those who kill their fathers or mothers, for murderers, for those who whore, for sodomites, for kidnappers, for liars, for perjurers, and for whatever else that is contrary to sound teaching, according to the esteemed Good News of the blessed Elohim which was entrusted to me.

Paul writes that the law is not laid down for a righteous being, but rather for the lawless and unruly. When God created mankind, He tasked them with ruling over the earth. Those who rule are those who have authority. Mankind was not under law when they were created. They were given authority over law to implement it upon the earth. They were in this position because God created them in His image, holy (set apart) and righteous. God is not under any law, and so when He created mankind in His image, mankind was not under any law either. Rather, mankind was given the authority of law to rule the earth, all creatures, including the beast.

When mankind disobeyed God, that put them under the law. Notice how, when God created the beast of the earth and all the animals, there is no mention of God giving those creatures rules or instructions. It is only mankind that God tasked with instructions because they were made in His image and therefore were held to a higher standard.

The beast of the earth was not given any instructions, and yet it was still *under* law—mankind had authority to rule *over* it. Do you see the distinction here? Law has application to both mankind and beast, but the two are distinct based on their relationship to law. Mankind was given law but created above it (in the image of God) with the authority to use it to rule. The beast was not given law, but it was created *under* law, with mankind ruling over it.

This is why I say that mankind is distinct from beast because of law. God gave mankind order, instruction, and expectation when He created them. We do not see this with the creation of the beast. Whereas mankind was created to have dominion, the beast was created to be dominated. When mankind disobeyed God, they demonstrated that they were more fit to be dominated than to dominate. That is why they were placed under God's law, alongside the beast.

And that is why God then did for us what we were originally supposed to do for the earth—be a perfect lawgiver. For our sake, He subdued us and dominated over us in order to teach us how we are supposed to be. He gave us the Torah, His holy law. His law is love, and it is a good thing if one uses it correctly (i.e., lawfully/lovingly).

When we disobeyed God, we had become rebellious and lawless. Therefore we were not fit to administer law, but rather we needed law administered upon us. First Timothy 1:8–10 says:

> And we know that the Torah is good if one uses it legitimately, knowing this: that Torah is not laid down for a righteous being, but for the lawless and unruly, for the wicked and for sinners, for the wrong-doers and profane, for those who kill their fathers or mothers, for murderers, for those who whore, for sodomites, for kidnappers, for liars, for perjurers, and for whatever else that is contrary to sound teaching,

God made clear to us through His law what we must do to be restored to our original position of perfect lawgiver. But we couldn't do what was required. Instead, God did it Himself through His son, Yeshua. Yeshua lived perfectly, and he died to satisfy the punishment for our sins. This was a necessary component of God's holy law—justice.

God created a new covenant with us through Yeshua's death. We can be restored to our position (created in God's image, above the punishment of the law) if we believe and obey, thereby having God's law written on our hearts (just like God gave Adam and Eve instructions at creation). The obedience here is not about legalistically over indexing on every single detail out of fear that we will lose our position. The obedience is about *desiring* to do what is good, according to God. It is that kind of obedience that distinguishes mankind (made in the image of God) from the beast.

Think about it. We can train animals to obey. But what is the primary motivation we use to teach them obedience? It is their *pleasure*. We offer them treats as incentives for doing good, and we give reprimands as incentives for not doing bad.

You may say, "Well people work this way, too."

Yes, and that's the point I'm trying to make. We currently live in a sin-fallen existence, and people, by and large, are taught, trained, and motivated through means of pleasure. This isn't a bad thing in itself, but if it is the extent to which a person experiences growth and development, it is a very sad thing.

Again, when there's nothing more to look forward to after this life, it makes sense to prioritize pleasure. When there is more life to come, however, we have reason to prioritize life itself. That reason is love.

Paul writes in 1 Corinthians 13:11-13:

> When I was a child, I spoke as a child, I thought as a child, I reasoned as a child. But when I became a man, I did away with childish matters. For now we see in a mirror, dimly, but then face to face. Now I know in part, but then I shall know, as I also have been known. And now belief, expectation, and love remain - these three. But the greatest of these is love.

If we live our entire lives only being motivated by pleasure, it is sad because it means we have never grown into spiritual adulthood and known love. Our relationships are still based on "what's in it for me?" When we come to know love, we are willing to serve in ways that don't necessarily bring us pleasure. Of course, there is still a certain type of pleasure associated with this kind of service, but it is different from the pleasure of the flesh. The pleasure of the flesh is beastly pleasure. When we serve out of love, it is Godly pleasure.

This is the distinction between mankind and beast, and it is the core narrative of the Bible. God created mankind in His image, instructing them to rule over the earth. Having been made in God's image, mankind possessed the ability to value life and love over their own pleasure. This is Godly law, and this is why mankind could be trustworthy stewards of this role.

The beast, on the other hand, needed ruling over, because its nature was to value its own, beastly pleasure over life and love. The beast needed right ruling from a loving overseer.

That loving overseer was supposed to be mankind, but when mankind sinned against God, they chose their own pleasure over love. That was the fall. Since then, mankind has been under a curse that causes our hearts to desire our own pleasure rather than love. Yeshua came as the antidote to the curse, enabling us to choose love over our pleasure.

When we choose love, we retake our role as image-bearers of God.

When we choose pleasure, we settle in among the beast.

I believe that these ideas are closely tied to the mark of the beast in Revelation, and that they're all part of the same narrative.

Revelation . . . Oh Man

HAVE YOU EVER thought about the irony around how most people approach the book of Revelation? The title of the book tells us something is being revealed, and yet it gets regarded as one of the most cryptic and weird books of the Bible.

What is Revelation supposed to be revealing?

Revelation 1:1–2 says:

> Revelation of יהושע Messiah, which Elohim gave Him to show His servants what has to take place with speed. And He signified it by sending His messenger to His servant Yoḥanan, who bore witness to the Word of Elohim, and the witness of יהושע Messiah – to all he saw.

This book contains the revealing of Yeshua. God gave this revealing of Yeshua to Yeshua so that he could show his servants what has to take place.

So what is this talking about? Why is this book revealing Yeshua and the things that have to take place? Furthermore, why is this information being given to John, who had already seen Yeshua in his lifetime?

Revelation shows us what has to take place leading up to Yeshua's second coming. It is not revealing Yeshua coming the first time. That's just about everything else in the New Testament. Revelation is revealing information about Yeshua's return.

Revelation 1:3 says:

> Blessed is he who reads and those who hear the words of this prophecy, and guard what is written in it, for the time is near.

Now between offering a blessing to those who hear its words and giving us information about the return of Yeshua, Revelation ought to have scores of people diving in and plumbing its depths. But it's often quite the opposite. Revelation seems to be the one book that many church leaders create fear or caution around. I've spoken with Christians who have told me that their pastor told them not to read Revelation. Some of them didn't even want to hear about it.

One night at work, James wanted to share something with me from the book of Revelation. He picked up a Bible from the bookshelves and flipped to the back.

"Oh man . . . " he murmured.

"What?" I stepped over to see what the problem was. Someone had ripped out the pages of Revelation from the Bible he was holding. That particular Bible ended with the book of Jude. People are serious about this.

There is a lot of fear around the book of Revelation. I'll be the first to admit that the book has some pretty weird stuff in it. But if we believe what it says to be true, then it doesn't matter how weird it gets. If we believe what it says to be true, then it is a good idea to read it and know it. Again, Revelation 1:3 says:

> Blessed is he who reads and those who hear the words of this prophecy, and guard what is written in it, for the time is near.

I'm not saying we must have a perfect understanding of everything Revelation talks about. We're not going to. But if we believe what it says, and it tells us that we're blessed for reading and hearing its words, then we should be reading and hearing its words.

I think one of the things that gets people into trouble is that those who do read Revelation often jump in and read it isolated from the rest of the Bible. Revelation—just like any other book of the Bible—cannot be interpreted in isolation. The book of Revelation consolidates a lot of Old Testament prophecy. By that, I mean Revelation quotes and refers to the Old Testament prophets (like Ezekiel, Daniel, Isaiah . . .) in such a way that it ties together various pieces of the prophets' messages into a seamless, consolidated narrative.

Now, if Revelation consolidates a lot of Old Testament prophecy, then it is no wonder why we end up with so many interpretations of the book. If we don't have a thorough understanding of the places from which all the pieces of Revelation come, then we're not going to be able to make much sense of it as a whole.

I am not going to be doing a deep dive into Revelation here. I am not the right person to do that. If you are looking for a good resource on this, I believe Michael Ohman of The OliveBranch Fellowship does a great job approaching biblical prophecy, including the book of Revelation. He approaches with certain biblically based principles, seeking to let the Bible interpret itself. If one portion of Scripture is unclear, rather than imposing his own assumptions, he seeks out other places in Scripture that can help bring clarity. In doing this, he establishes biblical cohesion based on what the Bible says as opposed to filtering everything through a preestablished human doctrine. Ohman's teachings are freely available on YouTube, and I encourage you to check them out.

Ohman has a twelve-part series called Biblical Prophecy, and in this series he establishes one of the principles he uses when approaching prophecy. He says something along the lines of, "If you want to talk to me about biblical prophecy without talking about the moedim [the biblical feasts], I'm not listening." Ohman shows how the feasts laid out in Leviticus and Deuteronomy create timetables and structures that are necessary for interpreting biblical prophecy. When you understand the timing and the themes of all the biblical feasts, much of prophecy begins falling into place without you having to do a bunch of mental gymnastics to make sense of things.

In his prophecy series, Ohman gives three teachings before getting into Revelation in order to lay the groundwork needed. Part 4 of the series is called "Connecting The Dots". When he goes into Revelation, he continuously connects back to Old Testament prophecy that is being quoted or referenced. In doing this, he allows *the Bible* to create the narrative as opposed to filling in the gaps himself with assumptions and opinions.

The Bible reveals a lot more information than we may realize *when we let it interpret itself*. However, in order to let the Bible interpret itself, we must be *immersed* in it. It doesn't work to read a couple verses here and a couple verses there, discuss what we feel God is saying to us, and call it a day. We have to voraciously consume and digest the words of God over and over again if we want to get the whole story straight. When we do that, we start seeing the different pieces connect, and the picture falls into place.

The Great Hour of Pre-Wrath Tribulation Rapture and Trial

THE TITLE OF this chapter reflects the kind of biblical understanding many have on the rapture. While they may have adamant opinions, most people, if they are honest, struggle with rooting their views on this subject in Scripture. Put plainly, most people don't really know what they're talking about when it comes to the rapture.

In Revelation, we read about the Great Tribulation. Like I said earlier, I'm not going to do a deep dive into Revelation, but I do want to address the topic of the Tribulation.

Much of Christianity has accepted that there will be a pre-Tribulation rapture, meaning that God will rapture up believers before the Tribulation starts. I had never had strong opinions on the matter, and I had never tried to understand it through a biblical lens. If I'm being honest, I never really believed Yeshua would return during my lifetime, so I didn't care very much either way.

Once I started caring, I began looking into what Scripture had to say about it. I discovered that it was really difficult to build a thorough doctrine around a pre-Tribulation rapture from the ground up using only Scripture.

Over the last year, I've heard several teachings express that there will be no pre-Tribulation rapture. To be clear, they were not teaching against a rapture (a catching up of God's chosen), but specifically when that rapture occurs in relation to the Tribulation. Using Scripture, these teachers independently of one another arrived at the conclusion that the rapture wouldn't take place until the end, or very near the end, of the Tribulation.

At first, when I started talking with other Christians about it, I was surprised to find how sensitive of an issue it was. The more I contemplated it, though, the more that sensitivity made sense. Maintaining a doctrine that I will be caught up and cleared out of here before *ish* hits the fan is a comforting contingency plan if I don't die before Yeshua's return. There's also a ring of human logic to it—if I already believe in Yeshua, then why would God allow me to go through all that distress?

But in spite of the comforting sentiment and the human logic, I've had to ask, "What does the Bible actually say about it?"

One of the main biblical justifications I've heard for a pre-Tribulation rapture is the notion that we are not appointed to God's wrath.

First Thessalonians 5:9 says:

> Because Elohim did not appoint us to wrath, but to obtain deliverance through our Master יהושע Messiah,

People also look to Revelation 3:10, when John is writing to the church in Philadelphia:

> "Because you have guarded My Word of endurance, I also shall guard you from the hour of trial which shall come upon all the world, to try those who dwell on the earth."

Those are the two main biblical "go-to"s I've heard defending the pre-Tribulation rapture model. We are not appointed to God's wrath, and He shall guard us from the hour of trial. These ideas are appealing because, well, who wants to be appointed to God's wrath?

These ideas are also appealing because they can be used as catchphrases. "Well, you know, we're not appointed to God's wrath." It's kind of like a flashy trick, something we can toss out there and feel good about without a whole lot of effort. But that's the thing about it—there's not a whole lot of effort or substance going on beneath the surface, and even mild questioning reveals that we don't have a really good grasp on what the Bible says about the Tribulation, even though it says quite a bit.

For example, we can look at Yeshua's words about the coming of the Son of Man, which looks to be the trigger event for God's chosen being caught up.

Yeshua says in Matthew 24:21:

> "For then there shall be great distress, such as has not been since the beginning of the world until this time, no, nor ever shall be."

This is the Great Tribulation. Yeshua then says a few verses later in Matthew 24:29–31:

> "And immediately after the distress of those days the sun shall be darkened, and the moon shall not give its light, and the stars shall fall from the heaven, and the powers of the heavens shall be shaken. And then the sign of the Son of Adam shall appear in the heaven, and then all the tribes of the earth shall mourn, and they shall see the Son of Adam coming on the clouds of the heaven with power and much esteem. And He shall send His messengers with a great sound of a trumpet, and they shall gather together His chosen ones from the four winds, from one end of the heavens to the other."

Yeshua says that His chosen ones will be gathered immediately *after* the distress of those days.

Yeshua says in Mark 13:24–27:

> "But in those days, after that distress, the sun shall be darkened, and the moon shall not give its light, and the stars of heaven shall fall, and the powers in the heavens shall be shaken. And then they shall see the Son of Adam coming in the clouds with much power and esteem. And then He shall send His messengers, and assemble His chosen ones from the four winds, from the farthest part of earth to the farthest part of heaven."

Again, the assembling of His chosen ones takes place "after that distress".

Yeshua says in Luke 21:25–28:

> "And there shall be signs in the sun, and moon, and stars, and on the earth anxiety of nations, in bewilderment at the roaring of the sea, and agitation, men fainting from fear and the expectation of what is coming on the earth, for the powers of the heavens shall be shaken. And then they shall see the Son of Adam coming in a cloud with power and much esteem. And when these matters begin to take place, look up and lift up your heads, because your redemption draws near."

In all three of these accounts, Yeshua says that the coming of the Son of Man will take place *after* the days of distress.

So why does Paul tell the Thessalonians that God did not appoint us to wrath? Well, maybe God's wrath and the hour of trial aren't synonymous with the Tribulation. We have to put more effort into understanding what Scripture says about these topics. We can't just look for feel-good catchphrases to pluck out and walk away with.

I'm not saying this subject is a simple one to understand. I'm saying the exact opposite, in fact. It can be complex, and it takes effort to look into. But I believe that is why Revelation tells us we will be blessed if we read and listen to its words. God reveals truth to us through His Word, but we have to want it. These catchphrase doctrines that we get so comfortable living with are just cheap knockoffs of the truth.

Maybe there is a pre-Tribulation rapture—but are you able to make a good case for it based on the Bible alone? If not, then who are you really putting your faith in?

For some, this subject may seem like nothing more than theological recreation, fun for those who enjoy that sort of thing. But the practical consequences of having a false understanding on this subject may very well be severe.

Based on what I read in the Bible, I don't believe there will be a pre-Tribulation rapture. The Tribulation and God's wrath are not synonymous. If Yeshua returns within the next decade or so, I believe we'll be going through the Tribulation, unless we die first.

That's the only point I'm wanting to make here, that the Bible doesn't seem to indicate a pre-Tribulation rapture. I encourage you to look into the Tribulation to develop your own understanding. Find good teachings that are based on the Bible. More importantly, go to the Bible and read it for yourself. Pray for clarity and discernment. Don't accept a doctrine just because it is comfortable and pithy.

I really didn't want to get into the Tribulation at all. In the same way that I'm not the right person to do a deep dive on Revelation, I'm not the right person to really dive into the Tribulation at this time. But if you are a firm believer in a pre-Tribulation rapture, or are on the fence, or never really thought about it at all, I wanted to present to you that a thorough reading of the Scriptures does not seem to indicate a pre-Tribulation rapture. Instead, the Bible presents a timeline of events in which believers will have to endure the Tribulation and the events that unfold during it. I want to encourage you to approach the next few chapters with these things in mind.

The Mark of the Beast at Four A.M.

A FEW WEEKS BEFORE Kendra and I left Raleigh, I was working a late shift on the prayer line. I finished up at four A.M., and I went to YouTube. Earlier that day I had come across a video I saved for later. It was posted by Tomorrow's World, and it was titled, "The Mark of the Beast Is Already Here . . . and It's NOT What Everyone Thinks…"

I chuckled at the fact that I was watching a mark of the beast video on YouTube at four A.M. I was that guy.

For context, during this season I had heard a couple theories about the mark of the beast. The COVID vaccines were being released, so there was that. Also, Bill Gates had recently released a microchip that happened to have three 6's in its patent number, so that got some attention.

Those kinds of theories are juicy, for sure, but there is something bothersome about them to me. I don't mean bothersome as in disturbing, like I am worried about accidentally getting the mark of the beast. I mean bothersome as in arbitrary and not biblically based.

Here are the verses in Revelation talking about the mark of the beast.

John writes in Revelation 13:16–18, talking about the second beast, the one coming up out of the earth:

> And he causes all, both small and great, and rich and poor, and free and slave, to be given a mark upon their right hand or upon their foreheads, and that no one should be able to buy or sell except he that has the mark or the name of the beast, or the number of his name. Here is the wisdom! He who has understanding, let him calculate the number of the beast, for it is the number of a man, and his number is six hundred and sixty six.

In Revelation 14:9–12, John writes:

> And a third messenger followed them, saying with a loud voice, "If anyone worships the beast and his image, and receives his mark upon his forehead or upon his hand, he also shall drink of the wine of the wrath of Elohim, which is poured out undiluted into the cup of His wrath. And he shall be tortured with fire and sulphur before the set-apart messengers and before the Lamb. And the smoke of their torture goes up forever and ever. And they have no rest day or night, those worshipping the beast and his image, also if anyone receives the mark of his name." Here is the endurance of the set-apart ones, here are those guarding the commands of Elohim and the belief of יהושע.

Revelation 15:2 says:

> And I saw like a sea of glass mixed with fire, and those overcoming the beast and his image and his mark and the number of his name, standing on the sea of glass, holding harps of Elohim.

And finally, Revelation 19:20–21 says:

> And the beast was seized, and with him the false prophet who worked signs in his presence, by which he led astray those who received the mark of the beast and those who worshipped his image. The two were thrown alive into the lake of fire burning with sulphur. And the rest were killed with the sword which came from the mouth of Him who sat on the horse, and all the birds were filled with their flesh.

Again, those other theories about the mark of the beast seemed arbitrary to me, particularly in light of what these verses seem to be saying about the mark of the beast. When we read the above verse, it's clear there's something more intentional going on within "those who received the mark of the beast". In contrast, theories about microchips and such pointed to something more accidental and, well, arbitrary.

When I watched this YouTube video at four A.M., I felt a sense of clarity. I'd say that maybe it was just a euphoria from sleep deprivation, but the clarity remained even after I'd slept.

The guy in the video did address some of those theories out there, vaccines, microchips, and tattoos. But then he said, "Let's let the Bible interpret itself." He made the point that those who receive the mark of the beast apparently experience God's wrath. Then he went to Colossians 3:5–6:

> Therefore put to death your members which are on the earth: whoring, uncleanness, passion, evil desire and greed of gain, which is idolatry. Because of these the wrath of Elohim is coming upon the sons of disobedience, in which you also once walked when you lived in them.

Colossians says that the wrath of God is coming upon the sons of disobedience. It also says we were once part of that group.

If Revelation says that those who *receive the mark of the beast* are those who are *subject to God's wrath*, and if Colossians says that those who are *disobedient* are *subject to God's wrath*, then there is a relationship between those who *receive the mark of the beast* and those who are *disobedient*.

Watching the video, I could track with this idea, because this was certainly not an isolated theme in Scripture. We read about the importance of obedience all throughout the Bible.

Then the guy said that, to understand the mark of the beast, we have to understand the mark of God. Revelation says that the mark of the beast will be given to people on their right hand or on their forehead. So what does the Bible have to say about the mark of God?

We already read about it in Scripture in Part 5. Deuteronomy 6:5–8 says:

> "And you shall love יהוה your Elohim with all your heart, and with all your being, and with all your might. And these Words which I am commanding you today shall be in your heart, and you shall impress them upon your children, and shall speak of them when you sit in your house, and when you walk by the way, and when you lie down, and when you rise up,"

Alright, pay attention to this next part:

> "and shall bind them as a sign on your hand, and they shall be as frontlets between your eyes."

The Torah tells us that we are to bind "these Words" of God as a sign on our hand and as frontlets between our eyes (i.e., our foreheads). So what are "these Words" of God? The words that Moses is commanding them that day make up God's law, the Torah.

Okay, so if the Torah tells us to bind the Torah as a sign on our hand and on our forehead, does it not seem to be more than coincidental that the mark of the beast in Revelation is given to people on their right hand or forehead? Furthermore, the mark of the beast seems to be associated with *disobedience*, whereas the Torah is God's law, which is associated with *obedience*.

If you think that incorporating those verses in Colossians was stretching the point about the mark of the beast being associated with disobedience, consider, once again, Revelation 14:11–12:

> "And the smoke of their torture goes up forever and ever. And they have no rest day or night, those worshipping the beast and his image, also if anyone receives the mark of his name." Here is the endurance of the set-apart ones, here are those guarding the commands of Elohim and the belief of יהושע.

Those who worship the beast or receive his mark are juxtaposed with the set-apart ones, those who guard the commands of God and believe in Yeshua. Notice, by the way, how it explicitly states "those guarding the commands of Elohim" *and* "the belief of Yeshua". I will touch on this more in a bit.

It seems to me that there is some serious connection between receiving the mark of the beast and disobeying God's commands.

The guy in the video asked, "Is there any commandment that is called out as being a sign between God and His people?" He said that there certainly is, and it is the Sabbath, the only commandment that receives this kind of recognition. Ezekiel 20:12 says:

> "And I also gave them My Sabbaths, to be a sign between them and Me, to know that I am יהוה who sets them apart."

Now I have to ask, is it not interesting how this has come full circle? The fourth commandment, remember the Sabbath, is the *one* commandment that is called out as a sign between God and His people, is the *one* commandment that tells us to *remember* something, and is the *one* commandment that we have effectively *forgotten* to keep. Again, we could go through each of the other Ten Commandments and recognize how it is intuitive moral logic for us to obey all the other nine. But for some reason, we're okay with not being concerned about not honoring the Sabbath.

That reason is simple: beastly pleasure. We can recognize the value of all other nine commandments through intuitive logic: have no other gods before God, have no idols, don't use God's name in vain, honor your parents, don't murder, don't commit adultery, don't steal, don't lie, don't covet. We understand why it's good to obey each of those. We comprehend that obeying them ultimately benefits us. Therefore, we don't argue against them. It's no different than a dog understanding that he's going to get a treat if he rolls over.

But when it comes to the Sabbath . . . well, it'd be easier if we could go into work, or if we could go shopping, or if we could do whatever else we feel like doing on whatever day we feel like doing it. We don't really see the logic behind obeying this commandment.

That's the divide between mankind made in the image of God and mankind taking on the image of the beast. Mankind made in the image of God will obey God's commands because they love God, and Yeshua told us that if we love him, we will obey him. It doesn't matter if we don't fully understand the value behind the obedience. If we love him, we obey him. End of story.

People who take on the image of the beast, on the other hand, will obey to the extent that they get a treat. This is why faith is the distinguishing factor. Those who have faith in God will obey God even when they don't understand how their obedience will lead to their pleasure. Those who don't have faith in God will obey up to the point that they can understand what's in it for them. God promises that He will bless us abundantly if we obey Him. Every person individually proves or disproves their faith by how they live their lives.

I want to point out a few more things about the mark of the beast as described in Revelation. First, notice what it says in Revelation 13:17:

> and that no one should be able to buy or sell except he that has
> the mark or the name of the beast, or the number of his name.

Buying and selling falls in the category of working and laboring. While some people today may consider buying and selling to be just a fun hobby, that does not take away from the reality that it is still contributing to the overall work that is taking place in the world.

For example, most people I know are at least somewhat adept at online shopping. With just a few simple clicks I can purchase a number of items and have them on the way to my door with next-day delivery. Those few simple clicks may not seem like much work, but in reality a simple purchase starts a long chain reaction of extensive labor for others. First of all, someone might actually be required to make the goods I've ordered. If the goods are already made, then someone must be working in a warehouse to find and package the items. Then a delivery or postal service (involving workers ranging from client services, warehouse managers, security, and drivers) must labor to transport the goods to my front door. What is only a few simple clicks for me ends up requiring others to do an extensive amount of work. God is clear that such commerce, and the resulting labor to support such commerce, should not take place on his Sabbath day.

We read this in Nehemiah 10:31:

> and that if the peoples of the land bring wares or any grain to sell on the Sabbath day, we would not buy it from them on the Sabbath, or on a set-apart day, and we would forego the seventh year and the interest of every hand.

Now consider this idea of not buying and selling on the Sabbath in connection with what Revelation 13:17 says: "no one should be able to buy or sell except he that has the mark . . . " If the mark of the beast is connected to disobedience specifically pertaining to the Sabbath day, then perhaps this verse is indicating that only those who have the mark of the beast are able to buy or sell because they are willfully neglecting observance of the Sabbath and disobeying God's command to not buy or sell on that day. In contrast, those that have the mark of God are not able to buy or sell out of conviction to uphold the Sabbath and all God's commands surrounding its observance, including refraining from commerce. I realize the Sabbath is only one day out of the week, but if the mark of the beast is connected to not honoring the Sabbath, then the Sabbath might be the only day that's relevant in the consideration of the mark of the beast.

I personally don't believe that this is the only reality around buying and selling about which this verse is prophesying, but I do think there is an interesting connection going on that's worth considering.

That said, look back at Revelation 14:11:

> "And the smoke of their torture goes up forever and ever. And they have no rest day or night, those worshipping the beast and his image, also if anyone receives the mark of his name."

They have no rest day or night. Again, I think there's more to this reality than people not having rest because they're disobeying the command to remember the Sabbath. But I do think there is a connection going on.

Finally, I want to return to the very next verse, Revelation 14:12:

> Here is the endurance of the set-apart ones, here are those guarding the commands of Elohim and the belief of יהושע.

Again, notice how it explicitly states "those guarding the commands of Elohim" *and* "the belief of Yeshua". This idea is reflected in Revelation 12:17 also:

> And the dragon was enraged with the woman, and he went to fight with the remnant of her seed, those guarding the commands of Elohim and possessing the witness of יהושע Messiah.

These verses explicitly call out guarding the commands (i.e., obedience) and guarding the belief/possessing witness in Yeshua. They're talking about both.

So what's the big deal with that? Go back to Deuteronomy 6:8, where we were looking at the mark of God and the words of the Torah:

> "and shall bind them as a sign on your hand, and they shall be as frontlets between your eyes."

The mark of God goes on the hand *and* the forehead. Now look at Revelation 13:16, talking about the mark of the beast:

> And he causes all, both small and great, and rich and poor, and free and slave, to be given a mark upon their right hand or upon their foreheads,

The mark of the beast goes on the hand *or* the forehead.

If the words of the Torah are on your hand, you are literally doing the commands of God's Word. If the words of the Torah are on your forehead, you are meditating on and believing in God's Word. Remember, Yeshua is God's Word in the flesh. The mark of God is on those who obey God's commands with their actions *and* guard the belief (or witness) of Yeshua. It takes both to have the mark of God.

It only takes failing in one of those two areas to receive the mark of the beast. Those who believe the deceit and deception of the beast receive the mark (on the forehead). Yet those who might not believe the deceit and deception of the beast, yet due to coercion or some other reason still perform the actions of the beast (buying or selling or another form of disobedience) still receive his mark, and the ensuing punishment that comes with it.

If I'm being honest, this makes me think of Judaism and Christianity. Judaism guards the commands of Elohim but rejects the belief of

Yeshua. Christianity disobeys the commands of Elohim but guards the belief in Yeshua. I wonder how many from each religion will allow their hate for the other group to prevent them from embracing the other key piece that they are missing.

    I believe that it's going to be very easy to receive the mark of the beast when the time comes (if it hasn't already). It's very logical: the beast prioritizes personal pleasure, and therefore the path of least resistance. The mark of God, however, will require perseverance and endurance, and a true love for our heavenly Father and His commands.

The Beast and the Horn

AT THE END of Part 3, I talked about the article in *The Catholic Record* of London, Canada regarding the Sabbath. Here, again, is a quote from that article:

> The Church is above the Bible; and this transference of Sabbath observance from Saturday to Sunday is proof positive of that fact.[1]

This quote was first brought to my attention by another video I stumbled across on YouTube: "Revelation's Mark of the Beast Exposed", posted by Three Angels Broadcasting Network. In the video, Mark Finley makes a case around the Roman Catholic Church being the beast from whom the mark of the beast comes.

Now, before you roll your eyes and dismiss this as just some conspiracy theory or eager accusation, watch the teaching. I was impressed with how Finley approached the subject with kindness and gentleness. He acknowledged how there is much sensitivity surrounding this topic for many well-meaning people, but he also recognized the need to be honest about what the Bible says.

Finley presented a good case through Scripture. I hope you'll watch his teaching, because I don't want to get into the beast of Revelation here as much as I want to look at one of the beasts in Daniel (though there does seem to be a connection between the two, which Finley addresses in his message).

In Daniel 7, Daniel speaks of a dream he had in which he saw four beasts. Daniel 7:17 says:

---

1. Anonymous, "Sabbath Observance," 2342.

> These great beasts, which are four, are four sovereigns which rise up from the earth.

The traditional view holds that these four beasts represent the following empires, respectively:

1. The Babylonian Empire
2. The Medo-Persian Empire
3. The Greek Empire
4. The Roman Empire

The fourth beast, then, is the Roman Empire, and Daniel 7:7 says that this beast "was different from all the beasts that were before it". We must understand history to see how the Roman Empire is different from those other empires.

The *Roman* Empire established the *Roman* Catholic Church, which in turn shaped the Christian religion—not just Catholicism, but *all* of Christianity going forward. This is evidenced by Sunday being embraced by Christianity as the day of worship, a decision made official by the Roman Catholic Church and not explicitly commanded in the Bible.

When the Roman Empire fell, Europe entered the Dark Ages, which developed into the Middle/Medieval Ages. Though it had once been a united empire under Rome, Europe became a conglomeration of kingdoms after Rome fell. *Roman* Catholicism was still practiced throughout these kingdoms even in the absence of a unified *Roman* Empire. In this way, the Roman Empire never perished. It shattered into pieces, but each piece became a remnant of the former empire, which was preserved through the religion and culture.

In the same way that Protestant Christianity came out of Roman Catholicism, America came out of Europe, which came out of the Roman Empire. The Roman Empire never died. This is proven here in America by the fact that Christians worship on Sunday and our culture celebrates Christmas and Easter. All these things point to the workings of the Roman Empire.

This is why the Roman Empire is different from the other empires represented by the beasts in Daniel's dream—the Roman Empire, though different in appearance, is alive and dominant today.

Daniel 7:23–25 says:

"This is what he [the Ancient of Days] said, 'The fourth beast is the fourth reign on earth, which is different from all other reigns, and it devours all the earth, tramples it down and crushes it. And the ten horns are ten sovereigns from this reign. They shall rise, and another shall rise after them, and it is different from the first ones, and it humbles three sovereigns, and it speaks words against the Most High, and it wears out the set-apart ones of the Most High, and it intends to change appointed times and law, and they are given into its hand for a time and times and half a time.'"

Did you catch what verse 25 said there: "'... it intends to change appointed times and law ...'" This isn't talking about the fourth beast itself, but rather one of the horns that comes out of the beast. The horn is a symbol of power or authority. So if the beast is the Roman Empire, the horn here is a power or authority that grows out of the Roman Empire. The Roman Catholic Church is an authority that came out of the Roman Empire. In this way, any authority that comes out of Roman Catholicism (whether it's a religious figure like the pope or the Christian religion today) can also be seen as an authority growing out of the Roman Empire.

Whatever this horn is specifically, it intends to change appointed times and law. So what are God's appointed times? The first one is the Sabbath, which the Roman Empire changed for the Christian religion from the seventh day to the first day. The next appointed times are Passover, Unleavened Bread, and Firstfruits, which the Roman Empire changed to Good Friday and Easter. As for the remaining appointed times (Weeks, Trumpets, Day of Atonement, and Tabernacles), Christian culture generally doesn't celebrate these, especially not as they are laid out explicitly in Leviticus. Christian culture in America puts more emphasis, instead, on Valentine's Day, St. Patrick's Day, and Halloween, all of which have origins in either Roman Catholicism or pagan rituals. I think it's safe to say the Roman Catholic Church effectively changed the appointed times for our culture.

But verse 25 also says that it intends to change law. Did the Roman Catholic Church also do that? It absolutely did that. The Christian religion today (again, an extension of the Roman Empire) considers the Torah null and void. The Torah is God's *law*, and yet Christians are under the impression that it is no longer relevant. Our culture, which has grown out of the Roman Empire, does not acknowledge God's appointed times nor His law. This appears to fit perfectly with what Daniel 7:25 is talking about.

All of this is cohesive with the notion that the mark of the beast is connected to the Sabbath. If the mark of the beast entails disobeying God, then it must be connected to disobeying a law or commandment of God (otherwise there's no case to be made for disobedience). The seventh-day Sabbath is both an appointed time and a commandment/law of God, and it was declared changed by the Roman Empire, which happens to be the fourth beast spoken of in Daniel 7.

If remembering the Sabbath (the *seventh* day) and keeping it set apart is like wearing a jersey declaring you are on God's team, then it is a mark of the authority of God's Word over your life. Just think about it practically. God's Word says to remember the Sabbath. When you remember the Sabbath by keeping it set apart, that is an outward demonstration, like a mark, that you submit to the commands of God as given by His Word.

Now let's revisit that quote from *The Catholic Record*:

> The Church is above the Bible; and this transference of Sabbath observance from Saturday to Sunday is proof positive of that fact.[2]

If remembering the seventh-day Sabbath is a mark of the authority of God's Word over your life, then honoring Sunday as "the new Sabbath" or "the new day of worship" is a mark of the Roman Catholic Church's authority over your life. If the Roman Empire is the beast, then honoring Sunday is, by the same logic, a mark of the beast.

I say *a* mark of the beast here because I don't know for sure what *the* mark of the beast in Revelation 13 is, and I'm not intending to suggest I do. I'm still on this journey for myself, and I'm not trying to give conclusions on these matters so much as I'm trying to relay ideas and connections I've come across that have made sense. I see some very curious connections between the Sabbath, the mark of the beast, and church history, and I believe we would do well to pay attention to such connections.

Again, watch Finley's teaching, as he goes much more into the Scriptures to make his case that the beast in Revelation is the Roman Catholic Church. I don't know that I agree with him on every point he makes, but he does present a good case overall. And, like I said earlier, he does it all in a good spirit, acknowledging sensitivities with compassion while still pushing forward to seek out truth.

---

2. Anonymous, "Sabbath Observance," 2342.

The Hundred-Dollar Intention

COMING OUT OF the last chapter, you may wonder, "How could these things be true when so many God-fearing Christians have spent their entire lives going to church to worship on Sunday?" That's a reasonable question. After all, the point here seems to be that anyone who doesn't remember the seventh-day Sabbath is disobeying God. That is true, based solely on what the Word of God says. But for the sake of addressing the question—"How can there be so many God-fearing Christians who get this wrong?"—we need to think in terms of *intentional* disobedience. It is one thing to disobey God when we are truly deceived about the disobedience. It is another thing altogether when we are aware of the disobedience and still make a conscious decision to go through with it.

Pretend a friend gives you a hundred-dollar bill and tells you it's a gift from him to you. You take the money (under the impression that your friend gave you his own money) and buy a new pair of shoes.

Now pretend a friend gives you a hundred-dollar bill and tells you it's a gift from him to you, but before you spend the money, you discover that your friend stole it from someone else. Not from just anyone else, but from your own father. With that knowledge in mind, you still go and use the money to buy a new pair of shoes.

I trust that the distinction in wrongdoing is clear here. Even if, in the first instance, the money was stolen, you didn't have that information when you bought the shoes. Buying the shoes was technically wrong because the money wasn't yours to spend. But you were deceived about whom the money really belonged to, and it was never your intention to purchase shoes *wrongfully*. Make no mistake, the purchasing of the shoes in this instance is wrong—good intentions do not negate objective reality, and the objective reality here is that the money did not rightfully belong to you. But because of the deception at play, any reasonable judge would entitle you to more grace and forgiveness than they would if you had knowingly used stolen money to purchase the shoes.

In the second instance, buying the shoes was wrong (again, because the money wasn't rightfully yours to spend), and your intentions in buying the shoes were also wrong (because you knew the money wasn't rightfully yours, but you spent it anyway). In this instance, a reasonable judge would be less forgiving because the crime was intentional.

That is the distinction I see at play in Christianity regarding the Sabbath. A lot of God-fearing Christians have observed Sunday as "the Lord's Day", genuinely believing this to be pleasing to God, disregarding the seventh-day Sabbath laid out in Scripture. Many may have gone their entire lives without the truth being revealed to them. I personally believe that God will allow such individuals grace and forgiveness around this matter due to the deception at play, though what I believe ultimately doesn't make a difference—it is a matter between every individual and God, as God is the judge of the heart.

The second category, however, is made up of those who have been given the truth concerning God's Sabbath and have rejected it. It is parallel to learning that the money you received as a "gift" was stolen from your father, and yet you still proceed to spend it on shoes for yourself, making no effort to correct the wrongdoing. Those who come to an understanding of the truth and decide to carry on in wrongdoing condemn themselves not necessarily through their actions, but through their intentions. They know what is right and *intentionally* disobey.

Do you feel like you fall into one of these categories? If you have any doubt whatsoever about whether God wants us to keep His Sabbath on the seventh day, I implore you not to simply dismiss the subject altogether. Lean into it and go to the Father directly. Ask for truth and clarity, and clear yourself of any disobedience in this area, whether it is mistaken or intentional. Don't count on religion's assurances coming through for you on judgment day.

There is a third category, and this might be the one you're in. Pretend a friend gives you a hundred-dollar bill and tells you it's a gift from him to you. You decide you're going to go out and buy a new pair of shoes over the weekend. As the weekend approaches, however, you start noticing clues that indicate the money was stolen. Your friend had gone over to your father's house a few days prior, and your father is now saying that he's missing a hundred-dollar bill. You find out your friend has a track record of stealing. You don't know for sure that your friend's gift was money stolen from your father, but you have some indications that it might be.

How do you respond at that point? Do you excuse yourself by saying you trust your friend and buy the shoes anyway? Or do you make an effort to uncover the truth to the best of your ability?

Let's say you go directly to your father to ask him about his missing money. When you do, he tells you the exact serial number of his missing hundred-dollar bill, and it's a perfect match to the one your friend gave you. What do you do at that point?

I believe this category applies to the Sabbath conversation. The Christian church has told the Christian that Sunday is now the Lord's Day. The Christian church is the friend giving the "gift". At some point, the Christian comes across the Ten Commandments in the Bible. They read that God told Moses that the seventh day (not the first day) is His Sabbath. They continue reading the Bible and see this idea reiterated over and over again, and they even find Yeshua remembering the Sabbath on the seventh day. These are all signs and indications that something fishy is going on with this new "Lord's Day" business.

Is there a point at which you decide to go to your Father directly on the matter? Do you go to God in prayer, asking for truth and revelation?

When I did this for myself, my confirmation came in the form of logic statements:

- I believe the Bible is God's Word.
- The Bible commands us to remember the seventh day as His Sabbath and keep it set apart.
- The Bible never commands us to alter that command.

I realized for myself that I needed to either keep the seventh day as God's Sabbath or stop saying I believe the Bible is God's Word. By calling the Bible "God's Word" while continuing to reject the seventh-day Sabbath, I was condemning myself because I was *intentionally* maintaining contradictory truths, one truth coming from church culture, and the other from Scripture.

I know there are many rebuttals to be made about the Bible being God's Word, rebuttals concerning the Christian church's role in canonizing Scripture, the issue of translation, and the distinction between "the Word of God" and "the *inspired* Word of God". I don't presume to have a satisfying answer to every question related to these topics. But when it comes to the Sabbath, I do believe these sorts of rebuttals can be addressed succinctly:

1. Is the spirit of your rebuttal seeking truth or seeking something else (argument, justification, etc.)?
2. Have you done your own research on your point of rebuttal, or are you just echoing things you've heard?
3. Does the rebuttal really discount any of the *fundamental* points I'm making about the Sabbath?

Again, I know there are many rebuttals about the Bible being the Word of God, but in my experience, when it comes to the Sabbath conversation, these rebuttals are typically flawed in the way of spirit, research, or fundamental points, and I simply don't want to get too off track here in trying to address every single rebuttal. The reality is every perspective on the Bible necessarily entails some degree of faith to maintain.

I have faith that the Bible is the Word of God. When I express that faith, I realize I need to acknowledge what the Bible says if I intend to obey God. When I go directly to God asking Him for clarity around the Sabbath, it's as if I hear Him telling me, "You claim to have My Word. So what do I say about it?" And that's that.

The Bible says that God's Sabbath is the seventh day—it is so clear and straightforward, just like the exact serial number on your father's stolen hundred-dollar bill.

Let's go back to that analogy. You just confirmed that it's your father's hundred-dollar bill because he gave you the exact serial number on it. Now it's the moment of truth—what do you do?

If you were in that situation, would you then go back to your "friend" and let them give you some run-around reasoning for how everything went down before returning the bill to your father? Pretend your friend said, "Well, yes, it was your father's *originally*, but remember how he said I was like a son to him, and so he basically gave me the authority to take his money."

Does that sound like bogus reasoning to you? It does to me. And yet, that's exactly what we've allowed the religious institution of Christianity to feed us for nearly two thousand years.

This is not a difficult thing to fix in our individual lives. If you know the hundred-dollar bill belongs to your father, how do you correct the wrongdoing? You return the hundred-dollar bill to your father. Because the money is in your possession, that is your responsibility. It is not your responsibility to fix your friend or get him to apologize to your father or anything like that. You can try. But you are accountable for the money that was put in your possession.

It's the same thing with the Sabbath. You might not correct all of Christianity or your church or even your family, but what do you do with yourself? Do you return the hundred-dollar bill by repenting and keeping the seventh-day Sabbath set apart? Or do you let your "friend" talk you out of it?

This is why it's important to understand the fourth beast spoken of in Daniel 7. The beast is the Roman Empire, and a power or authority that grows out of it intends to change the appointed times and law. We cannot be mistaken into thinking that this "horn" will *look* like an enemy. The power that comes from the beast is much more likely to be disguised as a friend, because that is the most effective way of accomplishing its intentions (changing the appointed times and law).

We need to ask ourselves, "Is someone really being my friend when they're causing me to reject my Father's words?"

Authority Complex

READ THIS QUOTE one more time:

> The Church is above the Bible; and this transference of Sabbath observance from Saturday to Sunday is proof positive of that fact.[1]

I don't keep bringing up this quote to make an accusation against the church. I keep bringing it up because, despite my disagreements with its position, it contains sound logic, and we need to see this. If we obey the church's commands when they contradict the commands of God's Word, we are proving that the church is above the Bible in our own lives.

This all has to do with a corrupted truth regarding authority.

Yeshua says in Matthew 16:18–19:

> "And I also say to you that you are Kĕpha, and on this rock I shall build My assembly, and the gates of She'ol shall not overcome it. And I shall give you the keys of the reign of the heavens, and whatever you bind on earth shall be having been bound in the heavens, and whatever you loosen on earth shall be having been loosened in the heavens."

Matthew 28:18–20 says:

> And יהושע came up and spoke to them, saying, "All authority has been given to Me in heaven and on earth. Therefore, go and make taught ones of all the nations, immersing them in the Name of the Father and of the Son and of the Set-apart Spirit, teaching them to guard all that I have commanded you. And see, I am with you always, until the end of the age." Amĕn.

Luke 9:1 says:

---

1. Anonymous, "Sabbath Observance," 2342.

> And having called His twelve taught ones together, He gave them power and authority over all demons, and to heal diseases.

It is true that Yeshua gave authority to his apostles and to those who believe in him. Unfortunately, the church took this truth and manipulated it into a false truth.

Paul writes in 1 Corinthians 15:24:

> then the end, when He delivers up the reign to Elohim the Father, when He has brought to naught all rule and all authority and power.

And then he writes a few verses later in 1 Corinthians 15:27–28:

> For "He has put all under His feet." But when He says "all are put under Him," it is clear that He who put all under Him is excepted. And when all are made subject to Him, then the Son Himself shall also be subject to Him who put all under Him, in order that Elohim be all in all.

Even at the end of Yeshua's millennial reign, Yeshua is still under Elohim, his Father. Paul writes that "He [Elohim] who put all under Him [Yeshua] is excepted," meaning Elohim is not put under Yeshua. We need to understand this truth because misunderstanding it leads to disastrous results.

Yeshua gave his followers authority, but the authority was not to be *over* Elohim the Father. If Yeshua remains under the Father, then there should be no question on whether the church remains under the Father.

The church started with the truth that Yeshua gave his followers authority, and then it made the false assertion, "Therefore we have the authority to make Sunday the Lord's Day instead of Saturday." The problem here is that this assertion runs counter to an explicit command of Elohim, the Father, and Yeshua never gave that kind of authority to anyone.

Elohim says in Exodus 20:8–10:

> "Remember the Sabbath day, to set it apart. Six days you labour, and shall do all your work, but the seventh day is a Sabbath of יהוה your Elohim. You do not do any work – you, nor your son, nor your daughter, nor your male servant, nor your female servant, nor your cattle, nor your stranger who is within your gates."

It was never the Bible, but rather the Council of Laodicea (i.e., religion) that said:

Christians must not judaize by resting on the Sabbath, but must work on that day, rather honouring the Lord's Day;[2]

When we look at the first millennium after Yeshua, the church embraced the authority given to it and truly did some good things. But it failed when its leaders considered it an acceptable use of that authority to change one of the Ten Commandments of Elohim, the Father. Bear in mind, this was not a "reinterpretation" of a commandment, but rather a total, quantitative, and admitted change—no longer day seven, but day one. In doing this, the church overstepped its bounds and abused its authority.

Paul writes in Romans 13:1:

> Let every being be in subjection to the governing authorities. For there is no authority except from Elohim, and the authorities that exist are appointed by Elohim.

We might say this is cause for obeying the authority of the church. If we go back to the book of Daniel, though, we can find two accounts of faithful men who stood up to authority when the authority demanded something contrary to the commands of Elohim: Shadrach, Meshach, and Abednego and the fiery furnace in Daniel 3, and Daniel and the lion's den in Daniel 6. These men were willing to defy specific laws of the governing authority to the point of death because they refused to compromise the commands of Elohim. That didn't mean they led rebellions to totally overthrow the governing powers. They just prioritized Elohim's authority over the earthly authority when the two were out of sync.

Some may argue that there's a difference between the secular authority in Daniel and the religious authority of the church. Acts 5:27–29 says:

> And having brought them, they set them before the council and the high priest asked them, saying, "Did we not strictly command you not to teach in this Name? And look, you have filled Yerushalayim with your teaching, and intend to bring the blood of this Man upon us!" And Kĕpha [Peter] and the other emissaries answering, said, "We have to obey Elohim rather than men."

Peter tells the high priest in Jerusalem that they must obey Elohim rather than the high priest and everyone else who strictly commanded

---

2. Schaff and Wace, *Nicene and Post-Nicene Fathers*, 148.

them. Religiously speaking, this would have been comparable to saying these things to the pope.

It's not a matter of which authority among men, be it secular or religious, but rather a matter of authority relative to Elohim.

The church has been given authority on this earth—theoretical philosophies aside, the Christian religion has real power in the world today. But just because it has authority doesn't mean everything it does with its authority is good.

We need to know the commands of Elohim so that we can know when we need to take a stand. It is good to have trustworthy, wisdom-filled brothers and sisters in the faith to look to for guidance. But if we find ourselves always deferring to others (whether it's the church, a pastor, an elder, or anyone else) and never seeking out and guarding the commands of Elohim with our own hearts and minds, then we are pigeonholing ourselves as children in faith. We are refusing to grow up, to become spiritual adults, and to be accountable for truth.

It's not hard to see how there might be an authority complex involved when the Roman Empire embraced Christianity. It was the most dominant world power at the time. If this was the foundation for the Christian religion we know today, is it that farfetched to think that same authority complex still exists in the church?

I see a demonic stronghold on the Christian church today, manifesting as an authority complex that is trying to compete with Elohim. It is not one person's responsibility to break that stronghold over the church. Rather, it is every person's responsibility to break that stronghold over him- or herself. How do we do this? Look at Shadrach, Meshach, Abednego, and Daniel. They respected the authority that was over them. But when it told them to do something that ran contrary to a commandment of Elohim, they refused to comply.

The Roman Empire is the fourth beast spoken of in Daniel 7, the same book in which we read about Shadrach, Meshach, Abednego, and Daniel refusing to disobey the commands of Elohim. This beast is said to grow a horn that intends to change the appointed times and law. Out of the Roman Empire grew Roman Catholicism, and out of Roman Catholicism grew the Christian religion we know today. This same Christian religion is telling everybody it is good to honor the first day of the week instead of the seventh-day Sabbath. The seventh-day Sabbath is *both* an appointed time and a law (Daniel 7:25).

I don't know how to make this any more clear. There is some spirit with an authority complex operating within the church that is using the fourth commandment of Elohim to try and demonstrate that it is above Elohim. Elohim warned us about this in Daniel 7:25. Elohim made His commandments very clear. It is the church that blurred the lines and made things more confusing than they need to be, and it appears that that was intentional.

I don't know every detail and reason surrounding this circumstance, but I have enough information to realize this is an important decision I must make for myself. Just like with Shadrach, Meshach, Abednego, and Daniel, just like with Noah, just like with Abraham, just like with Moses, and just like with so many other biblical heroes, it's not acceptable to think, "Everybody else seems to think it's okay."

If it's disobeying Elohim or challenging His authority, it's not okay.

Back to the Sixth Day

Okay, it's finally time to revisit creation Day 6 and its prophecy. Genesis 1:24 says:

> And Elohim said, "*Let the earth bring forth the living being according to its kind*: livestock and creeping creatures and beasts of the earth, according to its kind." And it came to be so.

If you recall, I held off on unpacking this prophecy because there was quite a bit I needed to cover first. Now it's time to connect some dots, and you may already be putting it together.

Remember, in the seven-day/seven-millennia model, at the time of the writing of this book in the year 2021, we are coming up on the end of Day 6, the sixth set of one thousand years.

Revelation 19:11–21 says:

> And I saw the heaven opened, and there was a white horse. And He who sat on him was called Trustworthy and True, and in righteousness He judges and fights. And His eyes were as a flame of fire, and on His head were many crowns, having a Name that had been written, which no one had perceived except Himself – and having been dressed in a robe dipped in blood – and His Name is called: The Word of יהוה. And the armies in the heaven, dressed in fine linen, white and clean, followed Him on white horses. And out of His mouth goes a sharp sword, that with it He should smite the nations. And He shall shepherd them with a rod of iron. And He treads the winepress of the fierceness and wrath of Ěl Shaddai. And on His robe and on His thigh He has a name written: SOVEREIGN OF SOVEREIGNS AND MASTER OF MASTERS. And I saw one messenger standing in the sun, and he cried with a loud voice, saying to all the birds that fly in mid-heaven, "Come and gather together for the supper of the

> great Elohim, to eat the flesh of sovereigns, and the flesh of commanders, and the flesh of strong ones, and the flesh of horses and of those who sit on them, and the flesh of all people, free and slave, both small and great." And I saw the beast, and the sovereigns of the earth, and their armies, gathered together to fight Him who sat on the horse and His army. And the beast was seized, and with him the false prophet who worked signs in his presence, by which he led astray those who received the mark of the beast and those who worshipped his image. The two were thrown alive into the lake of fire burning with sulphur. And the rest were killed with the sword which came from the mouth of Him who sat on the horse, and all the birds were filled with their flesh.

This is the scene of Yeshua returning as a conquering king. He throws the beast and the false prophet into the lake of fire. "The rest" are killed. Who are the rest? These verses mention the sovereigns of the earth and their armies, and they also mention those that were led astray and received the mark of the beast and worshipped his image.

If we keep reading, Revelation 20:1–6 gives us more clarity:

> And I saw a messenger coming down from the heaven, having the key to the pit of the deep and a great chain in his hand. And he seized the dragon, the serpent of old, who is the Devil and Satan, and bound him for a thousand years, and he threw him into the pit of the deep, and shut him up, and set a seal on him, so that he should lead the nations no more astray until the thousand years were ended. And after that he has to be released for a little while. And I saw thrones – and they sat on them, and judgment was given to them – and the lives of those who had been beheaded because of the witness they bore to יהושע and because of the Word of Elohim, and who did not worship the beast, nor his image, and did not receive his mark upon their foreheads or upon their hands. And they lived and reigned with Messiah for a thousand years (and the rest of the dead did not come to life until the thousand years were ended) – this is the first resurrection. Blessed and set-apart is the one having part in the first resurrection. The second death possesses no authority over these, but they shall be priests of Elohim and of Messiah, and shall reign with Him a thousand years.

At the end of Revelation 19, Yeshua returns as a conquering king, throws the beast and the false prophet into the lake of fire, and then kills the rest. We know this is the end of the sixth set of one thousand years

(Day 6) because in Revelation 20, a messenger, or an angel, comes down from heaven and locks up Satan in the pit of the deep for a thousand years. This is the start of the millennial reign, the seventh set of one thousand years (Day 7). We read that those who did not worship the beast, nor his image, and did not receive his mark upon their foreheads or hands live and reign with Yeshua for a thousand years.

In Day 6 of the creation account, God said "Let the earth bring forth the living being according to its kind". On Day 6 of the creation account, we find both the beast and man. Remember, man was created in God's image. The beast was not.

At the end of the sixth set of one thousand years, the earth will bring forth living beings according to their kinds. When Yeshua returns, there will be a separation process . . . according to kinds. Those who have taken on the mark of the beast will be of the beast kind. Those who have not taken on the mark of the beast will be of mankind, those who bear the image of God.

This will be the most significant event to occur during the sixth set of one thousand years—the earth bringing forth living beings according to their kinds—because this will be the separation of those who will live in the millennial reign with Yeshua from those who will not.

This is why it is so important to pay attention to these matters now. We are living at the end of the sixth set of one thousand years according to the Bible. These things will be happening soon. When they do, there will be even greater deception than there is now. There's no guarantee that we'll have the opportunity to think through these things clearly when the time is upon us. We'll be confused sitting ducks, hoping that the people feeding us information about what's going on are reliable. And they probably won't be.

I don't know exactly what the mark of the beast is going to be. I feel confident that it is tied to disobedience, so our best bet for not being deceived about it is knowing what God's Word says and obeying His commands. Do not be mistaken into thinking this is something you'll be able to muscle your way through when the time comes. The deception is going to be heavy. Even if we recognize the deception, standing up against it will likely be even heavier.

If you want to get serious about lifting weights, you don't start by lifting your end goal amount. You're not able to. If for some reason you are, you'll probably hurt yourself because you're not ready for it. Thinking that we're ready for all this stuff without bothering to get into spiritual shape ahead of time is just as foolish as trying to lift the heaviest weights when it's your first time in the gym. It's foolish and naïve.

We don't know exactly when all these things will come to be. People have theories, educated guesses, and biblical models. Some are better than others. But there is a reason God didn't spell out each piece exactly. We're not called to sit around and wait for the test of faith to come. This is the test of faith, right now. It's going to continue and get harder, but if you are reading this, the test has already begun. You are taking it. Are you acing it, obeying God's Words and living the kind of life He calls us to? Or are you flunking, putting more confidence in man's word than God's?

The Bible tells us that a time is coming when Yeshua will return. At that time, there will be death and destruction, and only those who have remained faithful to the witness of Yeshua and the Word of God will be brought into the millennial reign to live with King Yeshua. That is going to be a glorious time. But there is a lot that must happen between now and then, much of which is incredibly scary.

Do not sit around waiting for God to prove to you that these things will be taking place. He's already given you your life, your brain, and His Word, and He doesn't owe you anything. He calls us to faith, not skepticism. Believe me, I understand that all these things sound ridiculous at first, thinking that the end times are upon us and the earth is as old as the Bible says it is. But in a few hundred years, after these things have taken place, they will be just as much historical fact as all the other crazy stuff that has already gone down in history. That's our existence—it's intense and profoundly unbelievable, but it's real.

In the near future, the earth will be bringing forth the living being according to its kind. Some will go on to live with Yeshua in the millennial reign, and others will not. If the distinguishing factors are faith in Yeshua and obedience to God's Word, what kind of being are you at this moment—man made in God's image, or beast? If you need to change your kind, start working at it now. Repent. Obey His commandments. Follow Yeshua.

Chiastic Love

"Chiastic" refers to a certain kind of structure in which words or elements are repeated in reverse order. We find examples of this all throughout the Bible.

For example, in Matthew 6:24, Yeshua says:

> "No one is able to serve two masters, for either he shall hate the one and love the other, or else he shall cleave to the one and despise the other. You are not able to serve Elohim and mammon."

When we read it in paragraph form, it's not as obvious. But when we write it out like poetry, it becomes more obvious:

A	No one is able to serve two masters,
B	for either he shall hate the one
C	and love the other,
C	or else he shall cleave to the one
B	and despise the other.
A	You are not able to serve Elohim and mammon.

Do you see the repetition in reverse order? Again, this occurs throughout the Bible, and it's easy to do a Google search to find some cool examples.

You may be wondering why I'm writing about this. I'm writing about this because I'm wondering about you.

Have you seen the picture yet? It's not an accident that the chiastic structure is used throughout Scripture. God enjoys it. I must admit, I find it beautiful, myself. Why? Because it's the structure of the story that we are living. When we put together all the pieces of the puzzle, we have a picture that is beautiful. It is not beautiful by accident. It has symmetry, meaning, and intention. The chiastic structure proves this:

A	Day 1
B	Day 2
C	Day 3
D	Day 4
C	Day 5
B	Day 6
A	Day 7

Do you see it yet? Think about the days of creation, and the most significant event to occur within each respective one-thousand-year period.

A	Day 1	Light separated from darkness; God separated from mankind
B	Day 2	Firmament in the waters; flood destroys the wicked, Noah's family saved
C	Day 3	Waters gather, dry land appears; God's people go through the Red Sea, led out of slavery of Egypt
D	Day 4	Two great lights in the sky; John the Baptist witnessing to Yeshua, life and death of Yeshua
C	Day 5	Waters bringing forth life; God's people go through the waters of baptism, led out of slavery of sin
B	Day 6	Beast of the earth and mankind; fire destroys the wicked, Yeshua's family saved
A	Day 7	God rests from His work, blesses the day; the Son of God reigns, mankind reunited with God

Do you see it yet?

A	Day 1	Humanity separated from God
B	Day 2	The family of the righteous one saved from destruction of the wicked (flood)
C	Day 3	The people are brought out of slavery (Egypt)
D	Day 4	The life and death of the righteous one
C	Day 5	The people are brought out of slavery (sin)
B	Day 6	The family of the righteous one saved from destruction of the wicked (fire)
A	Day 7	Humanity reunited with God

Do you see it yet? This entire story is structurally, literally, and completely centered around Yeshua. He is at the center of everything. Like I said before, this is not The People Show. This is The Yeshua Show. It's all about him. Yeshua said if we love him, we will obey him. When we love and obey, we take on the image of God. When we disobey, we take on the image of the beast.

The life that we're living is all about Yeshua, though many people don't realize it. In Colossians 1:16–20, Paul writes concerning Yeshua:

> Because in Him were created all that are in the heavens and that are on earth, visible and invisible, whether thrones or rulerships or principalities or authorities – all have been created through Him and for Him. And He is before all, and in Him all hold together. And He is the Head of the body, the assembly, who is the beginning, the first-born from the dead, that He might become the One who is first in all. Because in Him all the completeness was well pleased to dwell, and through Him to completely restore to favour all unto Himself, whether on earth or in the heavens, having made peace through the blood of His stake.

All have been created through Yeshua and for Yeshua. You and I were created through Yeshua and *for* Yeshua. Look around you, wherever you are. It's all for him.

The Bible paints the most beautiful picture. At its center is one who loved and served to the death. As we move out from the center in either direction, we see the lesson of obedience, that we would follow in his footsteps to love and serve the world.

As we continue to move out in either direction, we see great destruction and miraculous salvation. It is intense and frightening, but it is glorious once we have aligned ourselves correctly. The destruction is for the wicked, those who refused the one who loved us. The salvation is for the family, those who embraced him and took heed of his lesson. Do you see how this is glorious? The injustice and the cruelty all around us will be taken out. That is wonderful news. But if we are part of the injustice and the cruelty when that time comes, we'll be taken out with it, because it's not about us—it's about Yeshua, and there will be no intentional disobedience and cruelty when he reigns. If that means certain people must go, then they must. But God does not desire that anyone would perish, but rather that everyone would come to repentance (Ezekiel 33:11).

Which brings us to the last piece of this picture, the peripheries. As we continue moving out in either direction, we see mankind living with

God. That's where we're supposed to be, with our heavenly Father, our creator. This picture tells the story of how we were lost from our Father, and then Yeshua came after us and led us home. This picture is all about Yeshua because we owe him everything. He owed us nothing, but he willingly went through agony for us. The Father is pleased to call him his son, and to place him on the throne, that at the name of Yeshua, every knee should bow.

This is a beautiful picture, and we are in it! We have a choice in the matter. The reason the Father has been able to lay this picture out so perfectly from the very beginning is because He knows us that well. The fact that God can tell us what's going to happen from the very beginning is not a statement about free will—it's a statement about the Father. He is marvelous, magnificent, majestic, and worthy of all praise, and his only begotten son carries the family resemblance. Revelation 4:8 shows us what recognition of the Father looks like:

> And the four living creatures, each having six wings, were covered with eyes around and within. And they do not cease, day or night, saying, "Set-apart, set-apart, set-apart, יהוה Ěl Shaddai, who was, and who is, and who is coming!"

This is a beautiful picture, and we have a choice in the matter: do we want to honor the creator and His son, or do we just want to seek our own pleasure?

The picture is almost complete. The photographer's about to snap the picture. This is your chance to choose how you want to pose for it. You know my advice.

Repent.

Obey.

Love.

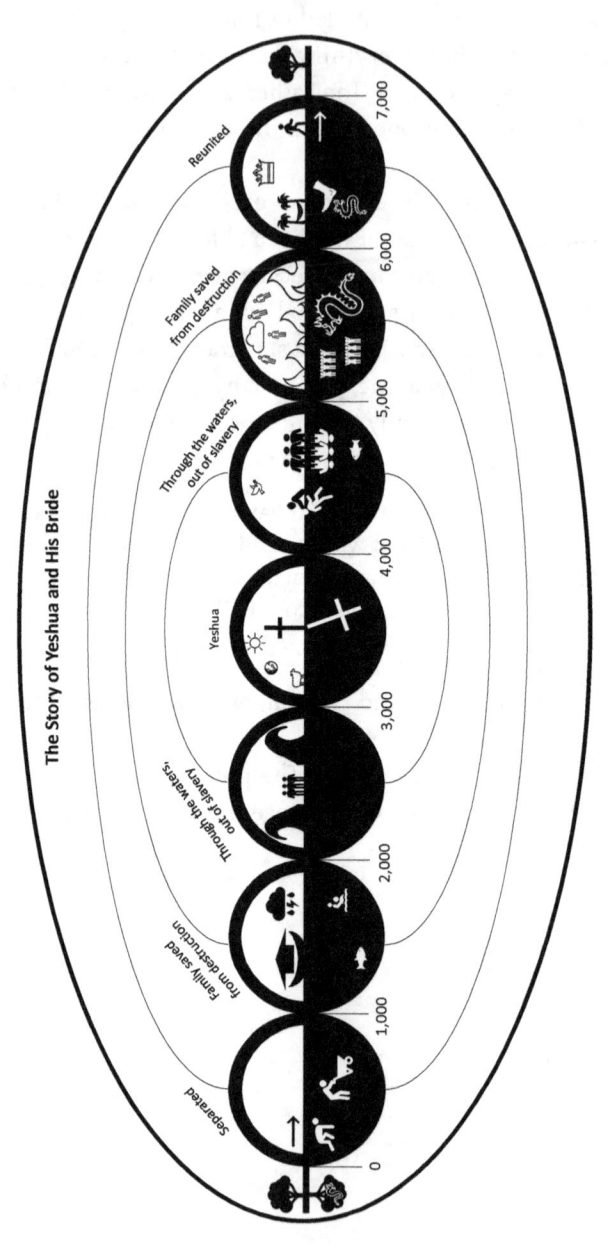

Closing Content

Are You Saying . . .

You may have a lot of questions that start with, "Are you saying . . . ?"

Are you saying that anybody who doesn't observe the Sabbath is going to get the mark of the beast?

Are you saying that everybody who has died and didn't obey the Torah is going to hell?

Are you saying that I have to believe in the seven-day creation account to be a follower of Yeshua?

I'm going to borrow one more line from Simons that I've really appreciated hearing: I'm saying I'm glad I'm not the judge.

I'm not trying to come to any conclusions that don't have biblical grounding, nor am I trying to say anything that isn't truthful. I am only trying to understand what the Word of God says and to help others see truth.

I am not attempting to invent false realities or conspiracy theories or anything that would layer further deception upon this world. We have been so deceived in this life that the truth sounds crazy to most people. I am hoping to help show that it may not be as crazy as it sounds at first.

All these topics are surrounded by sensitivity. These issues touch a lot of different nerves for a lot of different people. Some think about their loved ones who have died. What are the implications of their spiritual status if these things are true? Others think about all the people in the world and throughout history who would have had no way of knowing the things written in the Bible. And some people feel indignant at the idea that they have been wrong about certain truths throughout their life. Not only did they believe wrong ideas, but they taught and promoted those ideas to others, and so repenting of the lies they had accepted would cost too much.

For the first group of people, those who worry about the eternal state of their loved ones, this has always been a test of faith for everyone. When Abraham was called to leave his home, in addition to every other factor at play, he would have had to overcome the question, "If I listen to God and leave, does that mean all the rest of my family is wrong?" When God calls us, the step of faith we take isn't something that happens in a vacuum. If it were, that would be pretty easy: obey God in the specific thing He is asking you to do, and everything else in your life goes on unaffected. But that isn't how faith in God works. He calls us *out* of the world, and *out* of the lives we had been living into a different lifestyle. When we try to keep the life we've been living and just add in the God business as another piece, we're not truly taking a step of faith.

When we worry so much about the eternal state of our loved ones to the point that it is preventing us from moving further in the direction of truth, we're no longer seeking God. We're playing God. We are deceived into thinking that our views and beliefs might alter the spiritual destination for others. Ultimately, though, it doesn't matter what we believe when it comes to another person's relationship with God. The only thing we have any amount of real control over is our own relationship with God.

If you hold anxiety or sorrow for a loved one who has passed, knowing that they meant well in life but that they were deceived spiritually, then trust in God and submit those emotions to Him. He is good and loving, and He's the only one who knows our heart. Whatever takes place between that person and God is between that person and God. It is not our place to put our own spiritual journey on hold on behalf of someone else. We have to trust God, and we have good reason to do so: whomever it is that you love, He loves them even more.

For those who get caught up on everyone who has ever lived who didn't have access to the Bible, this is a similar circumstance. If that is our focus, we're not seeking God. We're playing God. It is not for us to reconcile every issue that every person might face.

Besides, Paul addresses this matter clearly in Romans 2:14–16:

> For when nations, who do not have the Torah, by nature do what is in the Torah, although not having the Torah, they are a torah to themselves, who show the work of the Torah written in their hearts, their conscience also bearing witness, and between themselves their thoughts accusing or even excusing, in the day

when Elohim shall judge the secrets of men through יהושע Messiah, according to my Good News.

God knows our heart. He is the only one who is able to judge every person perfectly, and He knows what standard is right to apply to each person. We don't, and we need to stop make believing that we've discovered a philosophical conundrum that God has overlooked. He knows what He's doing. It's time we backed off from His work and focused on our own hearts to make sure we are aligned with truth.

For those who are indignant at the idea that their lifelong beliefs haven't been completely aligned with truth, welcome to the club. We have all harbored and continue to harbor beliefs and ideas that are not aligned with truth. It is not a question of if we have false beliefs, but rather what we do upon recognizing false beliefs that we have been maintaining. Do we double down in obstinate pride, or do we repent before God and go forward in truth as best we can?

If you ever meet someone who has everything figured out with a perfect understanding of truth, either Yeshua has returned or you're mistaken about that person. I imagine there are things I have written in this book that are either flat-out wrong or worded in such a way that they are misleading from the truth. I certainly haven't intended anything to be like that, and I've tried my best to catch and correct those instances. But I realize that I am still living in this sin-fallen world that is terribly deceiving. I am not exempt from the deception. If and when I discover something I've written here or elsewhere is not aligned with truth, my intention is to repent and correct the error as best I can and then move on with my life.

That's what we should be doing when we discover we've been harboring false ideas. Repent, correct, and move on in truth. We should be doing this in a sincere way. Instead, we far too often allow our previous errors to direct our paths going forward. If we realize we've been doing something wrong, instead of correcting the wrong behavior, we seek out ways to justify the behavior, and we continue on in the deception. Repenting is the only way out of this mode.

Some may feel like they have no choice in the matter. They made their bed when they taught others to believe the same ideas they had accepted. If you feel like you have no choice in the matter, you are being played by some deceiving spirit. Yeshua is the truth, and the truth sets us free. You have a choice. Follow truth, or follow deception.

Creationism, the Torah, the Tribulation, the return of Yeshua... these are all sensitive issues. That isn't necessarily a problem. But if your sensitivity determines your decision making, then you've got a problem that needs dealing with.

Truth will remain truth no matter what we personally feel or believe. It is larger than we are. We should not be mistaken into thinking that we can alter truth by digging our heels into the ground and resisting the inevitability of true reality.

Some may ask the question, "Are you saying that nearly every Christian over the past couple thousand years has been getting it wrong in terms of the Torah?"

I am saying no such thing. The Christians that have come and gone over the past couple millennia are not my concern when writing these things, and I am not trying to cast judgment on anyone, especially those who are no longer with us. My concern is for those of us who are here today, alive and capable of looking at God's Word to see what it says.

Deuteronomy 30:1-4 says:

> "And it shall be, when all these words come upon you, the blessing and the curse which I have set before you, and you shall bring them back to your heart among all the nations where יהוה your Elohim drives you, and shall turn back to יהוה your Elohim and obey His voice, according to all that I command you today, with all your heart and with all your being, you and your children, then יהוה your Elohim shall turn back your captivity, and shall have compassion on you, and He shall turn back and gather you from all the peoples where יהוה your Elohim has scattered you. If any of you are driven out to the farthest parts under the heavens, from there יהוה your Elohim does gather you, and from there He does take you."

What has happened over the last couple millennia is exactly what God said would happen through Moses. God scattered His people throughout the earth, and He is going to gather them back when Yeshua returns. But notice what it says will happen first:

> "And it shall be, when all these words come upon you, the blessing and the curse which I have set before you, and you shall bring them back to your heart among all the nations where יהוה your Elohim drives you, and shall turn back to יהוה your Elohim and obey His voice, according to all that I command you

today, with all your heart and with all your being, you and your children,"

When His people bring His words back to their hearts, *then* God will gather them from all the peoples where they were scattered. I believe that God is pouring out His Spirit on His people today in preparation for the return of Yeshua. I'm not going to judge the Christians who lived before me, because God may have had different intentions for them. I can't say for sure one way or the other. But what I do know for sure is that I'm not the judge, and so I'm going to stay focused on what is happening in the here and now. When I read these verses in Deuteronomy, I see God's people returning to the words of God and then God gathering them back from where they were scattered. I believe that is what is happening right now in preparation for Yeshua's return.

This is our opportunity to return to God's law before Yeshua comes back. When he does come back, I know that I want to be well-acquainted with the law of God, not just in the way of head knowledge, but also in action. I want to do this as an act of love for my creator.

I don't know what to say about everyone else who has come and gone, or about all the crooked doctrines that exist today that so many others have subscribed to. I'm not required to give an account for every other person, and so I am not going to attempt to. I will have to give an account for myself, however. What did I do with the truth that was revealed to me? Did I lean into it and repent as needed, or did I look away from it and walk in the other direction? I don't know what to say about everyone else, but I want to be aligned with truth.

What If I'm Wrong?

I'VE HEARD THE QUESTION, "What if you're wrong about all of this?"

Let's work through this question. What if 2028 comes and goes, and nothing happens? And then the next couple of years come and go, and nothing happens. Suddenly, it's 2038, and I'm a fifty-year-old man who wrote a book that got it all wrong.

Yeesh, that would be embarrassing.

I think that would be the extent of it.

You might say, "Well wait just a minute. What about all that talk about the Torah? If you're wrong about this stuff, then that means you'll be misleading people around what God wants of them."

If years go by and we still haven't seen Yeshua, that will not change my views around God's law. I hope you can see that based on what I've written. My faith is not precariously balancing on a specific point in time by which I need Yeshua to return in order to maintain my faith. My prayer is that nobody else would find themselves in that position, either. If I live out my days and Yeshua ends up not returning in my lifetime, that means I misunderstood something about the timing of his return, and that's it. It would have nothing to do with the goodness of God's law or the perfection of His ultimate plan.

We're so eager to throw the baby out with the bathwater, and that can get us in a lot of trouble. We have to see that the whole point of thinking through and discussing Yeshua's return is to spur each other on to doing good and to prepare ourselves to be presentable before God. It is not so that we can get it all figured out, feel good about ourselves, and stake our reputations on our conclusions. That is a gross missing of the point.

When I feel confident that I'm going to see someone I love whom I haven't seen in a very long time, that gives me a special kind of energy. If they're coming to my home, I'm motivated to clean up the place and make sure the kitchen is stocked with foods and drinks that they like. I make sure I've showered and brushed my teeth (that typically doesn't require a special kind of energy for me to do; still, I make sure I've done it). I clear my schedule for their arrival and adjust it as needed leading up to their arrival to take care of the things I need to before they arrive.

It's the same idea with looking forward to Yeshua's return. We've gotten so comfortable thinking that there's no way he's going to return in our lifetime, or that we won't actually see him return because we'll be raptured up first. When we buy into that mentality, we end up living like spiritual slobs, not cleaning up or prioritizing our schedule around him.

This ought to be a motivating message, and if it feels condemning, threatening, or upsetting, then I would suggest there are some things in your life that need to get cleaned up. I'm not casting judgment over your life. I don't know what you've got going on in your life. But if you feel dread at the prospect of Yeshua returning, what is the reason for that?

The idea of Yeshua returning in the next few years gives me great joy. It has motivated me to go deeper with God. The blessings of looking forward to Yeshua's return far outweigh the supposed discretion of shying away from the topic. That supposed discretion is really just some form of fear. We fear that others will get carried away with an idea. We fear that we will believe something and end up being wrong, looking foolish in the end. We fear the reality of the future if the idea is correct.

If the years pass and Yeshua does not return, I will continue striving to increase my faith and enhance my relationship with God.

There may be some who immediately accept the ideas in this book and are like the seed that springs up quickly in rocky soil, soon after scorched by the sun because their roots have no depth. I cannot control them, and I cannot allow that reality to prevent me from sharing what is on my heart.

I can nurture my relationship with God, love others with biblical love, and speak truth to the best of my ability. I cannot micromanage another person's relationship with God. If I'm wrong about Yeshua returning in the near future, I will continue to nurture my relationship with God, love others with biblical love, and speak truth to the best of my ability. I'm not going to live in fear of being wrong. I'm going to live in pursuit of Yeshua.

What If I'm Right?

I DON'T CARE ABOUT being proven right. If I did, I wouldn't be writing this book. There'd be too much risk involved. Think about it. If I'm right, nobody will really care when it's all said and done, because so much stuff will have gone down between now and Yeshua's return that this will be the last thing on people's minds. But if I'm wrong, the world will be able to point at this book and ridicule me for having written it.

The point is, writing this book for the purpose of proving myself right is a pretty dumb gamble, and I recognize that. I don't care about being proven right.

I care about God and His people. That's why I'm writing this.

One of the teachers I've been listening to said that he doesn't have time to address all the questions and engage in all the emails he gets, particularly when it comes to the more basic matters, like the appointed times of the feasts. He said he has a flock to lead, referring to the congregation that he teaches on a regular basis, and had chosen to focus his energies on going deeper with his congregation in their spiritual journeys, instead of spending energy educating the masses about the basics.

At first, this was a bit offensive to me. It seemed hoity-toity and pretentious. But when I leaned into it, trying to understand where he was coming from, I realized that it wasn't pretentious at all. It was just genuine.

Coming from a Christian background, I had never received any kind of education or training around the appointed times of the feasts. It wasn't until I met James at the mission that I started learning about this stuff. When I began talking with my Christian friends about it, it was clear that, for us, these weren't "basic matters".

But when I started watching other teachers on YouTube that didn't necessarily subscribe to the Christian religion, I realized that the appointed times, for them and their congregations, were basic, foundational matters. These teachers approached their messages with an assumed knowledge of the feasts, to build up from the foundations laid by the appointed times. The more I listened to these messages, the more I understood. It would be impossible to lay the groundwork for the appointed times in every message they delivered and still be able to share what God had been revealing to them. They needed their flock to be rooted in the Word, just as they were. The flock needed to be walking alongside the teacher, not sitting back, expecting the teacher to cater to their every need.

I recognized the importance of this, but I still felt sad. So many Christians want to go deeper in truth, but they feel confined by the parameters that have been set by religion. Stepping out of those parameters to seek further truth can be daunting, especially if you end up tuning into a teaching that goes over your head. That's why I felt sad, because I was starting to see how there are some great teachers out there who are really going for it in the way of mining truth from God's Word. But because of how deep they're being called to go, they necessarily are unable to help others with some of the more basic matters, those who need help with that first step, simply jumping out of the boat and into the water.

I felt sad because pretty much all my loved ones were still confined by the parameters set by the Christian religion, and there seemed to be so few teachers who could meet them where they were and help them understand these basic matters. I decided there was no point in feeling sad and not doing anything about it.

I want to help others come into a deeper understanding of the Bible, because it is the truth. For some people, this book might feel overwhelming and sacrilegious. For others, it's barely scratching the surface of some of these basic matters. I'm writing this book for those of you who fall somewhere in between those two categories. My intent is that it would be a steppingstone and by no means a final destination.

I don't care about being proven right, but I ask you to think about the implications if the things I am saying here are true. Not just the idea of Yeshua returning in the near future, but everything about God's law, the history of the church, the history of the world, the appointed times, and the reality around the Tribulation. If these things are true, wouldn't you want to know about them before things go haywire?

Ezekiel 33:1–9 says:

> And the word of יהוה came to me, saying, "Son of man, speak to the children of your people, and you shall say to them, 'When I bring the sword upon a land, and the people of the land shall take a man from their borders and shall make him their watchman, and he sees the sword coming upon the land, and shall blow with the shophar and shall warn the people, then whoever shall hear the voice of the shophar and shall not take warning, if the sword comes and takes him away, his blood is on his own head. He heard the voice of the shophar, but he did not take warning, his blood is on himself. But he who takes warning shall deliver his being. But if the watchman sees the sword coming and shall not blow with the shophar, and the people shall not be warned, and the sword comes and takes any being from among them, he is taken away in his crookedness, and his blood I require at the watchman's hand.' And you, son of man, I have made you a watchman for the house of Yisra'ĕl. And you shall hear a word from My mouth and you shall warn them for Me. When I say to the wrong, 'O wrong one, you shall certainly die!' and you have not spoken to warn the wrong from his way, that wrong one shall die in his crookedness, and his blood I require at your hand. But when you have warned the wrong to turn from his way, and he has not turned from his way, he shall die in his crookedness, but you have delivered your being."

Notice how the imagery here is connected to the Feast of Trumpets. Watch. When you see, blow the shofar.

I care about God and His people. I also care about myself. God made clear to Ezekiel that if the watchman sees the sword coming and doesn't blow the shophar, the blood of those who are slain will be required at the hand of the watchman. But if the watchman blows the shofar when he sees the sword coming, even if the wrong do not turn from their way, the watchman has delivered himself.

You may ask if I believe this message to Ezekiel really applies to me. Yes, I do. I believe it applies to me and all who find themselves in a position of seeing disaster coming and having the choice of alerting the people or staying silent. If you see a child playing in the road, oblivious to the car heading in his direction, you are effectively the child's watchman. If you choose not to alert the child, you bear responsibility for what comes of the situation. That is the reality of the watchman's position.

We could argue about whether God considers us to be watchmen in the same way he considered Ezekiel to be Israel's watchman. I think the argument gets cleared up, though, in James 4:17:

> To him, then, who knows to do good and does not do it, to him it is sin.

This is one of those things where I'm not going to risk it. For your sake and for mine, I'm sounding the shofar. Yeshua is coming soon. For those who are in obedience, it will be a glorious day. For those who are in disobedience, it will be disastrous. Repent of the ways we have gone astray, not obeying God's Word and trusting in man's word instead. Return to God. Claim the righteousness that has been given to us by Yeshua and walk in it.

If I'm wrong about this, I'll look pretty silly. If I'm right about it, I might play a part in the saving of some. Either way, if I don't at least try to alert others, I'm condemning myself.

That said, what are the implications for you? What if everything I'm saying here is true?

Either Way, the World is in Trouble

WHETHER THE TRIBULATION and Yeshua are on their way in the next decade, the world is still in trouble. Have you looked at it lately?

Here's where folks will argue that there have always been doomsayers, claiming that the world's about to burn and destruction is nigh. I don't argue with that, it's true.

There are a ton of companies telling you to buy their product because you will like it. You probably won't like most of the products out there. Is that reason to believe you won't like any of them?

We shouldn't blindly accept any message that someone puts out there. But we also shouldn't blindly reject every message based on association, either. We should be engaging our minds, thinking about and testing the words that we hear.

Think about the world today and understand the differences between saying that it's in trouble now versus saying it's in trouble a hundred or two hundred years ago.

The population of the world in 1804 was one billion.
The population of the world in 1900 was 1.6 billion.
The population of the world in 2000 was 6.1 billion.
The population of the world in 2020 was 7.8 billion.[1]

Obviously, those are estimates, and, depending on the source, there may be some fluctuation, but nothing so substantial as to take away from the point. The human population didn't surpass one billion until after 1800, and since that point it has doubled nearly three times. This idea alone shows me that the time we're living in right now is uniquely different from every other previous period. The human population grew more in the past twenty years than it did from the time of the flood to 1800.

---

1. "World Population by Year," Worldometer, 2021.

Now keep that piece in mind.

When I lived in New York, I sometimes walked past the Metronome clock in Union Square. It was a giant digital clock that kept time by counting down on one end and up on the other. One night when I was working at the mission in Raleigh in 2020, one of our clients shared a *New York Times* article with me about this clock.

The gist of the article was that the clock has been reprogrammed to count down. The countdown represents "a critical window for action to prevent the effects of global warming from becoming irreversible." The article stated:

> On Saturday at 3:20 p.m., messages including "The Earth has a deadline" began to appear on the display. Then numbers — 7:103:15:40:07 — showed up, representing the years, days, hours, minutes and seconds until that deadline.[2]

This was in September of 2020, meaning that, according to the numbers shown, the clock is ticking down to somewhere right at the end of 2027.

Of course, the idea behind the clock is to alert people, hoping that humanity will change its ways in order to prevent the predicted disastrous effects of global warming. I am writing this as of July 2021, and the current countdown is at 6 years and 169 days, meaning that it is still roughly on track for the end of 2027.

Now we have to ask ourselves, between the population growth we've just looked at and this countdown, do we really believe humanity's going to pull this one off? I'm not trying to be a negative Ned here, I'm just curious about what we think is really going to happen with this.

The truth is most people are ignoring it and going on as usual. It's uncomfortable, and we prefer to just assume that things will work out one way or another. This is one of the reasons why I don't feel like the crazy one as I write about these things.

This clock in Union Square claims no affiliation with the Bible, yet both seem to be pointing at critical events happening around the same time.

Also, did you know there is an asteroid that is expected to pass awfully close (relatively speaking) to the earth in 2028? I'm not going to over-index on this, but I do find it interesting that it is expected to pass by the earth around October of 2028, which is right in the season for the

---

2. Moynihan, "A New York Clock," para. 4.

Feast of Trumpets. I wonder if there is any chance whatsoever that the calculations are incorrect or if something could change between now and then within the asteroid's trajectory. In other words, I wonder if there is any chance that the asteroid could hit the earth. Again, not over-indexing, just mentioning. If you get a chance, Google "2028 asteroid" and peruse the interesting content that's out there.

This leads me to another difference between saying the world's in trouble today versus saying the same thing a hundred years ago. The amount of information and communication available to us has sky-rocketed over the last century right alongside the population. We can reach more informed conclusions based on the information available. This has had positive and negative impacts. The positive is obvious: if we're curious about anything in particular, we can just sit down at a computer, type it in, and receive hundreds if not thousands of sources on the subject immediately. We can be better informed. The negative is a little more subtle: truth gets corrupted, and we often end up apathetic and cynical. With so much information, we feel drained from overload.

Unfortunately, that's the perfect condition for deception to reign. When we are sedated with information fatigue, we tend to acquiesce to the path of least resistance rather than put up a fight to find the truth. One of the benefits of prioritizing God and His Word is avoiding the snares of information fatigue. When we make the Word of God our priority, we have a standard against which we can measure everything else. Otherwise, we're responsible for creating and maintaining our own standard in addition to evaluating everything else. When we take that route, our standard tends to change over time, which leads to even more exhaustion and susceptibility to deception.

When we prioritize the Bible, the amount of information available to us is a beautiful thing, because we can effectively cut through the true nonsense and hone in on the pieces that contain real truth. The world would have us believe that this is a crazy approach. Again, when I look at the world around me, I don't feel crazy.

While some believe the Tribulation will be a seven-year period, many of the teachers I've been listening to recently teach that the Bible points to a three-and-a-half year Tribulation. If Yeshua returns in 2028 and there is a three-and-a-half year Tribulation, then that would put the start of the Tribulation right around the next United States presidential election inauguration, the beginning of 2025. This is another thing I'm not going to over-index on, but I want to mention it because America's elections have been getting increasingly nasty over the past decade.

When I look at the history of Rome, it makes me think of America. Rome started as a republic. After the leaders of the republic became increasingly corrupt, the people demanded that Julius Caesar be their emperor, because he actually seemed to care about the people, unlike the corrupt politicians. After Rome became an empire, though, it didn't take long for some cruel emperors to show up. Rome grew more and more powerful, and eventually the leaders grew lush and lazy. They got comfortable and careless. Eventually barbarians invaded, and the empire crumbled. When you look at all the reasons for its fall, you see that Rome had primed itself to implode.

The United States doesn't seem to be getting better. Most Americans seem to miss this point in its entirety because we have become so politically focused. If our party gets voted in, suddenly it feels like the world is on the up and up. Once the other party gets in, it's all falling apart. People will try to use this idea to argue that things aren't actually getting worse, we just see ups and downs. That's not what's happening, though. Yes, there may be minor ups and downs along the way, but the overall trajectory is headed in the direction of higher and higher volatility. We continue to move away from unity, creating more and more division. I believe this has made itself obvious during the last two presidential elections. Unfortunately, I think many Americans would read that last sentence and immediately defer to accusations of why the last couple of elections were the way they were, deferring to polarized positions and missing the overall point to be made.

Population is going up, resources are going down, and people are angry and disgruntled. Also, there's an asteroid on the way, but I'm not going to over-index on that.

You may have seen the show *The Chosen*. An article published earlier this year quoted the director, Dallas Jenkins:

> "We feel a sense of urgency," he said. "As you know, over the past year the world has gone crazy. From COVID to riots to political divides. All over the world. And our future, how solidified it is, is uncertain. And we feel the need to get seasons three through seven out to you as soon as possible."[3]

---

3. Holmes, "The Future of 'The Chosen,'" para. 10.

Please understand, I am not trying to pull Jenkins into everything I've been writing about here. I'm only using this quote to express the point that many people are feeling this sense of the world getting crazier and crazier.

Personally, I have enjoyed and appreciated watching *The Chosen*. Kendra told me one evening she feels like the show is an extension of grace from God to connect with people where they're at. I agreed with her, particularly in the way of portraying Jesus connecting with all sorts of personality types. We live in a culture that puts a lot of emphasis on personality. The media portrays likeable personalities. Villains in movies and television are often villainous solely because of their personality. We enjoy taking personality tests and discussing the results.

Personalities are fun and helpful in the way of understanding where people are coming from. But they can also be very polarizing if we're not mindful of the ways people are naturally different. *The Chosen* has done a great job in showing a realistic depiction of how Yeshua might have dealt with different personality types.

Again, I believe this show is an extension of grace from God to help the world see the realism surrounding our Messiah's life on earth. I don't think the timing of the show is any accident, nor do I feel it's coincidence that Jenkins feels a sense of urgency in making it. Right now, the world is in desperate need of these kinds of aids that give people an understanding of the reality surrounding the Bible. I say it is God's grace, because He doesn't owe it to us. He calls us to live by faith, and He's already given us His Word. Anything else that helps people step into a life of faith is a further extension of His grace.

I've been working on the prayer line I've mentioned for about eight months now, and this is probably the biggest reason I feel like our world is in trouble either way. Listening to all the types of people who call in has been eye opening. I do get calls that are very encouraging, and I'm thankful for those. But the majority of calls tend to be in the other direction.

Coming out of 2020, COVID quarantining, and the last presidential election, mass amounts of people feel discouraged, angry, lonely, betrayed, and depressed. Some people flat-out tell me they can't open up about their feelings to the people they know. The prayer line can be anonymous if they choose, so some folks are more willing to open up in this way.

Some people don't understand why God is letting such horrible things happen to them, and others understand exactly why God is letting such horrible things happen to them. Some people want permission to divorce their spouse, and others want permission to cheat on their spouse. Some people just want to talk, and some people just want to yell. Very few people call in with intentions of listening.

I have talked to people who know that God wants Trump in the White House, and I have talked to people who know that God wants Biden in the White House. I have talked with people who are certain Trump is the downfall of America, and I have talked with people who are certain Biden is the downfall of America.

I feel like I'm writing a Dr. Seuss book here. I get depressed callers, angry callers, upset callers, and prank callers.

I've been surprised at how many people have expressed some sentiment along the lines of being let down by their church. Others have told me they just haven't felt the same way since going back, after being away for so long during COVID. They feel a certain emptiness.

And then I get a lot of people who are sick, in the hospital or a nursing home, frightened and wanting prayers for healing.

All in all, it's heartbreaking.

The thing that stands out to me the most, though, is the reality that most people have a mental narrative that overrides the reality around them. People will call in and start telling me their situation. They'll tell me what's going on, how it is, and why it is. Most people don't call in with an open mind. Some do, but most call in with a confidence in what they've perceived and assessed. This isn't a problem, because the prayer line is explicitly for praying for people, not for counseling or analyzing them. But it's been eye-opening for me to see the similarities across different types of people, the way in which our minds all have an assuming confidence about completely different ideas.

Honestly, this is what scares me the most about the age we live in. Our technology, widespread information, and instantaneous communication have conditioned people to have a bizarre confidence in their own mental narrative, a confidence that will override the objective reality around them.

Some people will say, "You're assuming there's an objective reality around you." That's exactly what I'm talking about here. We've adopted these nonsensical thought patterns that allow us to feel smug in our own understandings while ignoring all the ways that we're being nonsensical. When people get to this way of being, there's no reasoning with them.

Most people don't think that way of being applies to them, and yet that way of being applies to most people.

I could go on with reasons for why the world is in trouble either way (I haven't even mentioned the sobering reality of nuclear weapons and EMPs), but for those who still insist otherwise at this point, I have a feeling it wouldn't make a difference.

Either Yeshua is returning soon, and there is a Tribulation on the way, or he's not, and there is still disaster on the horizon. Either way, get ready for a bumpy ride.

Population is going up, resources are going down, people are getting angrier and more depressed, and everyone is living according to their own mental narrative. Also, there's an asteroid on the way, but I'm not going to over-index on that.

So What Should We Do?

"Okay," you might be saying, "let's pretend for a moment that Yeshua's returning in the near future and the Tribulation is on the way. What difference does it make? What are you doing differently now as a result?"

I have come to find that these are trick questions when asked by those who aren't really convinced. If I answer with something substantial and grand, then I seem crazy. Pretend my response was, "I'm going to move to Montana." You'd say I'm crazy to alter my life in such a major way based on speculation.

If I answer with something noncommittal and minimal, then you feel justified in not being too concerned about the situation. Pretend my response was, "Well, I'm thinking through things and trying to get prepared." You'd say, "Gotchya," and carry on with life.

And if I respond with some sort of spiritual answer, then it's a big shame on me for not being of the right spiritual posture in the first place. Pretend my response was, "Well, I'm getting right with God, working hard to get *all* sin out of my life, praying to Him more often, and really getting into Scripture in a way I never have before." You'd say that we should be doing that anyway, regardless of whether Yeshua is coming back in the near future. And you'd be correct.

The point is, those are trick questions, whether intentionally or not, and they're seeking a simplistic satisfaction that doesn't exist.

That's why my answer is what it is. If Yeshua is returning in the near future and the Tribulation is on the way, it makes all the difference, and I am relying on God to show me if there are things I should be doing differently. But the things that I should be doing differently are not necessarily what you should be doing differently. If you are looking for some guidance around what you should be doing differently, then I suggest you start by spending some intentional time in prayer addressing it directly with God and spending some intentional time in His Word. If you feel like you don't have the time to do those things for yourself, then I don't want to share the things that God is showing me for myself, because it's clear you're not taking it seriously. In that case, I already know how you would respond to me.

If you are serious about this, then I will tell you that you shouldn't force anything. If you try and think your way through all the things you should do differently on your own, you're going to crash and burn. You have to spend time with God if you want reliable clarity. There's no shortcut around it. If you try and do things on your own, you'll just be perpetuating the mess we're already in.

Religion has conditioned us to think that getting into the Bible and spending time in prayer are tedious burdens. If that's how you feel about the Bible and prayer, then that's the first misconception you must correct in your life. I love getting into the Bible and spending time in prayer because those are the meat and potatoes of my relationship with God. It's a relationship that I enter into freely and joyfully, not out of obligation. The more I do this, the more He continues to pour freedom and joy upon me, providing an abundant return on my investment.

I can't tell you all the things that God wants you to do. Nobody can. It doesn't matter if they're behind a pulpit, wearing a collar, or carrying around an impressive degree. Stop playing around with religion, and start wrestling with God. If you're looking for helpful resources, I've already provided some names and ministries that I found helpful. Start with those, and see where God takes you. Wrestle through the night, and see if He doesn't bless you.

Gratitude

MY VIEWS DO not necessarily represent the views of those teachers I have mentioned, and vice versa. We should be seeking and looking out for truth, not another Messiah. Whether it's church, government, or any other institution, politics are polarizing. Just because someone has a political or other opinion you adamantly disagree with doesn't mean they don't have something valuable to teach you. I have seen the way in which people feel so let down when they discover that someone they esteem highly promotes certain politics. We must learn how to mature and not throw away everything a person has to say because of political disagreement. Feel free to disagree, but be mindful of the spirit of the matter when you do.

I want to close by thanking all the teachers who have had a role in my spiritual walk over the past couple years, those I have mentioned throughout this book and those I haven't. I am immensely grateful for their work. They are seeking God, seeking truth, and trying to help the world. That's the best any of us can do. Thank you to all of you.

Bibliography

Anonymous. "Sabbath Observance." *The Catholic Record, Volume XLV, London, Canada* 2342 (September 1, 1923). http://www.aloha.net/~mikesch/c-record.htm

Eusebius, *Life of Constantine, Vol. III, Ch. XVIII–XIX*. Translated by Averil Cameron and Stuart G. Hall. (1999) Oxford University Press, New York, NY. http://archive.eclass.uth.gr/eclass/modules/document/file.php/SEAD260/%CE%95%CF%85%CF%83%CE%AD%CE%B2%CE%B9%CE%BF%CF%82%2C%20Life%20of%20Constantine%20%28trans.%20Averil%20Cameron%20-%20Stuart%20Hall%29.pdf

Holmes, Joseph. "The Future Of 'The Chosen': Ambitious Plans And An Unconventional Season Two Premiere." *Religion Unplugged* (March 30, 2021). https://religionunplugged.com/news/2021/3/29/the-future-of-the-chosen-ambitious-plans-and-an-unconventional-season-two-premiere

Moynihan, Colin. "A New York Clock That Told Time Now Tells the Time Remaining." *The New York Times* (September 20, 2020). https://www.nytimes.com/2020/09/20/arts/design/climate-clock-metronome-nyc.html

Schaff, Philip and Wace, Henry, eds. *A Select Library of the Nicene and Post-Nicene Fathers of the Christian Church* 148. WM. B. Eerdmans, Grand Rapids, MI. https://www.ccel.org/ccel/schaff/npnf214/npnf214.i.html

"World Population by Year." Worldometer (2021). https://www.worldometers.info/world-population/world-population-by-year/

www.ingramcontent.com/pod-product-compliance
Lightning Source LLC
Chambersburg PA
CBHW050333230426
43663CB00010B/1839